The Helmand Baluch

The Helmand Baluch

A Native Ethnography of the People of Southwest Afghanistan

Ghulam Rahman Amiri

Edited and annotated by William B. Trousdale
With contributions by Mitchell Allen and Babrak Amiri
Translated from the Dari by James Gehlhar,
Mhairi Gehlhar, and Babrak Amiri

berghahn
NEW YORK · OXFORD
www.berghahnbooks.com

First published in 2021 by
Berghahn Books
www.berghahnbooks.com

© 2021, 2025 Estate of Ghulam Rahman Amiri
First paperback edition published in 2025

All rights reserved. Except for the quotation of short passages
for the purposes of criticism and review, no part of this book
may be reproduced in any form or by any means, electronic or
mechanical, including photocopying, recording, or any information
storage and retrieval system now known or to be invented,
without written permission of the publisher.

Library of Congress Cataloging-in-Publication Data

Names: Amiri, Ghulam Rahman, author. | Gehlhar, James Norman, 1945–
translator. | Gehlhar, Mhairi, translator. | Amiri, Babrak, translator,
contributor. | Trousdale, William, editor. | Allen, Mitchell, 1951–
contributor. | Carr, Helen Sorayya, editor. | Maurer, Cyndi, editor.
Title: The Helmand Baluch: A Native Ethnography of the People of Southwest
Afghanistan / Ghulam Rahman Amiri; translated from the Dari by James
Gehlhar, Mhairi Gehlhar, and Babrak Amiri; edited and annotated by
William B. Trousdale; with contributions by Mitchell Allen and Babrak
Amiri and editorial assistance from Sorayya Carr and Cyndi Maurer.
Description: New York: Berghahn Books, 2021. | Includes bibliographical
references and index.
Identifiers: LCCN 2020035008 (print) | LCCN 2020035009 (ebook) | ISBN
9781800730427 (hardback) | ISBN 9781800730434 (ebook)
Subjects: LCSH: Baluchi (Southwest Asian people)--Afghanistan--Helmand
River Valley. | Helmand River Valley (Afghanistan)--History.
Classification: LCC DS354.6.B35 A45 2020 (print) | LCC DS354.6.B35
(ebook) | DDC 305.891/5980581--dc23
LC record available at https://lccn.loc.gov/2020035008
LC ebook record available at https://lccn.loc.gov/2020035009

British Library Cataloguing in Publication Data

A catalogue record for this book is available from the British Library

ISBN 978-1-80073-042-7 hardback
ISBN 978-1-83695-059-2 paperback
ISBN 978-1-83695-181-0 epub
ISBN 978-1-80073-043-4 web pdf

https://doi.org/10.3167/9781800730427

Contents

List of Illustrations vi

Editors' Foreword ix
    William B. Trousdale and Mitchell Allen

Notes on Translation and Transliteration xvi
    William B. Trousdale

About the Author xviii
    Babrak Amiri

About the Editors xx

Preface xxi

Introduction 1

Chapter 1: History of Sistan 7

Chapter 2: Geography of the Helmand Basin 21

Chapter 3: Agricultural and Pastoral Production 37

Chapter 4: Crafts, Trade, and Travel 83

Chapter 5: Labor and Family Relationships 131

Chapter 6: Education, Health, Religion, and Cultural Norms 159

Conclusions 189

Afterword: *The Helmand Baluch* as Native Ethnography 197
    Mitchell Allen

Appendix A: Tribes of the Lower Helmand Valley 216

Appendix B: Climate Data from Zaranj and
    Deshu Meteorological Station 218

Appendix C: Monthly Water Flows at Charburjak Station 220

Glossary 221

References 227

Index 233

Illustrations

Figures
All uncredited photos are by the author.

0.1. Workmen at excavation camp at Shahr-i Gholghola xxi
0.2. Muhammad Haydar Rakhand-zadeh, mullah of Khwaja 'Ali Sehyaka xxii
0.3. Gholam Khan of Jui Nao xxii
2.1. Firing of reed beds in the *ashkin* around the Hamun-i Puzak 22
2.2. The Sar-o-Tar sand sea 28
2.3. The Helmand River near Qala-i Fath 35
3.1. Distribution point on the Qala-i Fath Canal 46
3.2. The seasonally dry bed of the Qala-i Fath Canal 46
3.3. Farmers returning from annual canal cleaning 49
3.4. Farmer cutting stubble to prepare the field for sowing wheat 51
3.5. Farmer plowing for wheat planting 52
3.6. The granary storage pits of Hajji Nafaz Khan 61
3.7. Hajji Nafaz Khan supervising the division of wheat 62
3.8. Shepherd with camel-hair cap and felt boots 65
3.9. Milch cows on the *ashkin* around the Hamun-i Puzak 66
3.10. Mud animal shelters in Asak 67
3.11. Transport camels loaded with wheat 68
3.12. Cowherds, *tavileh*, and donkeys in Asak 71
4.1. Framing of a Baluch dwelling 91
4.2. Baluch dwelling with woven reed mats placed over the tamarisk framing 91
4.3. A completed Baluch dwelling 92
4.4. Entry to a Baluch dwelling 92
4.5. Light-admitting panels on the sides of Baluch dwellings 93
4.6. Baluch dwelling in summer 94
4.7. Baluch house being dismantled 95
4.8. Tamarisk branches fencing private yards 96
4.9. Compound and house of one of the landowners of Hauz 96
4.10. *Palas* belonging to one of the Baluch *kirakesh* 97
4.11. *Palas* with attached mudbrick outbuilding 98
4.12. Dwellings of Asak constructed of rushes and mud 98

Illustrations

4.13. Carpenter sawing a rough plank into thinner boards 103
4.14. Carpenter and the objects he had made 104
4.15. Cradle made by a village carpenter 104
4.16. Carved doors of Baluch house 105
4.17. Blacksmith with apprentice at his smithy 106
4.18. Baluch woman spinning woolen thread with a *jilak* 107
4.19. Wooden handled shears for shearing carpet knap 107
4.20. Weaver beginning a *qilim* on a narrow ground loom 108
4.21. *Daup* or *dūp,* resembling a comb, used in beating back woof in weaving 108
4.22. Baluch *qilim* with typical local design 109
4.23. Portion of a *qilim* being woven on flat loom 109
4.24. Large wooden tub in which paste for tanning hides is prepared 112
4.25. Tanner scraping a hide with metal scraper 113
4.26. A treated sheep hide upon which rests the metal scraper 113
4.27. A *qurs* disc lozenge hat 114
4.28. Brass molds and jewelry made by silversmith 115
4.29. Smith fashioning jewelry on his *tayyak* 115
4.30. Migratory Baluch at Khwaja 'Ali Sehyaka 117
5.1. Bibarg Khan and several of his farmers 132
5.2. Hajji Nafaz Khan with his bodyguard 133
5.3. Hajji Nafaz Khan and bodyguards at boundary pillar near Jali Robat 134
5.4. Baluch workmen dancing during a night celebration 143
5.5. Baluch workmen eating their mid-morning meal of bread and water 146
5.6. Preparing *ghalu-i torsh* 146
5.7. Pulverizing the *qorut* in preparing the evening meal 147
5.8. Baking bread at the workmen's camp 148
5.9. Drawing water from a well 149
5.10. Swords from a khan's armory 152
6.1. The new *maktab* at Hauz 162
6.2. Baluch dwelling serves as the girls' school 163
6.3. Workman wearing a triangular *tumar* amulet around his neck 167
6.4. The Shrine of Adam Khan in Maktab 168
6.5. A typical regional grave near the Shrine of Adam Khan 168
6.6. Ziyarat-i Amiran, the Shrine of Amiran Sahib 169
6.7. Ziyarat-i Amiran, with the pile of horns marking the place of sacrifice 170

Illustrations

6.8. The horns of sacrificed goats at Ziyarat-i Amiran 170
6.9. Jahil Hakim in Delanguk 171
6.10. Itinerant holy man Sayyid Mostanshah 176
6.11. Holy man leading several camels 178

Maps

0.1 Main towns and villages in Afghan Sistan 3
1.1 Sistan and the surrounding region 14
2.1 Historical channels and major canals on the Lower Helmand River 26

Tables

2.1 Monthly evaporation rates 24
2.2 Helmand Basin climate 30
2.3 Wind velocities 31
2.4 Water flow in the Helmand River 33
3.1 Irrigation canals 44
3.2 Participation in canal cleaning 47
3.3 Distribution of harvests 60
4.1 Numbers of families in villages 84
5.1 Border distances 134
5.2 List of major khans 136
6.1 List of schools 161

Editors' Foreword

William B. Trousdale and Mitchell Allen

This manuscript, written in Dari, was delivered to William Trousdale by the late Ghulam Rahman Amiri in Kabul, September 1977 (1356 AH). A translation of the text to English was completed by James Gehlhar and Mhairi Gehlhar in November 1981. Amiri, then Director of Excavations at the Afghan Institute of Archaeology, collected the materials upon which this report is based during several autumn field seasons (chiefly 1973 to 1975) as a colleague and participant in the Helmand Sistan Project, a joint program of archaeological and other scientific investigations conducted by the Smithsonian Institution and the Afghan Institute of Archaeology.

The initiative to undertake this ethnography of the Helmand Baluch villages was Amiri's own, but he received every possible encouragement from the members of the mission. The work seemed important to us from two standpoints: 1) no similar studies had been conducted in the area since reports assembled by the Perso-Afghan Boundary Arbitration Commission early in the twentieth century, and 2) no such study had ever been undertaken by an Afghan scholar. Political events in Afghanistan since the completion of this study have brought such fundamental upheaval that no repeat study of the culture of Afghan Sistan that existed in the 1970s can ever be undertaken. This is an aspect of Amiri's work we could not have anticipated at the time, but it makes his work all the more important since it reports on a society now irrevocably changed.

Amiri was not an anthropologist, but he was deeply concerned with Afghan society for many years. His progressive attitudes more than once during his career as both educator and archaeologist were the cause of some anxiety for him, and these personally held beliefs could not but influence his observations and perceptions of village life in Sistan. For the most part, the text of the report has not been changed since it has value beyond the data it reports. Many of the observations in this report were subjects for lively discussions among the research team in the field, and on a number of occasions Trousdale made notes and observations of his own. It is on the basis of these that he annotated and augmented Amiri's text. To preserve the integrity of the original text, these comments are presented as endnotes, distinguishable from Amiri's own notes by the initials WBT.

Amiri conducted his research by observation and interview. We estimate that he conducted nearly one thousand hours of interviews with a hundred or more informants. These ranged from khans and members of the ulema to the poorest shepherds and laborers. With one notable exception,[1] these interviews were conducted among the men of the region, usually, but not exclusively, those employed by the mission. Amiri spoke Pashto and Dari. Most of the men interviewed were able to speak Pashto in addition to Baluchi and/or Brahui. Very rarely did he require the assistance of a third party interpreter.

Amiri's ethnographic research was conducted in two principal areas. When we worked in the Sar-o-Tar area east of the lower Helmand Valley, we hired workmen from nearby villages, chiefly Hauz, Qala-i Fath, Godri, and Jui Nao. Our archaeological field work in the Helmand Valley itself was conducted primarily in the villages at Khwaja 'Ali Sehyaka (but at the other Khwaja 'Ali villages to a lesser extent) and in the Lat, Lop, and Demarda districts of Rudbar, especially among the residents of Khel-i Bibarg Khan in the Lat district. A smaller amount of work was conducted at Deshu and at Malakhan, in the villages immediately to the south of Lashkar Gah/Bust, at the village of Asak on the eastern shore of the Hamun-i Puzak, and at the border village of Jali Robat, close to Kuh-i Malik Siah where the borders of Iran, Pakistan, and Afghanistan meet.

From Fieldwork to Publication: A Forty-Five Year Journey

In 1976 it was possible for Amiri to visit the United States for several months to access the meagre source materials pertinent to the work he was conducting and, free of other responsibilities, to commence the writing of his report. We know he would wish to express his gratitude to the Fulbright-Hayes Program for a travel grant, to the Smithsonian Institution for a research stipend, and to the Middle East Center at Harvard University for providing him with the facilities he required for his research. From the book's Acknowledgements, we believe he worked there with M. Hasan Kakar in organizing his notes and the text.

As noted above, by late 1977 the Dari manuscript was done. We are unaware of the steps he undertook to have the manuscript published in Dari in Kabul, but the volume came out from Ākadimīī-i 'Ulūm-i J.D.

Editors' Foreword

Afghānistān in that year. Trousdale commissioned James and Mhairi Gehlhar, specialists in Farsi, to undertake a translation to facilitate publication in English. This was delivered late in 1981.

Over the succeeding several years, Trousdale, who does not speak Dari, Farsi, Pashto, nor Baluchi, worked through the English manuscript, editing for style and lightly for content. For more substantive matters, he began an extensive series of notes that addressed some of the points of Amiri's manuscript that he thought required clarification or expansion. Many of these were based upon notes about village life recorded by Trousdale during discussions with Amiri while they were still in the field. Others stemmed from Trousdale's own observations during each field season. In some cases, it would have been impolitic for Amiri, a high ranking official in the Afghan government, to include his observations, but reasonable for Trousdale to make the same statement. In the mid-1980s, English publication of the manuscript ground to a halt as Trousdale focused on other parts of the Helmand Sistan Project. At some point in the early 1990s, Trousdale lost contact with Amiri after Amiri fled Afghanistan for India. The manuscript was shelved as Trousdale retired in 1996 and shipped his files, including the Dari text and the typed English translation, to his retirement home in the Los Angeles area.

Resuscitating the Baluch ethnography began when Allen, a junior field archaeologist on the original Helmand Sistan Project in 1974 and 1975, retired from a forty-year career in scholarly publishing in 2016. Discussions with Trousdale led Allen to volunteer to take the lead on completing publication of the work of the Helmand Sistan Project, including Amiri's ethnography.[2]

The typed draft of the Gehlhar translation was scanned and then edited by Cyndi Maurer, difficult because of the large number of non-English terms. Trousdale's lengthy handwritten notes were deciphered, transcribed, and edited by Sorayya Carr. Both Maurer and Carr are trained in anthropology. Various pieces—photos, charts, tables, introductory matter—were found within Trousdale's voluminous professional papers, collated, and then the entire manuscript was re-edited by Allen.

One of the key concerns was in finding Amiri himself, who owned the intellectual property to the book, but who hadn't been contacted in over two decades. Several web searches by Allen for him or a descendant turned up no firm leads. The book was once again stalled, this time for lack of a legal right to go forward. A later attempt turned up an online interview with a young Muslim woman, Geeti Amiri, living in Copenhagen

Editors' Foreword

and writing in Danish. Fortunately for us, Geeti was a public figure in Denmark, a political advocate for the Muslim minority and for Muslim women in the broader Danish society.[3] Not yet thirty years old, she had already published her autobiography, was very active on social media, and a regular blogger. Within the limitations posed by Google Translate from Danish to English, it appeared that Geeti's father had once been an archaeologist and an Afghan minister. One interview finally clinched it—she mourned the loss of her late father, Ghulam Rahman Amiri, and was seeking to find out more about him. We had found his family!

A Facebook message to Geeti provided an almost immediate response, not only from her but also from her oldest brother Babrak Amiri, an engineer living in Portland, Oregon. Amazingly, Portland was Allen's destination the following week for an applied anthropology conference. Dinner was quickly arranged, and Babrak became an invaluable partner in the process of getting the book completed and published. The Amiri family, consisting of ten children, his second wife, and various cousins scattered among the United States, Denmark, Sweden, and Afghanistan, has been enthusiastically supportive of the publication of the book ever since. Sadly, Amiri himself succumbed to ALS in 2003 after living his final years in Denmark.

Babrak Amiri reviewed the Gehlhar translation and improved on converting the colloquial Dari to English, as well as reviewing place names and personal names. The Gehlhars were re-contacted after forty years and gave their blessing to go forward. Carr and Maurer polished the text, tables, and images. Attempts was made to locate the publisher of the Dari work in Kabul without success, not surprisingly given the changes in Afghanistan over the past four decades. Allen secured the interest of Berghahn Books, a high-quality international publisher of anthropology books, for publication. He also presented a brief synopsis of the work at the American Anthropological Association annual meeting in Vancouver in 2019. Given that this was an innovative work both of Baluch ethnography and native ethnography, Allen added a chapter summarizing both literatures and placing Amiri's study within it (see Afterword). Trousdale, now ninety years old, reviewed all the elements as they were completed. The original Dari manuscript, long lost from view, was digitized by Babrak Amiri.

That there are a large number of names listed on the title page is no accident—numerous people contributed to converting Amiri's original manuscript into the book you have here. It took over forty years from writing the original manuscript until its English publication, but each of the participants is delighted to see that it finally happened.

Editors' Foreword

Measurement Equivalences of the 1970s in Afghan Sistan

Right Bank/Left Bank

The path of the lower Helmand River traces a large letter U in southwest Afghanistan, therefore traditional cardinal directions do not adequately describe on which side of the river places are located. The early European visitors solved this by labeling the sides as *right bank* and *left bank* as a person looks downstream toward the *hamun* lakes. Thus, the right bank would designate locations on the inside of the U, the left bank those on the outside of the U. Both Amiri and Trousdale use this designation regularly in the book, as do many of the sources they quote.

Currency

Afghanistan's national currency, the *afghani,* varied in value against the US dollar in the early 1970s when the fieldwork was taking place.

    1971 80 afghanis = US$1
    1972 80 afghanis = US$1
    1973 55 afghanis = US$1
    1974 52 afghanis = US$1
    1975 43 afghanis = US$1
    The *qeran* was worth 120 to an afghani

Crop Weights

    1 *satri* = a "handful" of sickled wheat
    1 *kisheh* = 20-25 *satri*
    1 *pav* = 452 gm = 1 lb of wheat
    1 *man* = 10 *pav* = 4.5 kg = 10 lb
    1 *kharvar* = 80 *man* = variously, in the text, 560 kg (1,232 lb)
        and 360 kg[4] (800 lb)
    1 *sir* = 7 kg = 14.4 lb

Land Area

    1 *jerib* = 0.2 hectare[5] = 0.5 acre

Notes to the Manuscript

Notes to the text are located at the end of each chapter. Amiri's textual notes from the 1970s are designated by the initials GRA. Trousdale's annotations to this text in the 1980s are shown by the initials WBT. Allen's and Babrak Amiri's 2020 comments are followed by the initials MA and BA respectively. Quoted passages from original English sources are not exact, having been translated by Amiri from English to Dari then back to English by the Gehlhars. The accompanying references can provide the exact quotes.

Data Preservation

Amiri's original field notes were lost in his rapid departure from Afghanistan in 1989. His manuscript from which the Gehlhar translation was made was preserved by Trousdale, scanned by Babrak Amiri, and is available online at https://sistanarchaeology.org/. The original print photos, manuscript, translation, Trousdale's handwritten notes, and other related items are being deposited with Trousdale's archives at the National Anthropological Archives of the Smithsonian Institution. The website of the Helmand Sistan Project (https://sistanarchaeology.org/) contains some of the material appearing in the book, as well the archaeological work of the project, of which Amiri was a full partner.

Acknowledgements

While Amiri provides his own acknowledgements below, the editors wish to thank the many people involved in bringing the English translation into reality. These include the original translators of the book, James and Mhairi Gehlhar, and Babrak Amiri. Maps were produced by the CAMEL Project of the Oriental Institute of the University of Chicago, by project geologist John W. Whitney, and by Joshua Allen. Editorial consistency was sought through a team consisting of Sorayya Carr, Cyndi Maurer, Ariadne Prater, and Babrak Amiri. Maurer scanned both the manuscript and the figures for publication and constructed the index. From the Helmand Sistan Project, the photographs of the late Robert K. Vincent, Jr., and the geological information from John W. Whitney were essential. Funding assistance toward publication was provided by the White-Levy Program for Archaeological Publication. Marion Berghahn and the Berghahn Books team has been an invaluable partner, as has the superb editorial team of Hannah and Michael Jennings. The Amiri family has been enthusiastically supportive of the project since we reconnected with them, and we are pleased to be able bring Ghulam Rachman Amiri's book to print in English at last.

Editors' Foreword

Notes

1 See chapter 5, note 20 concerning our worker Shaparai in the village of Khawja 'Ali Sehyaka. MA
2 The main field report of the project is still in process but expected to be published by 2021. MA
3 https://da.wikipedia.org/wiki/Geeti_Amiri MA
4 Neither figure matches the weight of a *kharvar* in Iran at the time, which was 300 kg (Kramer 1982, p. 37). MA
5 Amiri never defines the size of *jerib* in the volume at the time of the study, and its standard size has changed over time. Recently, the *jerib* in Afghanistan has been considered to be 0.5 acres/0.2 hectares (Grace 2005, p. i).

Notes on Translation and Transliteration

William B. Trousdale

Problems of transliteration and translation abound in the text. This might be anticipated in an area where Baluchi is the principal language, but where Pashto, Brahui, and Dari are also to some extent current among the Baluch, Pashtun, Tajik, and Brahui residents. In the late 1970s Iranian Persian pronunciations and speech patterns were increasingly prevalent as large numbers of the Baluch of Afghan Sistan crossed the border to work in a more prosperous Iran, frequently returning with deliberately affected speech mannerisms because it was thought fashionable to reflect cultural influence from Iran. Under the circumstances, consistency in transliteration is not to be expected. The Gehlhars used Iranian Persian pronunciation in their transliterations, which were occasionally modified by Babrak Amiri, a native speaker of Dari and Pashto. Where I know the local Baluchi, Pashto, or Dari equivalent in use during the years we were present in Sistan, I have changed (or added) this spelling to reflect current pronunciation. In one respect, this has had the effect of increasing the inconsistencies, but it seemed to me to be a price worth paying to correct proper names and terminology when I knew how these were pronounced locally at the time of this study. At any rate, this reflects the actual situation where what one may hear is in part up to the linguistic preference of the informant.

Let me cite one example of the multilingual nature of our field project. In October 1975 a boy of approximately fourteen years of age (few know except generally how old they are since no written records are kept) limped into our camp on one leg and a primitive wooden crutch. Several days before he had been severely bitten in the leg by one of those fierce dogs commonly kept by the rural populace of Afghanistan. Poultices of unknown substances had hardened on his leg, but had had no apparent healing effect. He spoke only Baluchi. What I know about him and his health was transmitted from Baluchi into Pashto by one of our workmen then into English for me by Amiri. The boy lived alone with his blind grandfather for whom he provided by collecting gifts of wheat for their

Notes on Translation and Transliteration

daily bread from various households of the diffuse and rapidly depopulating village of Khwaja ʿAli Sehyaka. At one of these hutches he was severely bitten in the area of the calf by a guard dog. By the time I saw the wound it was so infected that I despaired of the boy's recovery. He was, to be sure, very apprehensive of what might happen to him at the hands of foreigners such as ourselves. With much patience and boiled water, the caked poultices were removed from his wounds. The dog had grabbed his leg, and had held on for some time, twisting, shaking, and tearing at the leg. While there was a lot of skin damage, the dog had evidently not seriously injured muscle or severed a tendon. All of this the boy described as we plied him with popcorn. His apprehension subsided while I worked by lantern light on his leg. We could do little for him besides clean the wounds, then apply antiseptic and antibiotic cream and dressings. He returned each evening for several days for the dressing to be changed, but also, we suspected, for the popcorn. Then we saw him no more. Weeks later I once caught a glimpse of him some two hundred meters from where I was excavating. He was walking normally, without the aid of his tamarisk crutch. What Amiri learned from the bilingual local interpreter gave us enough information to properly treat him, as well as learn about his overall situation and blind grandfather. But this was an exception; normally Amiri was able to converse in Pashto with his informants.

About the Author
Babrak Amiri

Ghulam Rahman Amiri was born in 1934 in the village of Qualai Quazi near Kabul, Afghanistan. He attended Qualai Quazi primary school. He then attended the Teachers Training Academy in Kabul for his secondary education from 1951 to 1957. Afterwards, Amiri obtained a Bachelor of Arts degree in History and Geography at Kabul University in 1962. Amiri was a student the University of Ohio in 1965 and was awarded a Fulbright Fellowship to study at Harvard University in 1976. At the start of his career, Amiri taught history at Habibia High School and at the Teachers Training Academy in Kabul. He was also the Director of the Training Center at the Department of Civil Aviation and became an academic member of the Kabul Museum.

In 1970, Amiri became the Director of Excavation at the Institute of Archeology in Kabul. Part of this job required him to annually spend a few months in the field in different parts of Afghanistan. During this time, he worked on excavating historical sites, statues, and other relics that were buried underground. Amiri worked with the Helmand Sistan Project from the Smithsonian Institution for four seasons between 1971 and 1975, doing archaeological fieldwork in Afghani Sistan. He wrote several academic journal articles in Dari and in English about the project.

After his work in the Institute of Archeology, Amiri was the director of a special project titled "The Regional Development Project of Herat" in the Ministry of Information and Culture. This project aimed to highlight the history of Herat. After this job, Amiri initially worked as the Assistant Director, then as the Director, of the Tourism Bureau of Afghanistan. Before retirement, Amiri worked as a member of the Afghan Academy of Research.

Due to conflicts stemming from the Soviet Union invasion of Afghanistan, Amiri fled to India in late 1990 and eventually arrived in Denmark in 1993. During his time in Denmark, Amiri published parts one and two of his books, titled *The Complicated Dimensions of Wars' Duration in Afghanistan*. These were published in Dari in 1998 and 2003, respectively. The

About the Author

first part (covering the time before the Taliban) was printed in Iran, and the second part (covering the time during Taliban rule of Afghanistan) was printed in Sweden. Amiri passed away in 2003 due to Amyotrophic Lateral Sclerosis.

My father worked at the Institute of Archeology when I was in junior high school. After conducting his annual research in Sistan, he would return home for a few months. I particularly remember how he would sit on the ground in the corner of our living room, lay out the pictures in this book, and record his findings. He was always eager to show us his pictures and some of the different artifacts he collected. One of the few artifacts that I can remember is a spinning tool (*jilak*) that Sistan women used to make thread out of wool.

During this time, I remember that he would constantly talk about Baluch people, even when guests visited. He loved discussing the cultural differences between Sistan and Kabul, including the cuisine, housing, and traditions.

My youngest sister, Geeti, was not born when my father conducted his Sistan research; however, she is old enough to remember his work ethic. She adds:

> Without knowing a lot about my father's early life, before he became a political refugee, my father passed on the very fundamental principles that this book has been founded on. My father was an opinionated yet open-minded individual. He always emphasized the value of knowledge and taught my siblings and I to learn from our pasts to improve our futures. When I was a child, my father would spend countless hours with me visiting historical sites and telling stories about why the monuments had been raised. Now more than ever, I understand why he did it. My father passed on his curiosity in life about human nature by passing on his knowledge, as he did by writing this book.

About the Editors

William B. Trousdale is Curator Emeritus of the Anthropology Department of the National Museum of Natural History, Smithsonian Institution, where he worked for thirty-five years. Trousdale directed the Helmand Sistan Project in Afghanistan from 1971 to 1979. An expert on Afghanistan, he is author of six books and numerous articles on this country and on related subjects.

Babrak Amiri is a structural engineer at Associated Consultants, Inc. in Vancouver, Washington. Son of Ghulam Rahman Amiri, he was raised in Kabul but has been in the United States for thirty years. He trained in engineering at the University of Nebraska.

Mitchell Allen is a Research Associate in archaeology at both the Smithsonian Institution and the University of California, Berkeley. He served as field archaeologist on the Helmand Sistan Project before beginning a forty-year career in scholarly publishing.

Preface

Much of the information in this work has been gathered through conversations with excavation workers employed at various sites in this region (Fig. 0.1). Explanations were also sought from the inhabitants of the area adjoining the Helmand River at Qala-i Fath, Rudbar, Khwaja 'Ali Sehyaka and its environs near that region. Information in the work concerning other regions was obtained through contacts and conversations with the local people. Another portion of the information concerning the region was gathered from various clerics and khans of these locales (Fig. 0.2).

Figure 0.1. Excavation workmen at camp at Shahr-i Gholghola, Sar-o-Tar, Nimruz Province, 1974, being interviewed by G. R. Amiri. These Baluch men came from the Helmand Valley villages of Hauz, Godri, Jui Nao, Qala-i Fath. Muhammad Qasim (second from left) worked for the project for three seasons. Left to right: Abdur Rahim, Muhammad Qasim, Gel Ahmad, Muhammad Qudur, Ahmad Jan, Jan Muhammad, Abdur Rahman, 'Abd ul-Hamid, Eid Muhammad, Ghulam Mohai-ud-din, Muhammad Rasul. Photo by Robert K. Vincent, Jr. © Helmand Sistan Project.

Figure 0.2. Muhammad Haydar Akhand-zadeh, mullah of the small mosque at Khwaja 'Ali Sehyaka, Helmand Province, who supplied information about a mullah's religious duties and other activities in this region, 1975. Photo by Robert K. Vincent, Jr. © Helmand Sistan Project.

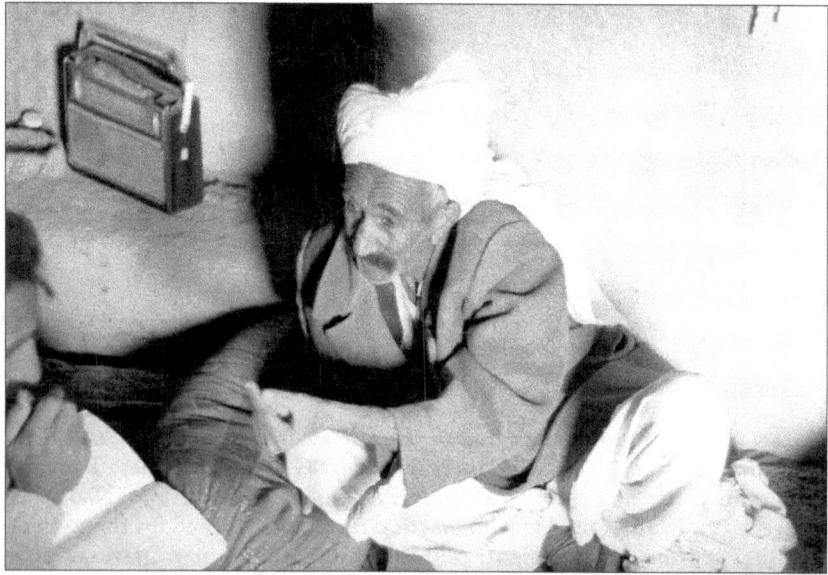

Figure 0.3. Gholam Khan of Jui Nao, reputed to be the oldest man in Sistan, being interviewed at Godri, Nimruz Province, November 23, 1973.

Preface

Some of this information comes from Khaghali Gholam Khan, reputedly the oldest inhabitant of the region,[1] who lives in Jui Nao (Fig. 0.3). In 1973 it was ascertained that he was between eighty-five and ninety years old, but the local people guessed his age as over one hundred.[2] In any case, an effort has been made to research the material thoroughly and to gather it accurately. The written sources, which can shine light on the historical roots of these issues, are very few and hard to find.

It must be noted that a large part of this research took place before the establishment of the Republic in Afghanistan. Since the Republic, conditions in the area have changed much more rapidly than before, and the development programs of the republican government have hastened these changes and had a profound effect on Baluch society.[3]

Finally, I must thank all those who have helped me in the collection of the material in this work, especially Dr. William Trousdale, the head of the expedition, who laid the groundwork for carrying out this research, and Dr. Hasan Kawun Kakar,[4] professor of history at Kabul University, who helped me with the arrangement and organization of the contents of this work.

Since no books or even articles have been found concerning Afghan Sistan and the way of life of its inhabitants[5] in Dari or Pashto languages, since knowledge of this area and the way of life of its inhabitants is necessary for the progress and prosperity of the region, or at least for the prevention of further destruction of it for Afghan youth, and since I find this research useful and enjoyable, I regret that these conditions have disappeared with the changing times and were never written down. It cannot be imagined that these data are free from error: I hope therefore that the scholarly community and my readers will be generous toward me in eliminating the defects and validating the truths.

Notes

1 The two-hour interview with Gholam Khan was held on 23 November 1973 while the mission was camped at Shahr-i Gholghola in the Sar-o-Tar region. Gholam Khan resided at Jui Nao, but because there was then no motorable way to reach this village, he came to the village of Godri on a horse led by a diffident attendant, and the interview was held in the reception room a

resident of Godri had made available for the purpose. Present at the interview, besides Amiri, were John W. Whitney, the mission geomorphologist who wished to question Gholam Khan on any environmental changes he might have observed during his life, Robert K. Vincent, Jr., the mission photographer, myself, and, occasionally, local residents who stayed for short periods in the room. Gholam Khan evidently once spoke English well, and certainly he understood it still. While his sight was failing, his hearing was still acute, and even *sotto voce* asides did not escape his attention. He had not had occasion to use English for many years and so preferred to respond to most questions to Amiri in Dari. He was venerated locally as a wise man, one of great knowledge, broad experience, and retentive memory. Hence, some greater measure of veneration is shown toward him than would normally be accorded a man of great age. The respect accorded him was evident in the attitudes and gestures of the host in whose house we sat, and in those of the few other Afghans present from time to time in the room. Gholam Khan was still a robust man of very firm hand grasp and though now slightly stooped and a bit unsteady (he carried a cane, seemingly more as a symbol and perquisite of age than as a necessity), he still stood tall, was slender, but with a sturdy frame. He complained that he did not know how old he was because such statistics are not recorded in Afghanistan as they are in other countries. On the basis of the interview, we estimated his age to be between seventy-five and eighty; Amiri thought him somewhat older. He stated that he was "Arab," but Amiri explained that he said so because Arabs are the people of the *Qur'an* and the original Muslims. Actually, he was Baluch, of the Arbab tribe.

The interview had been arranged primarily at the behest of John Whitney, who wished to query Gholam Khan about climate, water, and vegetation and agricultural matters in years past, and responses to these questions were recorded by Whitney. My own questions were designed to elicit biographical details. The meeting place was a 45-minute drive from our camp and within the dune field of Sar-o-Tar. Gholam Khan preceded us to the site. The mud-plastered rectangular room was furnished with qilims on the floor and bolsters around the walls, against which we could recline. Gholam Khan seated himself at the center of the wall opposite the entry.

Gholam Khan spoke slowly, deliberately, fluently, as though relating a tale told many times before, but one always listened to with fascination rather than forbearance or deference by his Afghan audience. He paused at regular intervals for Amiri to translate and complete his notes, and it is certain that the translation constituted only a brief summary of the tale, lacking the richness of detail and style it seemed to possess. I much regretted the lack of a tape recorder, which did not form a part of the expedition equipment until the following year.

In 1914, as a young man, Gholam Khan left Sistan, where he was born, and journeyed to Russia, where he was employed as a house servant in a town between Petrograd and Moscow. The circumstances of his departure from Sistan are unknown. When the First World War began, he, along with many non-Russians resident in that country, was inducted into the Russian

Preface

army. He was taken prisoner by the Germans and transported first to Warsaw and subsequently to Berlin, where after some time, the Germans freed the non-Russians (Muslims, he said) and made some attempts at repatriation when possible. Gholam Khan traveled through the Balkans and reached Constantinople, where he resided for six months. From this city he journeyed to Salonika, then still within the Ottoman domain. By 1919 he had reached Suez, and it was here that news of the assassination of the Amir Habibullah Khan, ruler of Afghanistan, reached him. He took a ship for Bombay in 1920, and there was first engaged as a stevedore on the docks and eventually as a dock foreman for Ardishar B. Karsatjee and Sons, handling especially cargoes from the Persian Gulf ships of the Pacific and Orient Line: dates, tea, rice, and motor vehicles. He remained intermittently employed in Bombay for about twenty years (until ca. 1940) before setting forth on travels to Calcutta, Penang, Singapore, and Kulaklang near Bangkok, and then again to Singapore. At Singapore he obtained a passport and a promise of a visa to the United States, providing he could go to Shanghai to receive it. But he was unable to go to Shanghai. The time frame of some of his wanderings is obscure, but probably they occurred during the 1920s, concurrent with his longer stay in Bombay and prior to his marriage. In Singapore, the French Consul provided him with a visa for Shanghai, but in the Singapore markets he observed Chinese butchering snakes, pigs, and cows with the same knives, and passing meat to Muslims and non-Muslims. This greatly disturbed him, and he developed a dislike for the Chinese and their chopsticks and feared he would not be able to survive among such pork eaters. Consequently, he returned to Bombay, from which city he finally departed in 1947, at the time of the partition of India and Pakistan.

He returned at last to Afghanistan. He declared that since his return to his native country everything had gone badly for him, he suddenly lost all his former excitement for life.

He was born in Jui Nao and he returned there via Quetta and Kandahar. Before he had left for Russia as a young man, his sister had married, and he had bought some land for her and her husband and had registered it in the husband's name, perhaps because land could not be held in this region in the name of a woman. His intent was that this land would revert to himself when he returned to Sistan, but he was unable to regain the land and now supported himself by selling his wife's jewelry. She was an Afghan woman he had married on a trip from Bombay back to Afghanistan. After the marriage, the couple had returned to Bombay. It was unclear whether his wife was still alive, but this seems unlikely. Now, he declared, he awaited only death.

He stated that there were three dams (*band*) on the Helmand once; at Rudbar, Bandar-i Kamal Khan, and Tap-pagao. Even when he was young there was much more *jangal* (wetlands with dense vegetation) by the Helmand River, up to a thousand meters on each side, though in places there was less. And there were many more boar. He claimed to recall the English members of the Perso-Afghan Arbitration Commission who were present in the area from 1902 to 1905 but declared that no one knew their purpose in being there. He had noted that since the building of the Kajaki Dam in the middle reach of the Helmand, the river has been scouring its channel, a point known because of the increasing difficulty in raising the water to the *juis* (canals). He believes the sand of the great Registan area now falls back into the Dori and Helmand Rivers and is carried back down the Helmand stream to the basin. He said there has been no water in the Gaud-i Zirreh in his memory. He stated that it was his belief that the sanding of this region was worsening.

He stated that in earlier times there were many, many old coins and other antiquities found in the Sar-o-Tar region. When asked what had become of them, he replied that they were all bought by the Germans and the French. This would indicate recent times. The French mission was briefly in Sistan in 1937, the Germans in the late 1960s and early 1970s. WBT

2   Exaggerated estimates of age form a part of the veneration of the old in Afghanistan, as they do in many other parts of the world. In 1972, an Afghan archaeologist in his early twenties, working with our mission for a few months only, repeatedly stated his father's age to be 125. One morning in November he revealed that he had dreamt in the night that his father had died. Only a few days later I received a letter from a member of our mission who had returned to Kabul at mid campaign; it contained the news that this young man's father had, in fact, died. I am not a believer in extra-sensory perception, but I am bound to acknowledge coincidence. WBT

3   Written in 1977, it reflects its time. We wonder how Amiri would view all of this today. MA

4   Dr. Kakar is one of the most brilliant Afghan intellectuals. An irrepressible proponent of progress and independence, he was later imprisoned by the Soviet-backed regime. See also the Afterword. WBT/MA

5   For all intents and purposes, this is an accurate statement. Some details concerning the inhabitants of the Helmand Valley and Sistan Basin are provided by early travelers in these regions, but their observations are generally incidental to the experiences of their flights or journeys. See the Afterword for some early European travelers' descriptions of the people of Afghan Sistan. It is indicative of the little attention generally paid this region that in G.F. Debets's *Physical Anthropology of Afghanistan* (1970), two lines only are devoted to the Baluch, whom he studied at Chakhansur on 19–20 December 1965, and six lines to the Brahui, whom he studied at Bakat (Bagat) on the Helmand 22–23 December 1965. In December 1977, J. Elfenbein conducted a brief linguistic survey along the lower course of the Helmand (Elfenbein 1979), but this investigation was too summary to have been of significant value. The most useful earlier data are contained in Tate (1910–1912) and Ward (1906), but the latter exists perhaps in only one complete copy in the Library and Records Department of the Foreign and Commonwealth Office, London, and is not easily accessible. Vol. I, pt. 3, of Ward, "Notes on herd-owners, flock-owners, wild fowlers, weavers and potters" (pp. 191–294), is especially pertinent. WBT

Introduction

In 1350/1971 an agreement was signed between the Afghan Department of Antiquities of the Ministry of Information and Culture and the Archaeological Expedition of the United States National Museum, the Smithsonian Institution, concerning historical excavations in Afghanistan.[1] According to this agreement, which would run for five years, the expedition was granted the privilege of conducting historical investigations in an extensive area of the provinces of Helmand and Nimruz. In the autumn of that year, the expedition, under the directorship of Dr. William Trousdale, undertook the survey of ruins and the historical sites in the designated region. The author, in the capacity of representative of the Department of Antiquities, also took part in this survey. The expedition's investigation covered the historical sites along the length of the Helmand River from Lashkar Gah to Deshu and Charburjak counties and similarly the historical sites of Sar-o-Tar[2] and other ruins along the road between Charburjak, Zaranj, and Lashkar Gah. As a result of this survey, the expedition chose two historical areas for excavation: first, the ancient region around the site of Shahr-i Gholghola, often called Sar-o-Tar, and the neighboring historical ruins in the province of Nimruz, and second, the historical site of Tepe Shishagi near the village of Khwaja 'Ali Sehyaka in the province of Helmand. Each of the sites was excavated by the expedition in subsequent years.[3]

In 1354/1975 in the course of the excavation of Tepe Shishagi and the survey of the surrounding area, the expedition succeeded in finding another historical site in Rudbar, which was called Kona Qala II. The discovery of this new site altered the expedition's previous plans. They set about excavating it with great enthusiasm, and by the end of the season, the excavation was completed.[4] Each year had one work season of approximately three months in the autumn.

1

During the first season of survey of the historical sites of that region, the people's lifestyle, the profound differences between the social classes, and their relationships to each other caught my attention. After a few enquiries among farmers and several of the inhabitants of the area, I found that the way of life of the Baluch people in that region—their customs and manners, the type of agriculture, the system of distribution of agricultural produce, and the relation of the landowners to the farmers—differs greatly from that of other regions in the country. Upon further investigation, I came upon more fascinating material that I felt was very important to record. Therefore, I decided that alongside the historical researches, I would also set about collecting sociological data concerning the Baluch people and the inhabitants of Afghan Sistan.

Unfortunately, by that time, the first field season (1349/1971) was almost over, and I knew that I was very short of time. I could not gather enough necessary information, and this research was left for a future occasion.

Luckily, in 1351/1973 the author was again assigned to the expedition as archaeological representative and took part in the digging. However, during this season, the expedition's research concentrated upon a very specific and limited area of the ancient city of Shahr-i Gholghola (Sar-o-Tar) and its environs. Therefore, it seemed appropriate that I undertake my research on the subject in a more circumscribed area that was easily within my reach.

The area about which I collected material during this time comprised the regions which are completely irrigated by a large canal that separates from the Helmand River in the vicinity of Karudi[5] and is called the Qala-i Fath Canal. This region, according to information in the Office of Finance there,[6] contains 42,000 *jeribs*[7] of agricultural land and includes eighteen villages or hamlets.

In 1352/1974 I again took part in the research with the expedition. In this season, the investigation of the historical site of Shahr-i Gholghola (Sar-o-Tar) and the historical ruins surrounding it took up much of the expedition's time, but approximately one third of the season was devoted to investigation of the historical sites of the northern portion of Sar-o-Tar and inspection of some of the ancient remains on the southern fringes of the Dasht-i Amiran, the historical ruins surrounding Hamun-i Puzak, Lash, Juwain, and Peshawaran. Accordingly, this plan gave me the opportunity not only to continue my research in the areas adjoining the Qala-i Fath Canal and to fill in the existing gaps, but also to extend this investigation to the northern areas of the Helmand Basin.

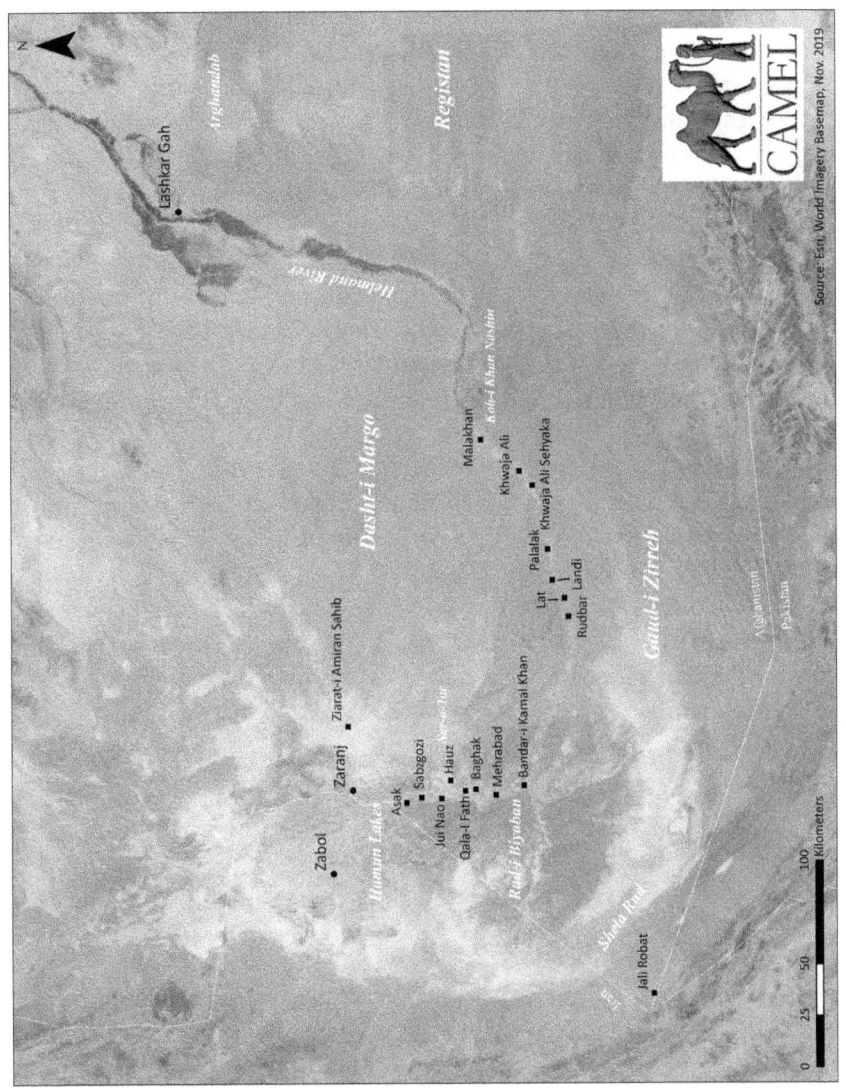

Map 0.1 Main towns and villages in Afghan Sistan. Map by CAMEL Project, University of Chicago Oriental Institute.

The expedition's fifth season of archaeological digging, in 1353/1975, was the last season of research according to the agreement. In this season, the expedition looked at some historical remains on the left bank of the Helmand River below Darwishan and on Tepe Shishagi at Khwaja 'Ali Sehyaka, which had been discovered as a result of the team's 1349/1971 survey. The Baluch people call *tikar* (clay pottery) *shisha*. Since many lumps of broken clay pottery can be seen on top of the hill, they gave it this name.[8] The excavation there took five weeks. Another five weeks of this season were spent in the excavation of the tepe Kona Qala II in Rudbar.

As a result of the plan of the investigations of the fifth season, I came into contact once again with the Baluch people along the length of the Helmand River from Lashkar Gah to Charburjak and Bandar-i Kamal Khan (approximately 150 km from Lashkar Gah),[9] and I was able to bring to a successful conclusion the research that I had been unable to complete in 1349/1971.

At the end of this season, a research trip was made to Rud-i Biyaban, to a fortress in the southwest corner of Afghanistan, which in that area was the marker of the common border between Fars, Baluchistan, and Afghanistan at the foot of Kuh-i Malik Siyah. The three day trip also included Trakhun, Bandar-i Kamal Khan, Charburjak, and Galudand.[10] As mentioned before, this monograph is comprised of information concerning the daily life of the Baluch and people native to the lower reaches of the Helmand River as far as the Basin and the surrounding areas, making up the present-day Afghan Sistan.

Notes

1 The contract was signed at Jalalabad in February 1971. The Helmand Sistan Project began work in September of the same year. The contract was composed by W. Trousdale in consultation with the Afghan Deputy Minister of Information and Culture. The contract was loosely based on one recently concluded with a German archaeological mission, but a month of negotiations was still required to develop a document acceptable to both parties. Subsequent to the signing ceremony at Jalalabad (noted on the front page of *The Kabul Times*, 1 March 1971), the government of Prime Minister Nur Ahmad Etemadi fell and all pending unratified contracts were subject to review and approval by a new Council of Ministers. The contract was

Introduction

approved by the Council in September and a Royal *firman* (decree) issued shortly thereafter. Subsequent changes in government, including establishment of the Republic in 1973, did not affect the operation of the mission. WBT

2 This toponym appears first in Western literature (as Sarotar) in McMahon 1906, p. 219f, where it is applied to the extensive ruins of the archaeological site of Shahr-i Gholghola. It next appears (as Sarotār) in Tate (1909) where it refers to a broad geographical area of ruin fields in Afghan Sistan, of which Shahr-i Gholghola is the southernmost complex, but the same author (1910–1912) erroneously limits this name to the ruins of Shahr-i Gholghola. In the brief report of the French mission to Afghan Sistan from mid-October to mid-November 1936, the term Tar-o-Sar is applied exclusively to the Shahr-i Gholghola ruins (Hackin 1959). Fairservis (1961, p. 20f.) seems to use the term in both senses, but on p. 52 refers to Shahr-i Gholghola as Sar-o-Tar and employs the toponym Ghulghula in reference to a concentration of ruins farther north. Fairservis did not visit sites in the sanded tract. If there is a correct application for the toponym, there is no correct form for it: Sar-o-Tar, Tar-o-Sar, even Sar-o-Sar are in current use. It refers not to Shahr-i Gholghola, but to the entire sand-covered portion of the eastern Basin where ruins occur. It is bounded on the north by the district of Chakhansur and the Dasht-i Amiran, on the east by the Dasht-i Margo, on the south by the Dasht-i-Jahanum, and on the west by the sometimes cultivated lands along the right bank of the Helmand River. The term is evidently Baluchi and means, insofar as we were able to elicit a concise meaning, "emptiness and desolation." In this sense, the order hardly matters.

Toponyms expressive of such bleakness exist elsewhere in the greater Sistan region; Conolly (1838, p. 713) cites a tract of land to the north of the Sistan *hamuns* then known by the name "Tug-i-Noomed," which he translates as "Waste of Despair." WBT

3 In 1971, archaeological and geomorphological surveys were conducted in the vicinity of Bust (at sites ancillary to this urban complex), in the Helmand Valley between Kuh-i Khan Neshin and the village of Deshu, and in the vicinity of Shahr-i Gholghola in the Sar-o-Tar area of the Sistan Basin to the east of the lower Helmand. Between 1972 and 1974, major efforts were confined to the Sar-o-Tar region. In 1975, excavations were conducted at two major sites on the left bank of the Helmand: Tepe Shishagi at Khwaja ʿAli Sehyaka and further west at Kona Qala II, in the Lat district of Rudbar, called Lat Qalʾa in the *Archaeologcial Gazetteer of Afghanistan* (Ball 2019, site 687). Additional surveys were conducted in 1975 and 1976 in the regions of the Gaud-i Zirreh, the Shela Rud, and the Rud-i Biyaban. During 1976 and 1977 additional surveys were conducted in bordering districts of Baluchistan in Pakistan and Iran. WBT. Our archaeological findings in Sistan will be described in the archaeological report of the Helmand Sistan Project still in development for publication in 2021. MA

4 In the records of the archaeological mission this site is recorded as Kona Qala II to distinguish it from another site of the same name near Deshu. Time

permitted the opening of only two exploratory trenches at Kona Qala II. It is the most substantial multi-period site we encountered in the five seasons of work. Unfortunately, virgin soil was not reached in either trench before the close of the season. Neither funds nor the expired contract permitted further work at this extremely important site. WBT

5 The point on the right bank of the Helmand River, north of Charburjak, where the Qala-i Fath Canal is drawn from the River. WBT
6 Probably Lashkar Gah, or Kabul. WBT
7 See Editors' Foreword for equivalencies of various sorts. MA
8 *Tikar* actually means shards, whether of glass or ceramic. This site was entered into the expedition's reports as Sehyak (Seh.), for it lies on elevated ground adjacent to the present village of this name. The site was known locally not only as *Tikar*, but as *dik*, meaning simply "mound," and as *Shishagi Ghundi*, "pottery mound." This last name appears on the U.S.T.C. Map Series 1501, Edition 1, Sheet NH 41-7, as Šišagi Ghundey. Amiri preferred to call this site Tepe Shishagi. WBT
9 The motor road ends several miles south of Darwishan. Below this point there is only a motorable track of reasonable quality in most places, except between the Bagat villages to the east and Malakhan to the west of Kuh-i Khan Neshin. WBT
10 The survey route was from Rudbar across the desert to the Gaud-i Zirreh, up the Shela Rud, and then south to Jali Robat on the Pakistan border. From here we traveled north to Trakhun in the Rud-i Biyaban, visiting several other sites in this dry channel, returning up the Helmand to Rudbar. For "Fars," read Iran; for "Baluchistan," read Pakistan. WBT

Chapter 1

History of Sistan

Ancient Sistan occupied a portion of present-day Afghanistan and part of the eastern edges of Fars. Although there is some dispute among historians and geographers about its previous borders, it is evident that in the past Sistan covered a much wider area than it does today.

The province which the Sakas occupied late in the second century BC, and which subsequently was called Sakastana after them, roughly included central Helmand. Of course, it cannot be stated with any certainty just which areas were considered Sistan during any particular period, but it is clear that even districts of Kandahar were at times included under this name,[1] and in the *Geography of Hafiz Abru*, the city of Bust (modern Lashkar Gah) is listed as the first city in Sistan.[2]

Present-day Sistan consists mostly of lowlands. This area is bounded on the south by the northern foothills of the Kuh-i Sultan and Kacha Kuh[3] and on the west by the ranges of the Palangan Hills and Bandan in Fars; on the north, the fertile areas of Qala-i Kakh of Farah and Sabzvar (Shindand of today) separate it from the fertile lands of Herat. On the eastern side, Sistan is bounded by the edges of the highlands, starting from the foothills of Zamindawar and Ghur, and extending to the south.[4] The maximum length of Sistan is approximately 100 miles, its width ranges from 70 to 100 miles, and its area is approximately 7,000 square miles (18,000 square km).[5]

Before the arrival of the Sakas in Sistan, the Amurjizis (Amurgisis), a branch of the ancient Sakas, inhabited Sistan. How and when they came to the region is not known for certain. Before the coming of the Sakas, this region was known as Drangiana.[6] G. P. Tate writes concerning this:

> Zara is a very ancient name for Sistan, from which the Greek and Latin authors derived "Drangiana." This name found its way to the West by writers of histories of Alexander's travels. At the time of the

conquest, the Arabs too found the name Zari in existence, and they called it Zaranj. The word Zirreh is now applied to a low-lying area in the south of Sistan, called Gaud-i Zirreh or Zirreh Hollow. This name was firmly established since the famous inscription of Darius uses Zaranka as the ancient name for Sistan.[7]

In approximately 175 BC and during the reign of the Graeco-Bactrian king Eukratides, the emigration of the "Siti" or Saka tribes began from the northeast. The Sakas moved down from beyond the Jaxartes to Sogdiana, their first wave taking Transoxania and subsequently crossing the Oxus to occupy the Bactrian territories. As this wave swept westwards, they were blocked by the Ashkanians of Parthia and had no choice but to go southwards and occupy both Sistan and Kandahar. Thenceforward in the ancient Drangiana, it was called by the name of Sakasthana after the Sakas. The Arab historians made this name into Sijistan, from which the present name Sistan is derived. The Sakas advanced gradually from Sistan and Kandahar into Sind. Due to the internal expansion of the Sakas and the attacks of the Parthian Ashkanians, the power center of the Graeco-Bactrian state moved in 135 BC from the north to the south of the Hindu Kush, and by the end of the first century BC, the Saka state was entirely extinct.[8]

Parthians and Ashkanians ruled independently from the last part of the second century BC (120 BC) to last part of the first century (75 AD). However, even with the evidence of their coins, their history is not clear.

In the Sasanian era, Ardeshir, the founder of the dynasty, incorporated Sakastan into his domain, but this relationship did not last, and in the Sasanian era, the Sakas were more their allies than their subjects. Bahram II (274–291 AD) conquered Sistan a second time, set up his own son as governor of the region, and proclaimed him Saganshah.[9] During the reign of Shapur II (309–379 AD), the Sakas again shook off the sovereignty of the Sasanians and became their allies.[10]

The Arab Conquest of Sistan

The important historical events in Sistan begin with the invasion of the Arabs.[11] At the time of 'Uthman (644–656 AD), the Arabs under 'Abdullah bin 'Umar invaded Ariana, besieged its capital Zaranj, and captured it. At first Rabi'a bin Ziyad was appointed by the Caliph to govern it, but the people of Sistan quickly rebelled against him and expelled him from Sistan. The Caliph appointed another man, 'Abdul-Rahman bin Thamara, as viceroy of Sistan. He reconquered Zaranj and Bust and made Bust the center of his administration. From then on, the Arabs took tribute, taxes, and revenues from Sistan and also used it as a base for their military campaigns and further conquests. During the period of Arab supremacy, the activities of dissidents and freedom fighters escalated. At first, these activities made it very difficult for the Arabs to govern.[12] Subsequently, under the leadership of Ya'qub-i Laith Safari, who was a native of the region, Sistan liberated itself from the Arabs and set up a state comprising Zabulistan, Kabulistan, Takharistan, Balkh, Nishapur, Kirman, Tabristan, and Khorasan. During the subsequent Saffarid period, Zaranj became the imperial capital and Bust the most renowned cultural center of the era.

In the Ghaznavis era, too, the importance of the region did not diminish. Sabuktagin, the father of Mahmood Ghaznavi, appreciated the geographical location of the region and paid great attention to it. Mahmood made Sistan his military headquarters because from there he could quickly and easily dispatch his forces to western Sistan, Ghur, and India.[13] In addition, the reed beds of the Helmand were apparently very suitable for the grazing of the elephants and horses, which were considered the most important means of transport. After the death of Mahmood, his son Mas'ud expanded his domains in Bust and built himself an elaborate castle, Koshk-i Soltani. Lashkar Gah came to be reckoned the heart of the country and the second capital of the Ghaznavis empire.[14] After Mas'ud, the Ghaznavis dynasty fell into decline and the fortunes of Sistan also slowly changed.

The first Mogul incursion into Sistan took place in 599/1221 when Tuli Khan was busy subduing the northwestern provinces of Afghanistan such as Nishapur and Herat. During these battles a number of Moguls turned in the direction of Sistan and besieged its center, which was the seat of King Nosrat ad-Din bin Bahramshah Harb. They returned unsuccessfully, but King Nosrat ad-Din was killed in those subsequent battles (600–601/1222–1223).

The second Mogul campaign into Sistan was carried out at the order of Ogatay by the command of his two lieutenants Mankadeh Charbi and Sa'adi Charbi. During this incursion the Moguls laid waste to the Helmand River valley and killed most of the population. King Rokn ad-Din Mahmood bin Harb, who had succeeded Nosrat ad-Din, was killed along with his entire family.

In 605/1227 the Mogul army again swept through Sistan. Niyaltegin was besieged in the Sistan fortress and fought for a year and seven months against the Mogul cavalry. During this siege, Niyaltegin was injured, captured, and eventually executed. The Moguls took the fortress, killed its defenders, laid waste the inhabited areas of Sistan as much as they could, and then returned home.[15]

Yet again during the period 610–631/1232–1253, Ogatay Khan appointed Tahir Khan Bahadur, an officer of the Mogul cavalry based at Badghis, to remove Faraja Hajib, one of the officers of Sultan Jalal ad-Din who had been conducting guerilla warfare against the Moguls. Faraja Hajib skirmished with Tahir Bahadur, but internal rivalry among the Mogul princes caused him to turn back from Sistan, occasioning instant relief among the people of Sistan.

After the repeated depredations of the Moguls in Sistan, the city of Jalalabad became the new capital of the local princes of Sistan,[16] until Amir Timur Gurgani (i.e., Tamerlane), the last of the Mogul conquerors, devastated Sistan in 761/1383. He not only destroyed Jalalabad and Band-i Rustam, which spanned the Helmand one day's travel from the city of Zaranj, but also totally destroyed the irrigation system of the area, so that no one was able afterwards to restore it.[17]

Sistan from the Time of the Timurids to the Twentieth Century

Accounts indicate that during the seventeenth and eighteenth centuries, little outside attention was directed at Sistan. The inhabitants of the area could not overcome the incursions of shifting sands, driven by the "Wind of 120 Days" from the northwest to the southeast with an average speed of 50 km per hour.[18] It is for this reason that those few irrigation networks which had been reconstructed following their destruction by Tamerlane became sand blocked, thus forcing a decline in the fortunes of Sistan that continues to this day.[19]

It is therefore to be noted that in the past Sistan has usually been a part of empires whose capitals have been at times in Afghanistan and at other times in Iran, but has also occasionally been independent and free from the authority of others. Neighboring territories have also from time to time come under the control of Sistan. During the Saffarid period, regions bordering Sistan—such as Zamindawar, Zabulistan, and Rokhj—were administered by the Saffarid kings, who themselves sprang from Sistan. Following the murder of Nader Shah Afshar in 1125/1747, Sistan came under the dominion of Ahmad Shah Abdali. Ahmad Shah appointed Malik Solaiman Kayani governor of Sistan and married his daughter. But in the ensuing change of authority between Malik Solaiman and the Sarbandi and Shohraki headmen, whom Nader had brought to Sistan from Fars, there was much discord. This trouble continued until finally Timur Shah seized power from the Kayani family and turned the province over to the Shohraki khans. After the death of Timur Shah, the governorship of Sistan was under the control and authority of the Afghan governors in Lash and Juwain,[20] restored to Malik Bahram of the Kayani line.[21]

The struggles between the chiefs of the Sarbandi and Shohraki Baluchi tribes and the Kayani family lasted until 1216/1838, when Jalal ad-Din, the last Kayani governor among Bahram's successors, was expelled from Sistan by the Sarbandis. Thenceforth, power in Sistan was in the hands of the local khans but influenced by the rivalry between the amirs of Herat and Kandahar. During the course of this dispute, 'Ali Khan, one of the Sarbandi leaders in Sistan, joined with the Iran government and raised the flag of Iran over his fortress in Seh Kuheh (Sahkuha).[22] 'Ali Khan acknowledged the authority of the government of Iran in that area and in 1231/1853 sent his son to Mashhad as surety. 'Ali Khan's governorship in that region so upset the Sistanis that he was killed and his wife wounded in an attack on his fortress in 1236/1858. Taj Mohammad Khan, son of Sardar Mohammad Reza Khan, who was 'Ali Khan's nephew and who had also taken part in the murder, assumed power in 'Ali Khan's stead. The wounded widow was taken to Tehran by a special agent of the Iranian government. No action was taken toward removing Taj Mohammad Khan from power for his suspected complicity in the murder. For a period, Taj Mohammad Khan ruled independently and without ties with the government of Iran, but when Dust Mohammad Khan, the Amir of Afghanistan, made advances towards Herat in 1240/1862, he took fright and declared his allegiance to the government of Iran. With the help of the Qajars, Sultan Ahmad Khan took control in Herat. For ten months Amir Dust Mohammad Khan fought with him, until Sultan Ahmad Khan and his two sons were defeated, and Herat fell to Amir Dust Mohammad Khan. In 1241/1863 Amir Dust Mohammad Khan died, and Amir Shir 'Ali Khan came to power in his place. At the same time, a falling out occurred between Taj Mohammad Khan and the officers dispatched there by the Iranian government, a circumstance that caused Taj Mohammad Khan to incline towards Afghanistan. Since Shir 'Ali Khan was preoccupied with internal matters, he was unable to offer significant aid to the people of Sistan, and so Taj Mohammad Khan again joined with the Iranian government.[23]

In 1243/1865 the government of Iran dispatched troops to punish the rebellion of Azad Khan, who in Sistan had fomented anarchy and unrest, particularly among the Kayanis. The governor of Kerman went there in 1244/1866 under orders from the government of Iran, and Mozaffer ad-Daula was sent from Neh, in the neighborhood of the Helmand Basin, at the head of two companies of soldiers. In this manner the major portion of Sistan gradually came under the military control of Iran. Eventually, a number of sons and kinsmen of Sistani khans were sent to Tehran. Similarly, Taj Mohammad Khan and his brother Kohandil Khan were seized during a visit with the governor of Mashhad and dispatched to the capital.[24]

Throughout this period in Afghanistan, tribal warfare and internal strife were rampant (e.g., the insurrection of the Mohmands in 1241/1863). Mohammadza'i brothers were at each other's throats for control; Sardar Mohammad A'zam Khan, Sardar Mohammad Afzal Khan, Sardar Mohammad Amin Khan, Amir 'Abd ur-Rahman Khan, and Amir Shir 'Ali Khan fought with each other nine times between 1241/1863 and 1245/1867.[25] Therefore Shir 'Ali Khan never had the opportunity to clarify his position vis-à-vis the Iranian government, who took the chance to occupy completely the major portion of Sistan. At the end of the internal disturbances, Shir 'Ali Khan intended to resolve the situation through the use of force. The British government undertook arbitration of the matter and put a halt to this plan of Shir 'Ali Khan's.[26]

British Rule and the Partition of Sistan

On 31 January 1872, the commission for establishing the boundary between Iran and Afghanistan, under the leadership of Sir Frederic Goldsmid, began its work. Included as members in the commission were: Major Oliver St. John, engineer; Beresford Lovett, of the Armed Forces of Madras; W. T. Blanford, of the Indian Geological Institute; Major Evan Smith of the Armed Forces of Madras; Sayyid Nur Muhammad Shah Fushanji, prime minister at the time and representative of the government of Afghanistan; Mirza Ma'sum Khan (and later Mirza Malkom Khan), representative of the government of Iran.[27]

The survey and work of the Commission continued until 25 April 1872 and took three months. After conducting investigations and polling the representatives of the two governments, Frederic Goldsmid, on 19 August 1872, elaborated his decision as follows:

Chapter 1: History of Sistan

The definition of "Sistan" is nowadays no simple matter. It has become vague and distorted, the previous borders of Sistan have disappeared, and the present definition of Sistan is merely that of the Helmand peninsula and Basin. In my opinion there are no more than two regions: one is a populous and fertile area that I call "Inner Sistan"; the other is arid and sparsely populated, and can be called "Secondary" or "Outer Sistan." Inner Sistan is in the north and west reaches of the Basin and its reed beds and is separated from Lash, Juwain, and Neh Bandan by the Basin. On the south it is bounded by the Basin, and later by the Sangbar Plain and the barren region of Sekuha and Borj-i 'Alam Khan. On the east it is bounded below the large dam by the old course of the Helmand River. Outer Sistan comprises the lands on the right bank of the Helmand River, and in the north it begins with the area of Charboli and the Khaspas River and extends southwards for 120 miles and reaches as far as Rudbar. The width of this territory is insignificant when compared with its length and, in fact, its limits are set in the west by the river and in the east by the agricultural regions. The width [of the area] near Chakhansur, from the old course of the Helmand River, including Nad-i 'Ali to Kadeh (Kadah), is approximately 30 miles.[28]

The Plain of Sistan, meaning the low-lying area known as Gaud-i Zirreh and Shela Rud formed by the flow of water from the Basin to Gaud-i Zirreh, may be added to Outer Sistan.

Inner Sistan, which is completely occupied by Iran, and whose governor is Mir 'Alam Khan, should, in my opinion, belong to Iran, and Outer Sistan, along with the Sistan Plain and Shela Rud, most of which is barren and unpopulated, should belong to Afghanistan.

In Outer Sistan, a few Baluchi *sardars* hold power, some of whom are supporters of the government of Iran, while others would not recognize anything but the authority of Afghanistan. I put no trust in the declaration of Kamal Khan and Imam Khan, the khans of Bandar and Charburjak, regarding the authority of the Iranian government in those areas. The fortress of Nad-i 'Ali on the right bank of the Helmand River which was recently occupied should be given up by the Iranian forces and handed over to Afghanistan so that some sort of balance may be maintained.[29]

Goldsmid's decision was rejected by the representatives of the governments of both Afghanistan and Iran, and the matter was postponed.

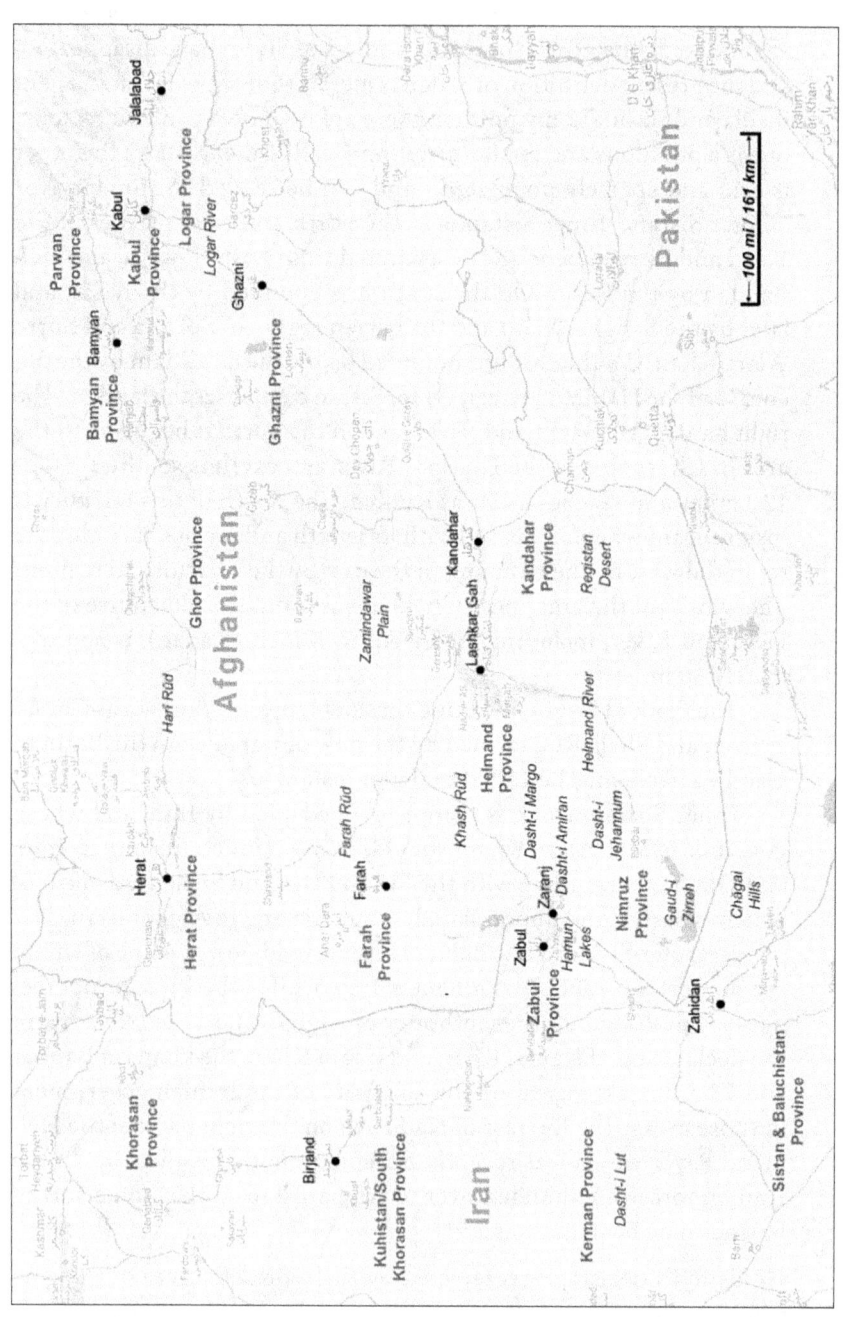

Map 1.1 Sistan and the surrounding region. Map by Joshua Allen.

Chapter 1: History of Sistan

In the summer of 1251/1873, the Shah of Iran journeyed to England, and the British queen obtained the Shah's agreement to Goldsmid's decision. Despite having reservations about the accord, the Amir of Afghanistan eventually announced his acceptance.

The imaginary border that had been established by Goldsmid's commission consisted of a single line beginning with Kuh-i Malik Siyah in the south and continuing north in such a way that the agricultural lands on both banks of the Helmand River up to Band-i Kuhak all became part of Afghanistan; thereafter the Helmand River forms the frontier and provides Iranian Sistan its eastern border. North of that, the edges of the southern reed beds of the Helmand Basin make up some of the border in the direction of Lash and Juwain, and another line from the reed beds to Kuh-i Malik Siyah near Bandan forms the border between the two countries.

It was noted in regard to the water of the Helmand River that neither party would take measures that adversely impact the amount of water required for agricultural use of the other side.

As the result of a massive flood in 1274/1896, the Helmand River abandoned its original channel, i.e., the Nad-i 'Ali Rud, and established a new channel to the west that came to be known as the Pariyan Rud. Contention, therefore, arose between Afghanistan and Iran over water distribution and the location of the frontier. The Iranian government, which according to the 1235/1857 Treaty of Paris with Britain was obliged to submit to Britain's arbitration in any dispute between itself and Afghanistan, sought Britain's decision. Afghanistan's Amir 'Abd ur-Rahman Khan also agreed to Britain's mediation. Britain appointed Colonel Henry McMahon to establish the groundwork with Afghan and Iranian representatives.[30] In January 1281/1903, McMahon set to work, and after placing border markers (110 miles in the plain and mountainous regions and 100 miles over areas such as lakes and rivers) delivered the final pronouncement of his mediation in February 1283/1905.[31]

Earlier in 1240/1862 on the basis of Goldsmid's mediation, the Iranian government gained a share in a 50 kilometer (31 mile) stretch of the lower Helmand River water. The amount of water that Iran got from the river was limited in Goldsmid's agreement to that required for agricultural needs. McMahon, however, specified that the Iranian government was entitled to one third of the Helmand River waters at Bandar-i Kamal Khan, and hastily recognized the old channel of the Helmand River as the border between Afghanistan and Iran.

In this manner and according to British dictates, one third of the Helmand's water and more than a third of the land of Sistan was severed from the body of Afghanistan and joined to the territory of Iran. Between 1272/1894 and 1274/1896, McMahon also established a border of about 800 miles (1,280 km) between Afghanistan and Baluchistan, from the banks of the Gomal River to Kuh-i Malik Siyah. The representative of the government of Afghanistan with McMahon was Sardar Gol Muhammad Khan. No direct consultations in this matter ever took place between them; they never even saw each other, in spite of the fact that in the previous agreement it was determined that the marking of the border would be done by a joint team. In the setting of this boundary line, McMahon removed from Afghanistan the 19,000 square mile (49,000 square km) Chaghi region,[32] which was occupied entirely by Afghans, and granted it to British Baluchistan.[33]

The British settlement, with the partitioning of Sistan and the apportioning of Helmand River waters to the government of Iran, was to have unfortunate consequences, for it became a source of contention between the two neighbors. The settlement, once in effect, would from time to time give rise to new protests on the part of the Iranian government. In 1316/1938, a new dispute arose and Baqer Kazemi, the representative of the Iranian government, had talks in Kabul at the Afghanistan Ministry of Foreign Affairs. The Afghan representative, Minister of Foreign Affairs 'Ali Muhammad Khan, and the Persian ambassador signed a sixteen-point agreement, the first point of which was as follows: "The two states of Afghanistan and Iran agree that throughout the year every drop of water in the Helmand River reaching Bandar Kamal Khan shall be divided equally between Iran and Afghanistan from Bandar Kamal Khan onwards."[34]

In this way half of the water of the Helmand River was ceded by Afghanistan to Iran, but the dispute was not completely settled. In 1344/1966, the subject of the division of the waters of the Helmand River between Afghanistan and Iran was again raised, and on 23 Hut 1351/14 March 1973 an agreement between the two states was signed, comprising twelve articles and two supplementary protocols.[35]

Chapter 1: History of Sistan

Notes

1 *The Encyclopaedia of Islam*, 1934, Vol. IV, p. 35. GRA
2 Heravi, *The Geography of Hafiz Abru*, Publications of the Iranian Cultural Foundation, 1349/1971, p. 51. GRA
3 The Chaghi Hills of Baluchistan in Pakistan. WBT
4 Tate, *Seistan*, 1910–1912, pp. 108–9. GRA. This is a broad delineation, including the Dasht-i Margo within Sistan. WBT
5 *The Encyclopaedia Britannica*, 11th ed., 1911, p. 593. GRA. The Helmand-Sistan Project contract concession area encompassed approximately 40,000 square miles, but its actual work was primarily dictated by the course of the Helmand River and the lands which at one time had been irrigated with its waters. We were unable within the time frame to conduct extensive surveys in the Registan to the south of Kandahar, nor did there seem much profit in investigating the Dasht-i Margo after crossing it eight times between 1966 and 1974. WBT
6 Kohzad, *The History of Afghanistan*, Vol. 2, 1325/1947, p. 142. GRA
7 Tate, *Seistan*, 1910–1912, p. 183. GRA. This is somewhat a paraphrase; the full quote goes thus:

> There are however two other, and probably more ancient, names for this country of Seistan. One is Nimruz and the other Zarī. The latter is more ancient than the first. From it was derived the form Drangiana used by Greek and Latin authors, and this form was introduced to the West by the writers whose records formed the basis of the detailed accounts which we possess of the expedition of Alexander. The Arab conquerors also found the name Zarī in existence when they added Seistan to the dominions of the Caliphs, but they altered the name into Zaranj and in this form the name appears in the early chronicles which mention this country. From Zarī we get Zirreh, a form that is still in existence, but which is in common use in a restricted sense. The Gaud-i Zirreh means the Hollow of Zirreh, but while it would apply to the whole of Seistan its use is confined to the depression to the south of the Lake ... The antiquity of the name Zarī is established by the discovery, in the famous inscription of Darius Hystaspes, of the word Zranka as the name for Seistan. WBT

8 Ghobar, *Afghanistan in the Course of History*, 1346/1968, p. 45. GRA
9 Ghobar, *Afghanistan in the Course of History*, 1346/1968, p. 46. GRA
10 *The Encyclopaedia of Islam*, Vol. IV, 1936, pp. 458-9. GRA
11 For the best study of the sources for the Arab conquest of Sistan see Bosworth (1968). WBT
12 Bahar, ed. *The History of Sistan*, 1314/1936, p. 148. GRA
13 His armies resided at Bust and Lashkari Bazar during the cool time of the year, and from this location they were within relatively easy striking distance of Sistan to the west, Ghur to the north, but rather less so India. WBT
14 Lashkar Gah is the contemporary town at the northern edge of Lashkari Bazar. The author means to refer to the metropolitan district of Lashkari

Bazar and Bust, which stretched for several miles along the east bank of the Helmand. WBT

15 Ghobar, *Afghanistan in the Course of History*, 1346/1968, p. 220. GRA. It is probably at this time that Shahr-i Golghola, the largest and most heavily fortified outpost city of Sistan, fell. Certainly there is ample evidence for its destruction at the hands of the Mongol army. WBT

16 Uncertainly identified. It may have been in the Iranian portion of Sistan, possibly near modern Zabul (formerly called Jalalabad), or the substantially fortified town of Zahedan in the delta, possessing a large and high *bala hissar* (citadel). WBT

17 Ghobar, *Afghanistan in the Course of History*, 1346/ 1968, p. 221. GRA. A popular but erroneous belief based on historical writings. The simple *bands* (weirs) of the Helmand may be destroyed (as they were almost every year in the annual spring flood), but they are easily repaired. Canals may be breached and lands flooded, but they are easily repaired. Man cannot easily destroy so complex and vast an irrigation system as had existed for millennia in Sistan, but human neglect can; since canals have constantly to be maintained. There is considerable evidence that the canal systems of Sistan were neglected for nearly a century after the earlier Mongol invasions, not because they had been destroyed, but because life had become too uncertain in this region to invest in labor-intensive activities of large-scale canal repair and the planting of vast fields of grain, vulnerable to any invader. By the time Tamerlane stormed through Sistan, there was probably not much of the irrigation network in operation. While he may have severely damaged what remained, in the following century the entire network was restored, and the archaeological remains studied by the Helmand Sistan Project indicate that the fifteenth century was one of extraordinary prosperity in the Sistan Basin. WBT

18 The *bad-i sad-o-bist ruz*, or "Wind of 120 Days," blows every year from late May until late September, day and night, sometimes abating for a few hours only. While 50 kph may constitute an average wind intensity over the full period, more violent periods of winds in excess of 100 kph are frequent. Nor are these violent wind storms restricted to this part of the year. In March 1905, the Perso-Afghan Arbitration Commission experienced a storm with an average wind over a course of 18 hours of 140 kph and a maximum velocity of 193 kph (McMahon 1906, p. 224). There is no evidence to suggest these winds are a phenomenon of historical times. Evidence of aeolian deposits may be read in the fault marking the western edge of the Dasht-i Margo, a cliff in places 400 feet high and exposing hundreds of thousands, if not millions, of years of geological history. Our project geologist, John Whitney, attempted to measure the impact of this constant, strong wind on sand dunes. Adjusted yearly, an average dune 4 m high moves approximately 30 cm per day, over 100 m per annum.

Our archaeological field season, normally from mid-September till mid-December, was selected for being the longest period of benign weather in the region. Yet severe storms were encountered at least once each month, and in 1974 winds of 24 kph to 40 kph plagued us two days out of three. WBT.

Chapter 1: History of Sistan

Wind of 120 Days is discussed further in Chapter 2. See also Whitney 2006 for more information on wind patterns. MA

19 The cause for the decline toward the end of the fifteenth century is more complicated than the presence of sand blocking the canals, but certainly this was a factor. The subject will be discussed in the archaeological report from the Helmand Sistan Project, expected publication in 2021. WBT

20 Lash and Juwain are two small towns to the north of the Hamun-i Sabari at the west and the Hamun-i Puzak at the east. Lash, now in ruins, clings to the sides of a high cliff at the west side of the Farah Rud, which flows into the Hamun-i Sabari. Across the river and in the plain slightly to the north of Lash is the modern village of Juwain. Captain Edward Conolly was the first European to visit Lash in 1839 (Conolly 1841). He describes it thus (p. 332):

> The fort is built on the edge of a high 'cliff' immediately under which flows the Furrah river; on the East face it has the perpendicular cliff, over which are erected buildings to a height of perhaps 400 feet; and a great deal of these will, I suspect, fall down the precipice in another year, for the water in the spring cuts below, weakening of course the upper bank, and already several ominous cracks may be observed. I pointed this out to the *Khan*, and recommended his turning the stream by a bank from immediate contact with the base of his castle; but he will doubtless forget the advice he promised to follow, till half his family are overwhelmed by the fall of his house. The N. and W. faces are detached from the high plain beyond them by a deep ravine; but the S. side offers but little obstruction to a regular army. Laush is an ancient place, though I do not remember its name mentioned in history. The cliff on which it stands has many caves cut in it, and there are said to be subterranean passages, to which perhaps the women of the garrison could retire in case of its being attempted to shell the fort; but most of these passages have neither fallen in, nor been stopped up.

Lash is twice mentioned in the *Tārikh-i Sistān* (Gold 1976, pp. 329, 331), here it is already considered to be of great antiquity. In the caves and passages cited by Conolly, whether mainly intact or collapsed (his text states the former but it is unclear that is what he intended), one is tempted to speculate that they might have been Buddhist in origin. But there is no corroborative evidence, and I know of no other traveler to have visited the site. Juwain, also mentioned in the *Tārikh-i Sistan*, may be of equal age. The possibility is that Lash and Juwain, so close and yet situated so distinctively geographically, may originally have been inhabited by the same people. Juwain, though fortified by a substantial wall, lies in the Farah Rud plain closer to agricultural lands. Lash may thus, in fact, have served as *bala hissar* to Juwain in times of attack. WBT

21 Heravi, *The Geography of Hafiz Abru*, 1971, p. 60. GRA

22 The modern village of Sehkuha, to the south of Zabul in Iranian Sistan, contains at its center a citadel, probably constructed on an ancient tepe. Small mud houses of the contemporary residents are clustered around the base of

this citadel. WBT
23 *Encyclopaedia of Islam*, Vol. IV, 1934, p. 460. GRA
24 Goldsmid, *Eastern Persia: An Account of the Journeys of the Persian Boundary Commission 1870-71-72*, 1876, pp. 406–7. GRA
25 Ghobar, *Afghanistan in the Course of History*, 1346/ 1968, pp. 511-70. GRA
26 Singhal, *India and Afghanistan (1876-1907)*, 1963, p. 10. GRA
27 Goldsmid, *Eastern Persia*, 1876. WBT
28 *Encyclopaedia Britannica*, 11th ed., 1911, pp. 592-3. GRA
29 Goldsmid, *Eastern Persia*, 1876, pp. 407–12. GRA. These paragraphs are a condensation and paraphrase of the original summary of the Boundary Commission arbitration decision appearing on those pages of the Goldsmid volume. MA
30 McMahon, "Recent Survey and Exploration in Seistan," *The Geographical Journal*, Vol. XXVIII. No. 4, 1906, p. 336. GRA
31 Singhal, *India and Afghanistan (1876–1907)*, 1963, p. 168. GRA
32 Yate, "Baluchistan," *Proceedings of the Central Asian Society (1906)*, 1906, p. 4. GRA
33 Singhal, *India and Afghanistan*, 1963, p.152. GRA
34 Ghobar, *Afghanistan in the Course of History*, 1346/1968, pp.735-37. GRA
35 Amiri's original Dari manuscript contained his translation of the full text of this agreement. Rather than reprinting here, readers are directed to an English version of this document online at https://www.internationalwaterlaw.org/documents/regionaldocs/1973_Helmand_River_Water_Treaty-Afghanistan-Iran.pdf. MA
The original document was published in Dari in Kabul from *Publications of the Public Relations Office, Ministry of Information and Culture, History and Documents Pertaining to the Helmand River Water*, 1352/1974, pp. 61–4. GRA/MA

Chapter 2
Geography of the Helmand Basin

The Helmand Basin region is situated in the southwest section of Afghanistan and embraces the areas adjoining the lower reaches of the Helmand River from Darwishan onwards and including Afghan Sistan. The region is located roughly between latitude 29°50' and 31°15' north and longitude 61°45' and 65° east.

The area is generally sloping from the northeast to the extreme southwest gradually with an altitude of 11,500 feet (3,500 m) near the source of the Helmand River to 1,500 feet (450 m) in the Sistan deserts where it ends. The flow of rivers in southwest Afghanistan is in line with that of the Helmand,[1] the waters of which collect in the Sistan Basin, covering an area exceeding 125,000 square miles (325,000 square km).[2] The lowest part is located at the Basin region in the environs of the Irano-Afghan border.

The Basin contains four water reservoirs, or *hamuns*. Chahar Kiseh Basin contains the deepest water reservoir. To the east is the Puzak Basin, and in the northwest corner, the Sabiri Basin. The Sabiri Basin was named after a king of Sistan known as Sabir Shah, and the ruins of his fortress may be seen at times of low water. The final reservoir, Kiseh-i Sivvomi, is to the north of Kuh-i Khwaja, separated from the Sabiri Basin by the Sangi River. This collection of reservoirs in the declivity forms the Helmand Basin. The Helmand Basin is situated within Sistan's borders and occupies a portion of it. In general, three rivers terminate in the basin after having irrigated the vast lands on their banks. The water reserve of the basin is dependent upon the amount of water deposited by these three rivers, especially the Helmand, and it is not constant. In 1280/1902, when the Helmand River was dry for sixty-two days, the Helmand Basin also dried up, and in the Sabiri Basin, which forms the deepest portion of the Helmand Basin area, the water also disappeared, and all the fish in the lake perished. In 1281/1903, the quantity of water in Helmand at Sistan reached 80,000 cubic feet (2,265 cubic meters) per second, and the area which the Basin covered expanded to 2,000 square miles (5,200 square km). In contrast, in 1282/1904, when the amount of water in the Helmand River was somewhat more than half the quantity of 1281/1903, the area of water coverage in the Helmand Basin reached only 1,200 square miles (3,100 square km).[3] During the period of high water, the Helmand Basin measures roughly 100 miles (160 km) in length and from 5 to 15 miles, (8 to 24 km) in width.[4] On these occasions, its waters flow from a channel called Shela Rud, the width of which is on average approximately 350 m (1,150 ft), and the shoreline of which in some instances has a height of about 50 m (165 ft), into Gaud-i Zirreh.

Like the Helmand, the Shela Rud at times of high water is wide and brackish. It flows in parallel to the Helmand but in the opposite direction because of the relative elevations. At times of low water, the Helmand Basin is limited to only two reservoirs, the Sabiri Basin and the Puzak Basin.[5]

As a result of the fluctuations of water in the Helmand Basin, sometimes a vast area is under water, sometimes a small one. Consequently, except in places where there are stone cliffs, the perimeters of the basin are constantly subject to change with the rise and fall of the water level. The areas surrounding the Helmand Basin temporarily under water are called *ashkin* (wetlands), and reeds of the best sort for animal fodder grow there in abundance (Fig. 2.1).

A detailed survey of Sistan and a study of long ridges of sand and traces of successive inundations in the upper portions of the depressions,

Figure 2.1. Firing of reed beds in the *ashkin* (wetlands) around the Hamun-i Puzak, Nimruz Province, autumn 1974.

Chapter 2: Geography of the Helmand Basin

meaning the shores of ancient lakes, clearly shows that the area of water coverage in the past was greater than at present and, likewise, that the depth of the water was greater. The area of water coverage today is, in fact, barely a third of what it once was.[6] The studied traces of water levels to the east are present along the edges of the Dasht-i Margo and to the west on the slopes and foothills of Kuh-i Khwaja. These traces, tied to various geological periods, are also present in the gravelly ridges of the Helmand delta area that occupy a significant portion of that area, indicating that much of the delta was once under water. Because the present level of sediment in the delta is approximately 400 feet (120 m) lower than the ancient level of sediment in Sistan, it is certain that the entire delta was for a while under water. According to McMahon, the reason for this disparity is the sinking of the level of the present-day sediment caused by the weight of sediments in the vicinity. The amount of clay and mud that the Helmand carries along during flood periods is roughly equivalent to one part in 127 parts of water, a figure rarely equaled in other rivers of the world.[7] The amount of sediment borne by the Helmand in a single year would cover an area of ten square miles (approximately 24 square km) with a layer one foot thick (about 30.5 cm).[8] Recently, after the construction of the Kajaki Dam, the greater part of the sediment is collected in the dam reservoir, and less is carried to the lower reaches of the Helmand.

A large amount of water gathers in the Helmand Basin in the spring flood season, whereas it is small at the beginning of winter. The most important factor here is the exposure of the lake to the extreme heat, dryness, and the strong winds of Sistan. It is calculated that in the course of an average year, a ten-foot layer (about 3.5 m) of the lake's water evaporates. Stated another way, in an average year, a lake having a depth of ten feet would dry up completely.[9]

Over the ages, the Helmand River, the Farah Rud, and the Khash Rud have each created a delta in Sistan that now form agricultural land and living areas for the people. Of these deltas, Lash and Juwain, along the Farah Rud, and Chakhansur, above the Khash Rud, are in Afghan territory. Inner Sistan, the great delta of the Helmand River, has since 1250/1872 belonged to Iran,[10] two thirds of it being alluvial land and the remaining third raised and covered with gravels. The Helmand River has also created a delta in Afghan Sistan, northward from the vicinity of Charburjak and Bandar-i Kamal Khan. The presence of the last-mentioned delta has shown the change in direction of the Helmand River towards the north. The history of this delta has been estimated to be from 3000 BC based on

Table 2.1

Evaporation Rates in Southwest Afghanistan, by Month

	Jan	Feb	Mar	Apr	May	Jun	Jul	Aug	Sep	Oct	Nov	Dec	Totals
Chah Anjir 1951–1955	60.0 (2.4)	88.0 (3.4)	138.0 (5.4)	242.0 (9.5)	338.0 (13.3)	474.0 (18.6)	342.0 (17.0)	386.0 (15.1)	286.0 (11.2)	214.0 (8.6)	149.0 (5.9)	71.0 (2.9)	2,994 (117.9)
Farah 1970	67.0 (2.6)	78.0 (3.0)	135.0 (5.3)	163.0 (6.4)	264.0 (10.4)	381.0 (15.0)	414.0 (16.3)	366.0 (14.4)	288.0 (11.3)	197.0 (7.8)	125.0 (4.9)	90.0 (3.5)	2,568 (101.1)
Lashkar Gah 1955–1970	85.0 (3.4)	100.0 (4.0)	169.0 (6.6)	227.4 (8.9)	332.7 (13.1)	430.3 (16.9)	441.0 (17.4)	398.0 (15.7)	309.0 (12.2)	216.0 (8.5)	118.0 (4.6)	93.0 (3.7)	2,920 (115.9)

First figure indicates evaporation in millimeters. (Figures in parentheses indicate inches.) Due to conditions of climate, evaporation exceeds precipitation. Source: Report of the *Survey and Study of the Land and Water of the Helmand River*, part one, pp. 2–15. Available online at http://scottshelmandvalleyarchives.org/docs/evl-76-11.pdf

Chapter 2: Geography of the Helmand Basin

evidence of excavations. Moreover, in the twists and turns of this river as far as Chakhansur, other older deltas have come to light. The thickness of the sedimentary layer in Afghan Sistan reaches 8 m; beneath this may be found a conglomerate layer from 3 to 6 m thick.[11]

The ancient channel of the Helmand River was that of the Rud-i Biyaban. Today, this channel is remembered on account of the existence of a large water source known as the Trakhun Canal. The route of the Helmand River above its delta has undergone numerous shifts, causing changes in the fortunes of the delta and in conditions of life. These fluctuations were merely local ones, however, and the more general situation was little affected. From brief descriptions of events connected with the Arab victories in Sistan, it is known that in the eighth century AD the Helmand River flowed above its own north delta, but it is not known with any certainty just when the changes occurred in its course. All that can be said is that the Helmand River probably towards the end of the eleventh century again followed the channel of the Rud-i Biyaban. Due to the need for water for the inhabitants, as noted in estate documents of the day, the Rustam Dam was built to divert the water to its old route. The dam was destroyed in 761/1383 by the forces of Tamerlane. Later, another dam was found necessary, and Band-i Balbaka was built from the right bank near Rudbar, although a large portion of the water still passed along the route of the Rud-i Biyaban toward the Gaud-i Zirreh. Later, during the thirty-year period between 1070/1692 and 1100/1722, the Helmand River reverted to its old northward channel and remains there to this day.[12]

The deltas of the Farah Rud and the Helmand River are joined by a ridge or raised area, being a result of sedimentation caused by the two channels coming together. At the north side of the ridge is the road to and from Sistan that carries much of Sistan's trade. Because the rise in this elevation is gradual, it is sometimes difficult to observe, but the opportunity to distinguish the rise and fall of water in the basin is clear. The other ridge connected with the Helmand delta and the small delta is formed by the flow of the waters of the Baluchan and the Trashap in the west. Also noteworthy is the fact that this elevated area was formed by the sedimentation of an extension of an ancient Helmand canal and became the barrier between the Sistan Basin and Gaud-i Zirreh. It is for this reason that it is only during periods of very high water with fierce winds that water from the Helmand Basin is able to flow over the above-mentioned higher elevation, through the channel named the Shela Rud, to the lower Gaud-i Zirreh area.[13]

If the delta of the Helmand and all other rivers that flow into the basin

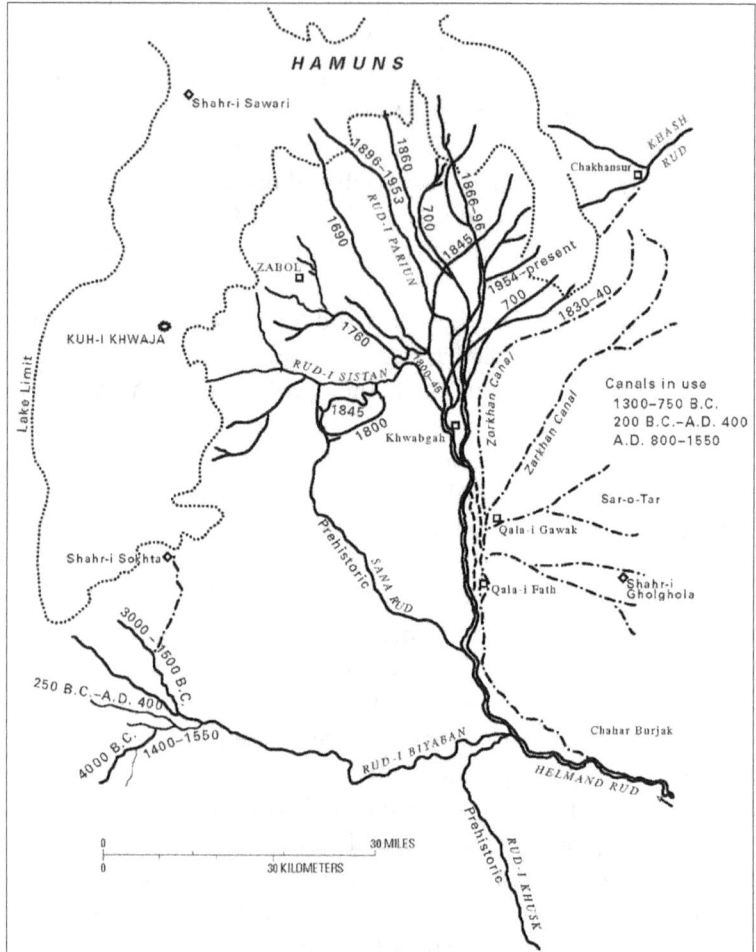

Map 2.1 Historical channels and major canals on the Lower Helmand River. Whitney 2006, Figure 18.

were looked at as a whole, it would be seen that the greatest portion of the area is taken up by the above deltas and, in fact, in all of the region under our consideration, those elevated areas, wind-eroded and covered with gravel, and those low-lying areas were each formed by sedimentation during various geological periods.[14]

Below Bust the Helmand has no tributary and from that point flows to Sha'ad, after a half circle towards the Sistan Basin, which is situated in the same latitude as Bust. The lower sections of the Helmand are along the southern edges of the plain, which starts from the foothills of the mountainous

Chapter 2: Geography of the Helmand Basin

region of Zamindawar and Ghur and descends to the south from there.[15] The left bank of the Helmand between Bust and the village of Landi Muhammad Amin Khan has little elevation and is silted from the sand dunes, after which the river changes course and goes steadily west. A little below Landi, the river enters a narrow valley, the sides of which have scattered stone escarpments; moreover, its northern side consists of a high plain with sharp rises and falls. On the southern side of the valley there is a high, level plain. From this point on for 36 to 40 miles (58 to 64 km) toward the Sistan delta, the river bed lies in a valley which is 1 to 2 miles (1.6 to 3.2 km) wide and is deeper by about 200 feet (60 m) than its surrounding plain.[16]

From the area of Khwaja 'Ali toward the delta, the Helmand Valley is separated on the left from the Gaud-i Zirreh declivity by a narrow strip of high flat desert. In the region of Rudbar, the river valley is approximately 300 feet (90 m) higher than the declivity of the Gaud-i Zirreh; however, at no time has the river found a route from here to the Gaud-i Zirreh.

At the point where the Helmand leaves the narrows it divides into two branches and is located on a plateau higher than the present Sistan delta. At the highest point of the plateau between two promontories on the sides of the river valley (which at this point opens out and comes to an end) and in the vicinity of a plain made up of sediment, there comes into sight remains of a small fortress built by Kamal Khan, one of the chiefs of the Sanjrani Baluchi tribe. This place was in the past a center or stopping place for caravans that came to Sistan from the border region, or even from Makran, to buy grains and exchange their animal products for wheat and barley. It is for this reason that the region was called *bandar* (port) and is still known as Bandar-i Kamal Khan.

The terrace that forms the southern bank of the Helmand here is abruptly broken, and the upper levels of it are approximately 200 feet (60 m) high. The northern bank of the Helmand River valley is formed from Deshu and Malakhan to near Bandar-i Kamal Khan by the southern slopes of the Dasht-i Margo. Near Bandar on the eastern side, the edge of the plain along the north changes, and in the vicinity of Qala-i Fath, its steepness increases. Later, the eastern edge turns back to connect with the desert declivities that form the limit of Sistan's eastern foothills. This tongue of desert, known as Meski, has an elevation 200 feet (60 m) greater than that of the Helmand river bed near Bandar.

After Bandar-i Kamal Khan, the Helmand turns north for a distance of 35 miles (56 km) and flows alongside a *dasht* to its west. Afterwards, it arrives above its present delta, where the village of Khwabgah is situated 34 feet (10

m) above the river bed in a position where floods cannot easily reach it.

Soil studies in Sistan indicate that on account of wind erosion the more elevated desert regions have become bare of soil and covered with gravel, locally called *dasht*. In the lower lying lands and a few other areas may be found fine mixed soils (clay mixed with sand) that in this countryside provide for abundant grass, thorns, tamarisk, and shrubs specific to alkaline areas. In other areas, clay mixed with sand has been transformed into a white clay that renders the areas devoid of grass and shrubs. Because the external crust of land having this sort of clay is bereft of fissures where seed might enter, in some areas the topsoil has been completely eroded by wind, and conglomerate layers beneath may be noted.[17] In the areas being examined here, approximately 34,000 square km (13,100 square miles) are sand-covered (Fig. 2.2) and another roughly 14,000 square km (5,400 square miles) of *dasht* are barren and uncultivated.[18]

Climate

The area of the Helmand and Afghan Sistan has a desert climate and is contiguous with Afghanistan's other arid and semi-arid regions. During the summer, its weather is unusually warm, and in the winter it is very cold, though the broader region generally has warm summers and mild winters. Here, there are two distinct seasons: summer and winter; spring and autumn are not really distinguishable. In the space of a few hours, in fact, the frigid temperatures of winter can be transformed into summer heat, and in the same way summer heat can suddenly give way to winter.

Figure 2.2. The Sar-o-Tar sand sea, Nimruz Province, 1974.

Chapter 2: Geography of the Helmand Basin

For this reason, the inhabitants call the region the "Land of fans and fur coats." The popular phrase "fan and fur coat" has come down because on the same day the heat requires a fan and the cold a sheepskin.[19] Because the area is surrounded by arid lands, it has very little moisture and a vast temperature range; for example, on one day in 1349 (October 1971) the high temperature was between 40° and 50° C while at midnight the temperature dropped to below zero. This temperature change was most noticeable at sunset. On the above date, in the space of fifteen minutes there was a temperature drop of 10° to 18° C.

There is the same extreme range of temperatures between summer and winter. In the summer the temperatures can rise to 60° C, and in the winter fall to minus 25° C.[20] The humid winter and early spring climate is derived largely from the Mediterranean in the west and in part from the Persian Gulf. In the winter not much snow falls, the average snowfall not exceeding two to five inches and melting rapidly away. (See Table 2.2[21] and Appendix B.) Rain is heavy and of short duration; in one hour, 40 to 50 mm (1.6 to 2.0 in) may fall, and at such times the Helmand River and Khash Rud overflow their banks. Because of the heaviness of the rain on the region's soft soil, a hard crust is formed. Since the underneath layers are very hard and impenetrable, the amount of water absorbed into the soil is very small, and about 70 percent of the rainwater runs off the surface. The rain which occasionally falls during the summer is less heavy, in one hour about 10 mm may fall. The rains of summer are associated with the monsoons of the Indian subcontinent that on occasion reach the region. The annual precipitation in this region is from 70 to 150 mm (2.6 to 5.9 in), almost 90 percent of which is in the months of December to May (Appendix B). In contrast, the annual precipitation in Kandahar is 300 mm (11.8 in), in Kabul it is 500 mm (19.7 in), and in Kuh-i Baba where the Helmand starts, it is 800 mm (31.5 in).[22]

An important and noteworthy factor in the climate of this region is the wind. Local and intermittent winds begin during the month of October and continue until the end of May, but during June, July, August, and September, the climate is affected by the "120-day winds" that blow ceaselessly from the northwest, from 316.5° and 333.25° on the compass, meaning a little west of north.[23] At first, the direction of the wind is variable, but when it strengthens, the direction becomes fixed and does not change more than 5° in any direction. In the initial days these winds are dirtier because material loosened by winter freezing and subsequent thawing is carried away, along with dust and soil. Sometimes, it becomes

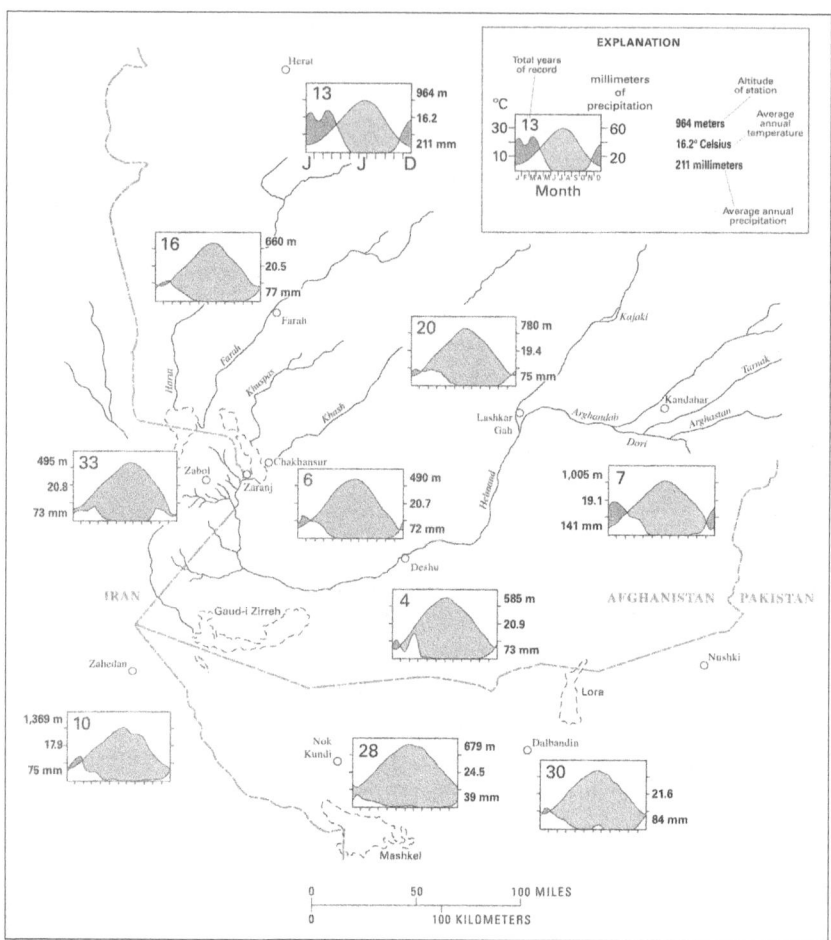

Table 2.2. Climate diagrams for the Helmand Basin and adjacent areas, from Whitney 2006, Fig. 10

stormy and visibility is reduced by the dust and soil to five to ten meters. This wind combined with dust and sand makes a very strange noise upsetting to those who hear it. The area covered by these winds is approximately 100 miles (160 km) wide and in the north reaches as far as Mashhad. The height of their ferocity is said to be at Lash and Juwain in the north, where the maximum speeds are about 70 mph (112 kph). On the other hand, in the south of Sistan their force and speed are less, and in the vicinity of Noshaki and Rabat, they are not felt. To the east they are sometimes felt in the plain of Delbandan.[24] Anyone who has travelled to Sistan or who has studied the area is no doubt familiar with these winds.

Chapter 2: Geography of the Helmand Basin

The effects of the wind on most places in Sistan is apparent, for hardly anything escapes its assaults; the homes of the people of Sistan, along with their historical buildings, are surely and ceaselessly ground down by these winds. Baked bricks, stone, mud, and other materials face the onslaught of the wind when unprotected, particularly those on the windward side of structures. They become polished and pitted, eventually becoming so diminished that they disappear. The wind and sand threaten the abodes of most people and so oppress the inhabitants that they leave those places. In the past, the people of Sistan were facing their homes according to the direction of the prevailing winds. The existence of these winds was also the reason for establishing windmills in this area. In addition to burying the houses and buildings under piles of sand, the winds occasionally have the opposite effect in that they sometimes uncover buildings and historical ruins that had long been buried beneath the desert. Each year in our investigations we came across at least one large or small structure that during the course of the year had been uncovered from the sand. It is certain that if we were to return now, there would be several newly uncovered structures waiting.

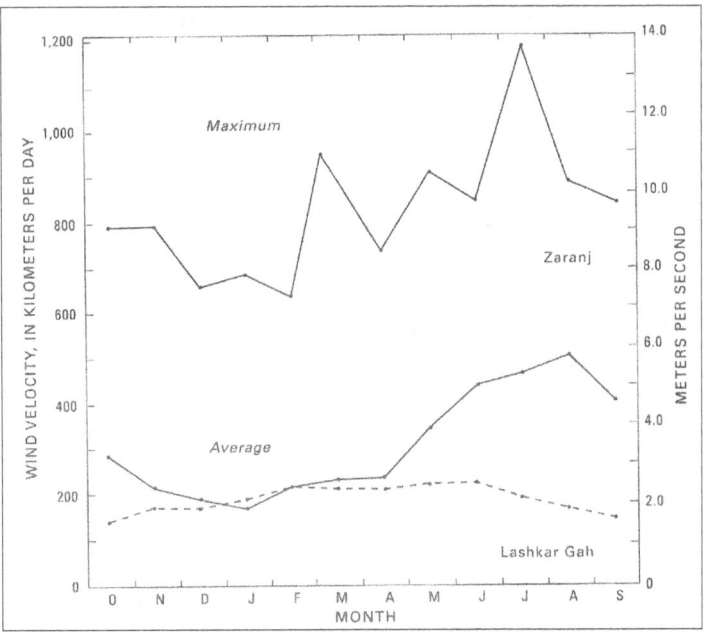

Table 2.3. Mean monthly wind velocities for Zaranj and Lashkar Gah. Maximum monthly wind velocities are shown for Zaranj, from Whitney 2006, Figure 11.

There are other winds besides the 120-day winds. During the winter there are occasional stiff, cold winds that the natives dub "black winds" that are severe and dangerous. In 1905 during the month of March, a barometric anemometer recorded maximum gust speeds of 120 mph, with an average speed during a 16-hour period of 88 mph (140 kph).[25] During the winter time, the ferocity of this black wind is such that large rivers freeze over and the rapid flow of their water is halted. In 1343/1965 during the month of January, the Shela Rud, with all its breadth and rapid movement, froze as a result of the black wind so that quadrupeds slipped and only with much difficulty were able to cross the river. Sometimes even towards the end of the month of April, the dangerous black wind begins to blow so that great damage is done to the animal herds; if perchance the cattle should at this time be in the reeds, the injury to the herds is particularly great, so much so that the inhabitants of the region have named the wind the "one in five cow killer."[26] This cruel factor of the climate and the accompanying change in water and the sudden extremes of heat and cold in Sistan occasion much loss among the livestock.

Because of the tremendous winds, it is only under extraordinary circumstances that trees grow naturally straight in Sistan. Those trees, which sometimes take root in the shelter of tamarisk or other shrubs alongside the rivers or lakes, lose their bark or moisture to the wind as soon as they rise above the surrounding foliage, and they therefore perish. For this reason, in most places in this area there are no trees to be found.

The Rivers

Of all the rivers found in the Sistan Basin the greatest is the Helmand. This river finds its origin in the southern branch of the Hindu Kush mountains, known as Kuh-i Baba, 60 km west of Kabul, near the wellspring of the Kabul River at an altitude of 11,500 feet (3,505 m).[27] The Kabul-Bamiyan road crosses the Helmand River about 20 miles (32 km) below the headwaters, and from the headwaters to this crossing the river bed falls approximately 100 feet (30 m), a drop of approximately 1.5 m per mile.[28]

On the northern edges of the Urt Plateau, the Ab-i Siyah creek, which derives from the Hajigak pass declivity, joins the Helmand. Later, the Helmand enters a deep wadi running alongside Baba mountain, about 35 miles (56 km) from Goch-i Khul (Ghaoch-Khol). In this area, the shores are adorned with roses and willow trees, and the waters of Trin and Garmab, which flow from the vicinity of Trin and Nish (Nesh) in the hills of Mt. Paghman, join it from the left. In this manner, the Helmand emerges onto

Chapter 2: Geography of the Helmand Basin

the flat plain of Zamindawar 40 miles (64 km) from Girishk, after boring through the gorges of great wide mountain valleys. From the vicinity of the main Kabul-Bamiyan road onwards to Girishk, the Helmand's elevation drops by about 35 feet (10 m) in each mile.[29] Here its other tributary, the Bugran, which has its headwaters in Siyah Kuh and waters the whole of the Zamindawar Plain from north to south, joins the Helmand. It is here that this joined river has a width of 900 m and flows at a rate of 35 to 50 cubic meters (1,250 to 1,750 cubic feet) per second (Appendix C and Table 2.4).[30]

During the years 1325/1947 to 1332/1954, a dam was built across the central channel of the Helmand near Kajaki. This dam forms a reservoir used particularly in new agricultural projects. About 45 miles (72 km) downstream from Girishk, the Arghandab River, a large tributary of the Helmand, joins it. Now it is possible to use the electrical energy of the river for the cities of Kandahar and Lashkar Gah. From Girishk to this point, the river bed drops approximately six feet (1.8 m) per mile.[31] From Bust onwards, the Helmand first takes a southerly course and enters a cultivated region, then turns west, separating the Dasht-i Margo from the cultivable areas. From Bust to Khwaja 'Ali the descent of the river does not exceed three feet (90 cm) per mile.[32] The Helmand contains abundant water during the dry seasons so that along its lower reaches much use is made of its water for agriculture. Towards the end of autumn when there is little snow in the mountains, the water level of the Helmand also goes down. At the

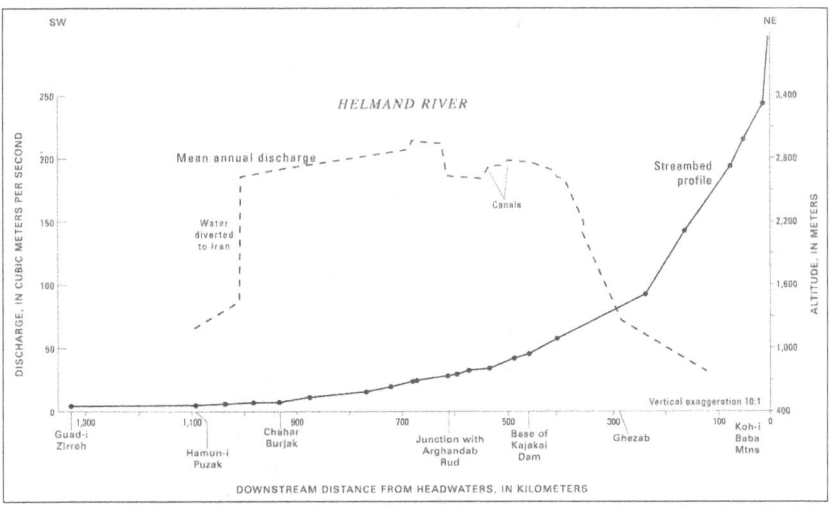

Table 2.4. Stream profile of the Helmand River with mean annual discharges shown along the profile, from Whitney 2006, Figure 14.

end of spring when the snow on the mountains begins to melt, the water level of the Helmand rises. (See Appendix C.) Before the construction of the Kajaki Dam, the Helmand, during times of normal flooding, flowed at a rate of from 50, 000 to 70,000 cubic feet (1,415 to 1,980 cubic meters) per second. In times of exceptional flooding, for example in 1233/1855, the rate was from 60,000 to 70,000 cubic feet (1,700 to 1,980 cubic meters) per second. In normal non-flood seasons, the flow is at 2,000 cubic feet (55 cubic meters) per second.[33] Previous floodings and dry periods of the Helmand are not precisely known, and the people of the area themselves cannot distinguish the history of its past floods, except when an important event coincident with one of them gave it prominence. Given all this, it can still be said that one of these dry periods took place over 100 years ago in the 1840s. As a result of this drought, for a period of four days there was no water in the lower reaches of the Helmand above the delta. Similarly, in the year 1280/1902 the river was dry for 62 days.[34]

After a long stretch the river makes a big loop and reaches its delta in Sistan (Fig. 2.3). From Khwaja 'Ali to the delta of the Helmand, the level of the river bed drops approximately two feet (60 cm) per mile, and above the delta the drop is no more than one foot (30 cm) per mile.[35]

From Kuhak Dam, south of the historical city of Zaranj, the Helmand once again curves west and through the Pariyan Rud route flows into Sistan Basin. Another branch of it, known as the Nad-i 'Ali Rud, goes straight north for several miles and about two miles north of Nad-i 'Ali, in a place called Burj-i As, divides in two: one branch is the Sikh-sar Rud, all the water of which goes towards the irrigation of the agricultural regions around Bazar-i Kang. The other branch, called Shela-i Charkh, is broader, more full of water, and swifter than the Sikh-sar. The Shela-i Charkh flows east and, after a long stretch encompasses the arable land of Minu and Shirabad in its southern reaches and flows close to the village of 'Ali Abad on its northern side. On the east it passes near Bazar-i Kang, passes on the west near Chakhansur, and flows into the Puzak Basin. When the basin becomes full, it makes its way north by the district of 'Alaqeh-Dari (Mayl-i Kuraki) and south by Saliyan to the Sabiri Basin.[36]

Thus the Helmand, after making a journey of 1,400 km (870 miles) and assimilating the waters of a region of 151,300 square km (58,400 square miles), flows with its tributaries into the Sistan Basin.[37] Another river of secondary importance that reaches the Sistan Basin in times of high water flow is the Khash Rud. The length of this river from its source in the Hazareh and Imaq Mountains to its end in the Sistan Basin is 380 km

Chapter 2: Geography of the Helmand Basin

Figure 2.3. The Helmand River near Qala-i Fath, Nimruz Province, 1974.

(236 miles). The Khash Rud plain is 2,300 square km (890 square miles) and from June to December is dry down river from the fertile regions of Delaram as the water is absorbed into the sandy plains.[38]

A number of other rivers, such as the Farah Rud, the Adarsakin, the Khaspas Rud, etc., also flow in the spring into the Helmand Basin. The combined area of the plains of these rivers comes to 4,200 square km (1,600 square miles).

Notes

1 Ghobar, *Afghanistan in the Course of History*, 1346/1968, p.4. GRA
2 McMahon, "Recent Survey and Exploration in Seistan," 1906, pp. 217–8. GRA. Amiri's conversion between various measuring systems is not always accurate; inaccurate conversions have been corrected and generally rounded off by the editors. Some of his measurements were originally expressed using the metric system, others were not. We have not attempted to standardize those. MA
3 Tate, *Seistan (A Memoir on the History, Topography, Ruins and People of the Country)*, 1910–1912, pp. 107–8. GRA
4 McMahon, "Recent Survey and Exploration in Seistan," 1906, pp. 217–8. GRA
5 Seltzer, *The Columbia Lippincott Gazetteer of the World*, Morningside Heights, New York, Columbia University Press, 1952. p.1728. GRA
6 Tate, *Seistan (A Memoir on the History, Topography, Ruins and People of the Country)*, 1910–1912, p.111. GRA
7 McMahon, "Recent Survey and Exploration in Seistan," 1906, p. 222. GRA
8 McMahon, "Recent Survey and Exploration in Seistan," 1906, p. 350. GRA

9   McMahon, "Recent Survey and Exploration in Seistan," 1906, p. 222. GRA
10 *Encyclopaedia Britannica*, 11th Edition, 1911, p. 36. GRA
11 Rademacher, *International Commission for Irrigation and Drainage Bulletin*, 1974. GRA
12 Tate, *The Frontiers of Baluchistan*, London, Witherby and Co., 1909, p. 251. GRA. The Helmand Sistan Project geologist John Whitney deals with this question at length in Whitney 2006. MA
13 Tate, *Seistan (A Memoir on the History, Topography, Ruins and People of the Country)*, 1910–1912, p.129. GRA
14 McMahon, "Recent Survey and Exploration in Seistan," 1906, p. 216. GRA
15 Tate, *Seistan (A Memoir on the History, Topography, Ruins and People of the Country)*, 1910–1912, p.109. GRA
16 McMahon, "Recent Survey and Exploration in Seistan," 1906, pp. 217–8 GRA
17 Rademacher, *International Commission for Irrigation and Drainage Bulletin*, 1974. GRA
18 Service Corps of Engineers, Scale 1:100,000. GRA
19 McMahon, "Recent Survey and Exploration in Seistan," 1906, p. 36. GRA
20 Rademacher, *International Commission for Irrigation and Drainage Bulletin*, 1974. GRA
21 Amiri's data, drawn from official Afghan government sources in 1975, is presented in Appendix B and C. Helmand Sistan Project geologist has collected substantial additional climatological information, presented in Whitney 2006. His Figure 10 is reprinted here as Table 2.2, his Figure 11 reprinted as Table 2.3, and his Figure 14 as Table 2.4. MA
22 Rademacher, *International Commission for Irrigation and Drainage Bulletin*, 1974. GRA
23 McMahon, "Recent Survey and Exploration in Seistan," 1906, p. 351. GRA
24 Tate, *The Frontiers of Baluchistan*, 1909, p. 162. GRA
25 McMahon, "Recent Survey and Exploration in Seistan," 1906, p. 224. GRA
26 Sistani, "Natural Geography of Sistan," *Aryana*, Joint Issue 274, Dalv-Hoot 1346/1967. GRA
27 Ministry of Publications, Department of Afghanistan Studies, *Afghanistan*, 1342–1343/1963–1964, p. 139.
28 Tate, *The Frontiers of Baluchistan*, 1909, pp. 238–9. GRA
29 Tate, *The Frontiers of Baluchistan*, 1909, p. 241. GRA
30 McMahon, "Recent Survey and Exploration in Seistan," 1906, pp. 389–400. GRA
31 Tate, *The Frontiers of Baluchistan*, 1909, p. 241. GRA
32 Tate, *The Frontiers of Baluchistan*, 1909, p. 241. GRA
33 McMahon, "Recent Survey and Exploration in Seistan," 1906, pp. 217–18. GRA
34 Tate, *The Frontiers of Baluchistan*, 1909, pp. 246–7. GRA
35 Tate, *The Frontiers of Baluchistan*, 1909, p. 241. GRA
36 Sistani, "The History of a Great River," *Aryana*, Joint Issues, 1966, 266, 267. GRA
37 Ministry of Publications, Department of Afghanistan Studies, *Afghanistan*, 1342–1343/1963–1964, pp. 217–18.
38 Sistani, "Sistan in Farsina Literature," *Aryana*, Joint Issue 275, Hamal/ Saur 1347/1968. GRA

Chapter 3
Agricultural and Pastoral Production

The Organization of Tribal Chiefs or Khan-i Khani

The feudal or tribal chieftain system has manifested itself in several forms in human societies, depending upon the time and place. Today, too, this system presents many contradictions based upon disparate local conditions. These contradictions can lead researchers into error and aberration unless they follow some specific and established principles. Researchers into this matter, after much investigation of the system, now feel certain of the following definition. "In a society whose livelihood is in crop production and the greater part of whose land is controlled by a small number of people who themselves never work that land, the social organization will be that of tribal chieftains."[1] Without due attention to this definition and by researching the system of local chieftains in the countries of Asia based only on the classic European model, we will certainly meet with confusion and doubt. With this in mind it can be said that evidence of feudal elements in Afghanistan begins with the first century AD. By the third and fourth centuries AD, after the disintegration of the Kushan Indo-Greek states, i.e., at a time when slavery was disappearing,[2] the country entered a stage conducive to the establishment of feudalism.[3] With the coming of Islam, the conquered agricultural lands were declared state lands, and afterwards they were given to feudal lords and wealthy local and Arab families in exchange for taxes. In this way, the feudal system was established, and the social and economic feudal structures were developed in the Islamic period. During the 'Abbasid period,[4] the local feudal lords gradually began to exert influence upon the Arab administration and to take a share in the benefits of the Arab states. With this association the taxes and burdens on the peasants became even greater, and popular uprisings, which in the Umayyad period had been mostly political, became popular economic insurrections against the Arabs and the local khans.

The Helmand Baluch

The feudal system was prevalent in Afghanistan from the seventh to the thirteenth centuries and the appearance of the Moguls, and the oppression of the peasants increased during this time. From the appearance of Islam until the arrival of Genghis Khan in Afghanistan, the social system was based upon three classes. The first was the feudal class (the nobles, the wealthy, and the clerics) who comprised the ruling class. Second was the urban middle class (merchants, civil servants, and artisans). The third class was the peasants and shepherds.

Feudal power was in inverse proportion to the power of the king and the central government; increase of influence of one side would result in decrease of influence of the other side. In Europe, where the feudal lords were more powerful than the kings, peasants were sometimes not considered to be subjects of the king. The European peasants also more closely resembled serfs, and control of their lives and property was in the hands of the feudal lords. In Afghanistan, the influence of the king and the central government was greater than was the case in the European feudal system. In order for the governments of Afghanistan to shake off the influence of the Arabs, they centralized and placed clerics and feudal lords in positions of power. Furthermore, according to both Afghan tradition and Islamic teaching, the peasants were free, were allowed by law to choose professions and trades, and were not tied to the land. But during these centuries, a portion of the agricultural land of Afghanistan was given in fief to the ruling class, or in the form of religious endowments to the clerical class. Timur-i Lang [Tamerlane] (738–782/1360–1404) established rules concerning taxes and alleviated them. Scrub land became the property of whoever cultivated it and for two years was free of taxes. But Tamerlane did away with the tribal chiefs and local leaders who ruled separately and independently and who had disunited Afghanistan. And once again, after one and a half centuries, he gave to Afghanistan a centralized government.[5]

Throughout the succeeding Kurgani period (758–884/1380–1506), feudalistic tendencies held sway, and the vast agricultural lands that had been granted to the feudal lords became hereditary property. Initially, the people who received land grants did not have military status, but once civilian government gave way to military rule, the military leaders used their status to reinstate the previous system of land distribution in order to protect their power. The reason for this was that once the gold-based economy collapsed, it became difficult to raise funds to pay the soldiery. Military governors had little choice but to adopt the previous diffused feudal system of land distribution.

Chapter 3: Agricultural and Pastoral Production

Thus, we see that this distribution method differed from the feudalism of western Europe, both because of differing origins and bases and because those who received the land in Afghanistan initially had no military status. Here, the feudal lords were concentrated in the cities; by contrast, western lords secluded themselves in castles. During the 'Abbasid period, when the central government could not perform normal governmental functions, the right to collect taxes was granted to notable individuals. In order to protect their own wealth, the common people were increasingly forced to support such receivers of land, and as a result, the populace became more than ever before dependent on them. In the Seljuk period, it became common for some kinds of land grants—court grants, military grants, and so on—to be distributed as personal property. Court grants, in fact, consisted of the gift of a governorship of a province. They were like the pre-Islamic land grants that were given to various people and were known as *to'ma*, "bait." The land was given for a person's use in perpetuity. He had the right to sell it, and succeeding rulers did not have the right to deny the heirs the use of the land. At first, the court land grants were different from military ones in that the latter were not inheritable. But gradually the distinction between the two types of land grants became blurred, and in the Seljuk period, the Court grants were just like military grants. At the time of Sultan Sanjar, military divisions were formed and equipped and sent to the sultan's court by the receivers of these land grants In addition to the land grants that we have been discussing until now, there was another type of grant: a personal grant called a "gift." Grants given to the clergy were such gifts.[6]

Pashto speakers who lived in the Soleiman Mountains region and who were divided into hundreds of big and little tribes were slower to adopt feudalism compared with the other valleys and towns of Afghanistan.[7] The social organization of the Pashto-speaking tribes of Afghanistan was two-fold: the tribal way of life and the movement towards feudalism. But the principles of feudalism were varying and uneven in their stages of development. In one place, the feudal system was weak and subordinate to tribal law, but elsewhere it was stronger. In the latter case, the tribal councils gradually succumbed to the authority of the khans, whereas in other cases, the councils were truly tribal assemblies that convened to discuss and solve tribal affairs. Simultaneous with the maturation of feudalism, these councils were transformed from their original simplicity—discussion among tribal elders—into assemblies of nobles and lords, and from the nineteenth century onward, the governments of Afghanistan also reorganized these councils. Between the eleventh and eighteenth centuries, because of conditions in the fertile valleys surrounding the Soleiman Mountains, groups of Afghan Pashto speakers had passed beyond the stage of simple nomadism and were well on the way to feudalism. In the seventeenth century, the feudal government of the small tribe of Khatak was formed, and subsequently the Ghilza'i and Abdali tribes in the south and west spread this model further.

In the central section of the country, the peasant class, which formed the majority, and the artisan class suffered for many years from the rule of the tribal chiefs and from local and foreign army invasions, taxes, requisitioning and so forth, and they sought a more secure, powerful central government. For this reason, the government of the central section attracted, without compulsion, all the oppressed from everywhere into the feudal system. The feudal lords of this area had unlimited authority. The feudal lords controlling this region, by means of allegiance and the payment of taxes to the central government of Afghanistan, fought stubbornly to retain their own local authority relative to that of the central government until the end of the nineteenth century.

For a quarter of a century during the eighteenth century reign of Ahmad Shah Durrani, the power of the Abdali tribesmen was so great that the feudal lords were in conflict with the central government to expand their territories, and they were prepared to start civil war. Ahmad Shah, however, put a stop to these tendencies. When Ahmad Shah died, before Timur Shah had established his rule among all those groups, an uprising of the powerful feudal lords on the one hand, and resistance among the peoples of the subjugated regions on the other hand, weakened the power of the Abdali government. Amir Sher 'Ali Khan (1246–1256/1868–1878), after establishing his rule, began to institute a program of reform. He turned his attention to the realms of politics, culture, military, administration, animal husbandry, roadhouses, and the facilitating of trade to the extent that it might be said that for the first time in Afghan feudal society, the stage was set for the seeds of capitalism to grow.

The feudal system in Afghanistan that had been developing for centuries changed in form during the reign of Amir 'Abd ur-Rahman Khan (1258–1279/1880–1901), who was able to centralize the feudal powers and establish security throughout the country. He established the exchange of goods and money and inaugurated trade over a wide area. In the span of twenty years, the bourgeois trading class became established, and along with it a whole new system emerged, so that an entity that had been done

Chapter 3: Agricultural and Pastoral Production

away with in the period of Amir Sher 'Ali Khan came back into existence. Trade missions in Mashhad and Peshawar, consulates in Karachi, and trade representatives in major towns of Afghanistan came into being. Medium-term loans of from 5,000 to 50,000 rupees were given without difficulty to merchants at home. The Afghan trade mission in Karachi was able to give financial aid to other Afghan merchants up to 150,000 rupees (Kaldar). Handicrafts such as *kark, bark, bashruyeh, qanaviz, ilcheh*[8] and rugs, qilims, sheepskins and the like were produced. Artisanship, which had stagnated during the reign of the Abdali and the Muhammad Za'i *sardars* (nobles) and during the wars against the British, again sprang to life. With the establishment of security and trade, cities became prosperous, and internal markets came into being throughout the country.

Along with the dominion of feudal organization during the reign of Amir Habibollah Khan (1279–1297/1901–1919) the commercial bourgeoisie established itself, while most of the population, i.e., the farmers, herdsmen and various artisans, were firmly under the thumb of taxes, state grain levies, feudal lords and masters, land lessors, and revenue collectors. The lower classes became responsible for the feeding of the ruling class and for providing free service to state and private enterprises. The government forced these people to build roads, bridges and the like, but paid them nothing.[9] Ranking officials exacted as many goods as possible from them at the lowest rates. Landlords benefited from farmers to the maximum extent possible. The state was the defender of feudal lords and land lessors. During peacetime farmers furnished the government with soldiers, and during war they personally marched beneath the government banner. There was no more than a handful of factories at that time nor more than a few thousand laborers. The commercial bourgeoisie, seeking its own development and propagation, complained about the state's support of foreign (i.e., Hindustani) brokers and money changers and sought the expulsion of the Hindustani merchants and the establishment of a free area for their own trade.[10]

Private ownership of land in Afghanistan was for the first time officially proclaimed following the seizure of independence during the period of Amanullah Khan (1297–1307/1919–1929). Amanullah Khan was desperate for money in order to reform and equip the army. He determined when government monetary reserves had been depleted that all state lands be put up for sale, thereby making land ownership legal. Prior to the issuing of this decree and the order to sell state lands, the state officially had control over land in Afghanistan. In practice, a significant portion of the agricultural and pastoral land was in the possession of individuals and tribes. Afterwards as well, a portion of the state lands was granted in reward for services rendered to the state by the representatives of the Afghan nobles during the liberation, and the remaining properties were leased to the local feudal lords. At present, roughly 40,000 landowners have deed to 70 percent of the land, while approximately 580,000 peasant families own 27 percent of the land. Of the peasant families, 40 percent have no more than two *jeribs* of land, and 43 percent have from three to twenty *jeribs*. The lucky peasant is the one who owns from twenty-one to fifty *jeribs*.[11] Perhaps one of the reasons for all these have-nots and malcontents in the natural course of the economic arrangements in the country is that the affairs of present-day Afghanistan have their roots in the invasions and assumption of power throughout the centuries by outsiders who swept this land with fire and sword and left nothing standing except ruined towns and villages.[12] After each attack the conquerors established new economic systems that were overlaid over existing ones. As a result of these assaults, the Afghan lands were divided into several sections, each under a separate government. This disorder destroyed the economic links between the peoples of the various regions of the country and created economic disarray and imbalance in different regions. As a result of these calamities, there arose in Afghanistan various economic and social systems—feudal, natural resources, commercial, investment, governmental—none of which resembled any other.

One may conclude that various systems are extant in the present-day economic structure of Afghanistan, most predominantly the feudal system, which today still follows its traditional course. It must be noted that feudalism in Afghan Sistan appears stronger than that in other regions of Afghanistan, and the system is firmly established from Darwishan down to the lower reaches of the Helmand River to Khwabgah and Sabzgozi.[13] In the vicinity of Zaranj and the Helmand Basin, most of the small landowners favor it, and above this region, towards Farah, the continuation of ownership of land appeals to the big landowners. As a result, this research in Afghan Sistan has concentrated on land, agricultural production and the lifestyles of landlord and peasant.

Irrigation

In the lower reaches of the Helmand River, for the irrigation of agricultural lands a series of dams and weirs (*band*) have been built across the

Chapter 3: Agricultural and Pastoral Production

river, and a few irrigation channels have been cut. Since these dams have been built by the landowners of the vicinity, no strong materials were used in their construction, and they were built with traditional materials to old designs, as the dams from Darwishan to Bandar-i Kamal Khan attest.

The people of this area were not lacking in technical expertise. They chose a place to build a dam upstream, and from that spot they cut a ditch that was two to three meters wide and at a depth maintaining the slope from the mouth of the canal to the place in question. Certainly, the width would vary according to the volume needed, and the depth of the canal would be determined by the difference in elevation between the dam and the ground to be irrigated. Usually, the place on which the dam was built was five to ten miles from the agricultural lands. The river bed in this area falls approximately three feet per mile.[14]

The width of the valley between Darwishan and Bandar-i Kamal Khan averages two miles, and on both sides of the valley are high plains on which the digging of the above-mentioned kind of canal is not possible. In the few areas where it is possible, the digging of canals is beyond the financial means of the local people.[15] Since in this valley the Helmand River twists like a snake and sometimes flows on one side of the valley, sometimes on the other, the possibilities for building watercourses are limited. It is because of this and another whole series of economic and technical difficulties that several areas of the valley alongside the river are still uncultivated.

After the digging of a canal, in order to construct a dam, the people of this region drive poles into the bed of the river in a row at intervals of approximately one meter so that the row extends about one third or one half of the way into the river from the bank on which they have dug the canal. These piles are driven at an angle parallel to each other, and every second one is crossed, occasionally every third one, so that in effect these wooden posts form the skeleton of the dam. The term for this in the Baluchi tongue translates to a "horse"[16] in English.

In order to lessen the pressure of water above the dam, they arrange the line of stakes in such a way that they make an acute angle with the side of the river on which the channel is to be cut. Then they securely fasten closely woven reed mats to the stakes and behind the mats they pile branches, wood chips and whatever else they can heap up before this wooden dam. In any event, mud, silt and especially *cham* (sod) is stuck to both sides of the dam. This system of dam-building has been prevalent for many centuries in Sistan, and its existence is attested from the time of

Table 3.1

Irrigation Canals Drawn from the Helmand between Darwishan and Nad-i 'Ali

	Name	Canal Source	Side of River	Places Irrigated
1.	Darwishan	Sorkh Dez	left bank	Darwishan, Laki, Safar, Banadar
2.	Khan Neshin	Diwalak	right bank	Khan Neshin
3.	Qala-i Nao	just below Diwalak	right bank	Qala-i Nao, Khairabad
4.	Taghaz	Qala-i Nao	right bank	vicinity of Taghaz
5.	Upper Landi	Taghaz	left bank	Bagat and Upper Landi
6.	Malakhan	Khairabad	right bank	Malakhan
7.	Deshu	opposite Taghaz	left bank	Deshu
8.	Khwaja 'Ali	Qala-i Sirak	left bank	Khwaja 'Ali and Khwaja 'Ali Sehyaka
9.	Lower Khwaja 'Ali	between upper Khwaja 'Ali and Deshu	left bank	Lower Khwaja 'Ali
10.	Pulalak	Deh Muhammad Sharif Khan	left bank	Lower Landi, Pulalak
11.	Upper Rudbar	Niluki	left bank	Upper Rudbar
12.	Lower Rudbar	Deh Bibarg Khan	left bank	Khalmuk, Lower Rudbar
13.	Guludand	Bajundi	left bank	Guludand
14.	Khajau & Charburjak	Nil opposite Guludand	right bank	Khajau, Ashkanak, Charburjak
15.	Bandar-i Kamal Khan	Lundau	left bank	Bandar, vicinity of Trakhun
16.	Qala-i Fath	Garudi	right bank	Mehrabad, Baluchan, Qala-i Fath, Hauz, Godri, Jui Nao, Sabzgozi
17.	Lashkari Canal	above mouth of Khwabgah Rud	right bank	Zaranj, Nad-i 'Ali, portion of Khwabgah
18.	Shahi	below Bandar-i Kamal Khan	right bank	joins Lashkari C. after 11½ km
19.	Khwabgah	below Lashkari Canal	right bank	about 10,000 *jerib* of Khwabgah lands

the earliest historical writings up to the era of the depredations of Timur-i Lang.[17] The work of enlarging the dam goes on until the water flows into the side channel. At the same time, the water is made to run along the

Chapter 3: Agricultural and Pastoral Production

main river channel, and the flow current is the means of sending the requisite amount of water from the mouth of the canal to the agricultural lands. Its proper flow is observed by individuals in charge of it. If the water is impeded, effort is made to fix it until the water flows freely. Because of the design and materials of these dams, their durability is limited. At times of flood and high water most of the dams under discussion are destroyed, and as soon as the water level goes down, people set about rebuilding them. The problems of irrigating the agricultural lands of this region will not be solved solely with the building of such dams and channels.[18]

The irrigation canals in Sistan require constant care and attention. Dredging the water channels is necessary every year because of the sand deposited by the 120-day winds and sedimentation of river silt in the canals.[19] The time taken and the amount of work involved in dredging depends on the number of people involved and the length and width of the channel, but usually it requires from one and a half to two months. The farmers perform this heavy work themselves. The number of irrigation channels which flow from the Helmand River between Darwishan and the Helmand Basin is so great that it would take too long to mention them all. Therefore, I shall take the dredging operations of the Qala-i Fath Canal as an example to describe them.

The Qala-i Fath Canal splits off from the Helmand River in the vicinity of Karodi of the county (*waliswali*) of Charburjak and irrigates the fertile agricultural lands of Mehrabad, Maluchan (or Baluchan), Qala-i Fath, and the villages of Hauz, Godri, Jui Nao, and Sabzgozi. This channel feeds two other rapid offshoots that separate from it in the area of Mehrabad and Maluchan/Baluchan, until the main channel reaches the vicinity of Qala-i Fath. There it splits up into small rivulets (Fig. 3.1). The distance between Karodi and Qala-i Fath is 32 km (20 miles).[20] The width of the channel before the second division in the area of Qala-i Fath is approximately 6 m and its depth (prior to the dredging of 1353/1975) was 2 m. (Fig. 3.2) In recent times at Qala-i Fath, a dam made of fired bricks was built to the northeast about 500 m (1,650 ft) above the aforesaid channel to divide the water and to ensure an adequate supply to the lands and villages with water rights. The apportioning of water for every area of the region is done here. The longest of all the canals is the Sabzgozi Canal, which two years before 1353/1975 was blocked up, and during our research period no water flowed.[21] The dredging of the canal from the river to Mehrabad and Maluchan/Baluchan is carried out every year as a cooperative effort among all the localities that use the water, contributing

Figure 3.1. Distribution point on the Qala-i Fath canal, dividing the water into the canals for the villages of Hauz, Godri, and Jui Nao, Nimruz Province, 1974.

Figure 3.2. ʿAbd ar Rahim, a farmer, in the seasonally dry bed of the Qala-i Fath canal. The bridge supports the road between Zaranj and Charburjak, Nimruz Province, 1974.

Chapter 3: Agricultural and Pastoral Production

labor in proportion to their distance from the Helmand River and the benefit they derive from it.

Only publicly used canals are cleaned by communal effort as described above. After the public canals have been dredged, each region sets about clearing its own canals from the source to their own lands. If occasionally a canal is shared by two or three areas, they share in the clean-up operations for the distance the canal is shared, and afterwards, in the manner described, every locale cleans only the portions pertaining to itself.

As Table 3.2 shows, if one of these locales changes its number of workers, it affects the number of workers coming from another area. Thus, the total number of workers varies from year to year. As some of the farmers said, in the past the number of people engaged in this work was very high compared with now; in the 1950s, meaning the lifetime of Colonel Duran Khan and even up to 1335/1957, when ten sons of the colonel had not yet left home and the major portion of the lands that are now subdivided still belonged to that family, the number of farmers who were engaged in this

Table 3.2

Village Participation in Canal Clearing for the Year 1975

Village	Proportion Participating in Canal Clearing		No. of Participants	Water amount (cm/year)	
Modi ⎤ Qala-i Fath	equivalent to Hauz		75	68	⎤ 173
Na-'Illaj ⎦				105	⎦
Hauz	equivalent to Godri		75	195	
Deh Godri	equivalent to Qala-i Fath		75	210	
Sabzgozi	1/3 Jui Nao	together half of people from Hauz, Godri, and Qala-i Fath	112	145	
Jui Nao	3x Sabzgozi			350	
Mehrabad ⎤ Maluchan/ Baluchan ⎦	together ¼ of the people from Hauz, Godri, and Qala-i Fath		75	?	

work varied from 1,000 to 1,200, whereas in 1353/1975, a mere 300 people took part in it.²² As a result of this reduced manpower, dredging and clearing of canals and channels takes a lot of time nowadays, and in times of need the water does not always reach the agricultural lands. As a result, the fields do not yield their accustomed crops. In the year 1353/1975 until mid-October, there was absolutely no water in the channel. The factors which caused this and resulted in the decrease in the number of farmers are listed in part below:

1. The khans and landowners of the above-mentioned area demanded money from the farmers who could pay 3,000 afghanis or somewhat less, and excused them from this duty in exchange for the money. By way of example, in 1353/1975 in the village of Hauz only 75 from a total of 120 farmers were sent to ditch-digging; the remainder had been excused from work through the payment of money.²³

2. Both of the regions of Jui Nao and Sabzgozi were in 1351/1973 unable to send a single person for this work because on the one hand the annual level of income of the farmers, which by no means met their basic needs, fell, and on the other hand the agricultural unemployment resulting from the drought years of 1349/1971 and 1350/1972 throughout Sistan was especially bad in this area of the Helmand River. The result was that a great number of farmers from the area migrated to other areas. At the end of the drought, the people of Sabzgozi procured necessary water by means of tractors and diesel water pumps from the Helmand River and did not use the canal. The region of Jui Nao remained uncultivated after the drought because of the paucity of inhabitants. In compensation, in 1353/1975 the people paid the sum of 30,000 afghanis ($535.71) for the farmers to divide among them. With it, they employed people for dredging the canals. A number of the local farmers confirmed this to me. They expressed their dissatisfaction with the state of canal dredging, saying as follows: every time a farmer for some reason cannot or will not take part in ditch dredging, he must pay 3,000 afghanis to the *zamindar* (landowner). But the zamindars of Jui Nao sent only 30,000 afghanis, the equivalent of the wages of ten people, instead of 225,000 afghanis ($4,017.86), or the wages of 75 people. The farmers did not agree with this, but despite their dissatisfaction, in view of the pressure exerted by the khans and zamindars of Jui Nao, this was forced upon them.

Chapter 3: Agricultural and Pastoral Production

3. In the past, the khans of each *pagao* (a group of six people who cooperatively till the land) took at first one and later two people into their own service, calling them "dead men," exempt from communal labor in exchange for service to the khan. This system is described in greater detail below. In recent times these khans have refrained from taking two such people and instead take the equivalent of their salaries from the other four farmers. In the past these two "dead" people, in addition to the services rendered to the khan in times of need, would also help the four other farmers as well as being obligated to help with the ditch digging. Now that the khans do not have the services of the "dead" people, the duties of those "dead" people in canal cleaning have fallen on the shoulders of the remaining farmers, whose burden has thus been doubled. Therefore, in 1975 the farmers demanded that either the khans refrain from taking the "dead" laborers away from the work group or that they give the wages of the "dead" to the farmers who do the canal cleaning.[24]

But not only was no attention paid to the farmers' first complaint; no one took any notice of the second one either, and the same few farmers

Figure 3.3. Farmers returning to their homes from the yearly canal cleaning, near Qala-i Fath, Nimruz Province, 1974.

undertook the work of cleaning the canals even though it required greater effort and took longer.

The difficulties of the farmers in the ditch-cleaning season are increased because the work is far from their homes and they have no transport. They have to carry their daily necessities with them and spend day and night at the work site. For most of them, bed is an old quilt and food a small amount of wheat, some *ghalu-i torsh* (a mixture of yogurt, whey, wheat flower, turmeric, potato and onion), and tea. The better off among them also bring a bit of oil. A few tin bowls for mixing dough and cooking the *ghalu-i torsh* and a tea kettle suffice for two or three people. Some of the farmers carry these articles to the worksite on a pack animal, while others make their way there unaided (Fig. 3.3). At the end of the day after their labor of canal cleaning some of them collect firewood for cooking;[25] others busy themselves with food preparation. They usually cook their bread in the sand in this way: first they build a fire on top of the sand until it becomes red hot. Then they remove some of the hot sand, spread their dough on the remainder, and replace the hot sand on top of the dough. In this way the dough is cooked in about fifteen or twenty minutes in the hot sand.[26] Naturally the bread contains a bit of sand, but the farmers pay no attention to that. Mostly *dugh* (a drink made of yoghurt or whey) or water, sometimes unsweetened tea, and occasionally *piyaveh*, or soup from *ghalu-i torsh*, helps the dry bread to go down. *Piyaveh* is a kind of local food made from oil, onions, water and *ghalu-i torsh*. Usually, for lunch, for which there is no time for cooking, they eat bread with water, *dugh*, or tea. For the evening meal, they eat mostly *piyaveh* and *ishkineh*, a local food made by cooking oil, onions, eggs, water, and dried apricots in a pan and eaten with bread. Because the day's toil is so great, they are very tired and usually go to bed early, at eight or nine in the evening. As mentioned, they are far from their homes and from the comfort of their wives and mothers. Their clothes are not washed for three weeks or a month. Most of them do not have a change of clothing, so they do not change their clothes during this time.[27]

Towards the end of the month of October, due to the cold winds, the cold weather, the lack of adequate bedding, and the sand blowing in their eyes, the discomfort of the farmers is greatly augmented.

As a result of natural deterioration and the dissatisfaction of the farmers, the maintenance of the irrigation network in Sistan has now been rendered very difficult, and from day to day it decreases. As a result of the construction of the Kajaki Dam in the central course of the Helmand River, the deposit of sediment in the lower reaches of the river has lessened,

Chapter 3: Agricultural and Pastoral Production

and the distribution of silt in its delta has been slowed. The deposit of less sediment results in the river maintaining its existing course to a greater extent. On the other hand, since the water is clearer, the flow of the river is faster and scours the channel more rapidly than before.

In this way the irrigation canals dug from the above-mentioned channels to the farm lands now often have a higher elevation than the river level, and therefore the flow of water into them has been cut off. As a result, the crops of this region diminish year by year, and the livelihood of the farmers and inhabitants of the area is threatened.[28] This diminishment also adversely affects the general agricultural productivity of the country.

Mode of Agriculture

In this region agricultural methods are ancient and primitive, with arable lands being cultivated in rotation. The available land and the lack of any modern farming methods have obliged the landowners to divide their lands into two or three sections, and each section is left fallow for two or three successive years. In areas where the agricultural lands are divided in two and each year one part is cultivated, they call it "One Bora"; and if two years intervene they call it "Two Bora" (Fig.3.4).

The farmers of this region knew nothing about the use of fertilizers until 1348/1970. Even now, fertilizer is used only in Darwishan, Laki,

Figure 3.4. Karamshah, a farmer, cutting stubble to prepare the field for sowing wheat, near Khel-i Bibarg Khan, Lat, Nimruz Province, 1975.

Safar, and the region of Lashkar Gah.[29] In some areas animal dung (in the Baluchi tongue *hashm*) and ashes are used to revitalize the ground.[30]

Tractors and other agricultural machinery are rarely used.[31] Usually tilling is by means of an ox and plow (Fig. 3.5).[32] Irrigation from the Helmand River by means of water pumps is not generally seen. For reasons of kinship and the paucity of crops, the people have not yet been able to step beyond their fields. In most of the rest of the country, agricultural lands are plowed before the spring planting of the same year and are plowed five or six months prior to cultivation; in this way the land is

Figure 3.5. Dadshah, a farmer, plowing for wheat planting, near Lop, Rudbar, Nimruz Province, 1975.

more fit for subsequent planting. But in this area the land is plowed just before planting.

At the end of October and the beginning of November, farmers begin to irrigate for the wheat planting, and this continues until the end of March. If good land is plowed by the end of March, it will yield a good crop, but poor land must be planted prior to the month of March, otherwise the crop will be bad. After two or three days, the land which has been irrigated becomes *vatar* or *guyi*. Land that has sufficient moisture for germinating seeds is called *vatar*, or *guyi* in the local tongue. If the land has too much moisture, seeds sown in it will bloat, then rot and not

Chapter 3: Agricultural and Pastoral Production

germinate. If it is too dry, seeds will not sprout. *Vatar/guyi* is the happy medium between these two extremes. The seed is scattered by hand on the prepared ground; in order to cover the seeds, the land is plowed and then harrowed. After planting, good land is watered after about 35 days and poor land after 20 to 25 days. If good land is watered more than this, the wheat will grow abnormally tall and fall over, which ruins the grain. Moderately good land, which constitutes the majority of land in this area, yields a crop with two or three waterings after planting. In poor or infertile land, there must be six or seven waterings before it yields a crop. Surrounding the basin and the *ashkin* there are very fertile lands that can be cultivated without any irrigation.[33]

In areas of fertile land the canals are built at intervals of approximately 30 meters, and water runs in them from four to six days. Seed in the area between two canals is sown as in dry land and the seed germinates by means of moisture from the adjoining canals. This land does not quickly lose its water, and wheat planted there grows without irrigation. Land such as this is largely to be found in Shirabad, Panjdeh, Hasanabad, and other places surrounding the basin. Land which is sown by the end of February will yield a crop during May, and land sown by the end of March will yield during June.

The ripened wheat is harvested by means of a hand sickle (*mangal*) and is cut by the handful. Each handful is called a *satri*. Approximately 20 to 25 *satri* make up a *kisheh* and it is threshed using an animal.[34] In some places the harvested wheat is collected in a cloth (*saruk*) and carried on the farmers' heads to the threshing floor. A *saruk* is a square cloth, 50 by 50 cm, made of wool or cotton, each corner of which has a string 1.5 m long, in which harvested wheat is carried. The wheat is ground beneath a sled pulled by the plow animals, yielding dehusked kernels of grain. The process of dehusking on an average threshing floor takes ten to fifteen days for six *kharvars* of wheat. In some places (the area around the Hamun-i Puzak, Chakhansur, Kang, etc.) several head of cattle are yoked together (*rusteh* in the local language) and driven over the wheat without a sled, thereby threshing the wheat until it becomes dehusked. The threshed grain is thrown up in the air with a wooden fork (*rashtan* in the Baluchi tongue), and the chaff is separated from the grain by means of the wind. The pile of separated wheat is called *rash*.[35]

As agriculture has not been mechanized in Afghan Sistan, the battle against agricultural difficulties is not being fought as it should be.

The principal difficulties in farming identified by the local people are as follows:

1. *Zardi*

    In the course of the month of April, when the wheat fields have been moist for a few days and the weather is warm and muggy and there is no wind, the leaves, stems, and ears of wheat turn yellow. As a result, the wheat dries too quickly and the grain does not attain its normal size.

2. *Patun*

    From the middle to the end of April, sometimes a kind of worm (called *lulak* in the Baluchi tongue), yellow in color and shaped like a fingernail, appears in the wheat fields. This worm has fourteen feet and resembles a small caterpillar. There are usually five to eight of these worms to be found in the nearly ripe ears of wheat, eating them. The cure for this is in the wind. The wind's rustling the wheat stalks causes the plants to strike one another, causing the worms to fall. As a result of the motion of the wheat, the worms have no chance to climb back up the ears of grain.

3. *Shireh*

    This disease attacks the melon-beds and consists of a kind of worm that eats the tendrils and vines of the watermelons. After the leaves have been eaten, the vines dry up. Once the worms have gone, some leachate from the worms remains in the vines. As a result of this, the vine becomes sticky. Melon fields which are watered less are more secure from this disease.

Agricultural implements in this area are also very crude. They are made of wood and sometimes of iron or part wood and part iron. All of these implements are made by carpenters and smiths in each locality. The usual implements are the yoke (Baluchi *chogh*), plowshare (*tish*), trowel, spade (*rakul*), sickle (*mangal*), winnowing fork (*kesheh*), wooden *kesheh* (*mangarsheh*), and grain sieve (*raugir*). Farmers make great use of ox-drawn plows. A wooden plow consists of a shaft (*rakht*), made of wood and sometimes harnessed to two oxen, which is attached to the yoke. It is crooked, and in the angle a plow share is placed (Baluchi *banak*), and there is also a perpendicular wooden handle. A wooden platform, about 2 m long by 0.5 m wide, is fastened to the yoke by a chain and is called a *maleh* (harrow). This implement is used to level the plowed ground. If this implement is not heavy enough, the driver stands on it while using it.

Chapter 3: Agricultural and Pastoral Production

A *rakul* is another wooden implement (about 75 cm by 75 cm) the center of which is depressed and the edges raised. On one side, which touches the ground when it is in operation, there are triangular iron blades or a hooked iron strip along the length, and on the opposite side there are two handles. This implement is also attached to a yoke by means of a chain. The driver moves the high bits of earth which would not be covered with water into the hollows by means of this implement, and this is how it is used on farmlands.[36]

The spade, like its English counterpart, is used in the irrigation of agricultural land and is another of the tools making up the line of Baluch farm implements.[37]

Farming Systems

The agricultural lands in this district belong to a small minority, three to four percent of the people. The other 96 percent of the people own no land. Most of the landless group are farmers whose returns from agriculture by no means suffice for their needs. Several types of farming arrangements between land owners and farmers may be noted, some of which are not common in other parts of the country, but most of the farming in this area is *pagao, kashtmandi, mamateh, galgir* or *bagri*.

Pagao Farming

In this agricultural system, six farmers work on one piece of land that is called a *pagao* or *pagav*. The amount of land granted by the landlord to these people for agriculture is usually 150 *man* of seed worth, which is sufficient for approximately 60 to 70 *jeribs* of land. The land, the water, the seed, and the farm animals belong to the landlord. The six farmers who share the agricultural work of the *pagao* each has his own title and duties, and since the roles of the *pagao* members are specialized, each of them can in his own work try out his own skills and innovations to his own best advantage. The members of the *pagao* are as follows:

1. The *salar* (the head of the group of farmers on one piece of land). His duty throughout all the agricultural year is to tend to the watering and preparation of the land for crops. This man rebuilds the little walls and ditches that were destroyed in the previous year's planting. In addition, during harvest he takes part in the threshing and storage of the grain.

2. The *ghaminha* ("sorrowful ones"). Three other members of the *pagao* are called *ghamin*. They are employed in levelling and plowing the land and collecting the seed, and as they do virtually all the work, are in truth the essential farmers.
3. The *bighamha* ("carefree ones"). The remaining two people in the group are known as *bigham* or the "dead men." As noted above, their original duties were services to the landlord, such as the collecting of cooking fuel, guard duty, care of the animals, and similar tasks. Today, the landlord no longer employs these people but instead exacts their salary from the remaining four farmers. Formerly, in addition to services to the khan, these two people helped the other four farmers in times of need. Local people believe that in the past each of the six people performed these services for the landlord on a daily basis. In addition they tilled another piece of land separately for the landlord, called a *tawil* or *tuyul*, and the harvest from this land went entirely to the landlord without the farmers taking a share of it. Later, members of the *pagao* agreed that instead of all of them being in the service of the landlord, they would excuse two of them from agricultural work and place them directly in the service of the land owner. This is an unusual arrangement. In other areas of the country, the taking of the two *bigham* or "dead men" is not customary. With regard to the origin of this tradition, much research has been done. Unfortunately, the documents and evidence that could truly shed light on the origins of this arrangement have not been found. But one can surmise that when these lands were under state control, the government of the time gave them to farmers in exchange for a specific number of horsemen and foot soldiers in the forces of the local khans and notables. Two people in every *pagao* were placed under the authority of the khans and, in times of need, were given over to the authority of the state. With the passing of time this custom was abandoned, and probably the landlords availed themselves of the services of these two people for their own purposes. Now, this tradition has changed, and the landlords content themselves with appropriating the salary and share of these two people from each *pagao*.

In Chakhansur and Kang and the environs of the basin, there is one *bigham* in each *pagao* and the total number of people in a *pagao* is five. The

Chapter 3: Agricultural and Pastoral Production

taking of a *bigham* by the landlord has fallen from use and will perhaps soon disappear.

The *pagao* system of farming is the most common one found in the province of Nimruz, and especially in the environs of the Qala-i Fath Canal. In the province of Helmand eastwards from Rudbar to Hazar Joft, Laki, Safar, and Darwishan, the agriculture is of a different sort. The landlord gives only land and water to the farmer. The recipient hires two other farmers to do the farm work and he himself for the most part does not participate in the agricultural work. In the event that he does himself participate in farming work, he hires only one farmer. There are no *bigham* in the above areas. Two farmers do the work of one peasant plowman, which is about 300 *man* worth of seed. The size of the *man* differs in various parts of this area. In this region, a *man* equals 10 *pav*, with each *pav* equaling 452 gm.

Kashtmand Farming

A *kashtmand* is a farmer, but he is the owner of the farm tools and equipment and also obtains his own seed. The landlord puts a piece of land at the farmer's disposal. If he cannot complete a *pagao* with six farmers, he hires other farmers. He is obliged to provide two *bigham* to the khan or the landlord or reimburse him from the profits of the land, in which case four people make up the workforce. If a *kashtmand* has one plow ox, he shares it with another man who also has one. They also share seed in this way. The two people hire two more people as farmers. The landlords of this region do not like this method of farming and try their utmost to hire farmers themselves, because in this system the landlord's share of the produce is less than if he hires farmers directly. As a result, the landlords or khans are willing to give their land to the *kashtmand* only during times of scarcity of animals or seed, or when there are difficulties caused by a shortage of farmers or other limitations. Otherwise, they prefer to hire farmers themselves.

Mamateh Farming

A portion of the land of the khan or landlord that is situated around the houses of villagers or farmers is tilled according to the *mamateh* method, with the landlord granting 20 to 30 *man* of seed worth of land with its irrigation water to the *mamateh* farmer. In exchange for each ten *man* received, the farmer is obliged to spend three days cleaning the canals.

The landlord leases the *mamateh* harvest to the *mamateh* farmer when the grain is still green, with the terms of the agreement being more favorable to the landlord. The landlord leases the *mamateh* harvest in this way so that he will not suffer from any damage by the livestock of the *mamateh* farmer on and around the land. The *mamateh* farmer himself has to provide the necessary tools, and if there should be a shortage of plow oxen, the *mamateh* farmer pays with his labor those people who have spare cattle that he uses.

Galgir Farming

In the past when the land was controlled by the state, the government received about 60 *qeran* (0.5 afghani) in tax for each *pagao* farm. Pieces of land that were granted to people tax-free were called *galgir*. Usually, these pieces of land were given by the government to the clergy to profit from, but they were sometimes given in return for other services, too. In Sistan there were approximately 100 *galgir pagaos*, and roughly 800 families used them.

Today, the meaning of *galgir* has changed in Sistan. It now consists of land given by the landlords to individuals who, because of misfortune, are unable to farm. The amount of land is equal to share of one farmer in a *pagao*. The canal-cleaning duty of a *galgir* is the same as that of a *mamateh* farmer. Agricultural implements, seed, and livestock are provided by the *galgir* farmer.

Bagri Farming

The equivalent of about two to three *man* of seed worth of land in addition to the *pagao* is allocated by the landlord to each farmer for tilling, this being called *bagri* farming. Because in every *pagao* there are four farmers and two *bigham*, the farmers till the *bigham* share for the landlord, but they do not share in the harvest of it. The landlord receives no share of the profit of the other four farmers on *bagri* land.

Kinds of Land and Agricultural Products

In the lower reaches of the Helmand River, which consists of parts of the provinces of Nimruz and Helmand, there are generally two kinds of agricultural land, the dry and the watered. The exact extent of wet and dry lands in this area has not been ascertained, but in general in the entire province of Nimruz which measures 41,725 square km (16,110 square miles)[38]

Chapter 3: Agricultural and Pastoral Production

there are 301,500 *jeribs* of wet land and 927,520 *jeribs* of dry land,[39] and in the province of Helmand, which has an area of 62,337 square km (24,068 square miles)[40] there are 813,610 *jeribs* of wet land and 1,100 *jeribs* of dry land.[41] To give perspective, all of the agricultural lands in Afghanistan, according to statistics from the year 1345/1967, total 2,274,500 *jeribs*, of which 1,192,600 *jeribs* are wet lands and 1,081,900 *jeribs* are dry lands. The area under wheat cultivation, according to the statistics of 1352/1974, is roughly 223,600 hectares, and its total production reaches 2,750,000 tons.[42] The wet lands of Sistan derive their water from canals cut from the Helmand River. Lands watered solely by streams do not exist in this region, except for some areas on the southern borders.

The history of land ownership in Sistan is not known for sure, but this much is known, that in the period of Amir 'Abd ur-Rahman Khan, a number of the elders and leaders of the Sanjrani tribe, a branch of the Baluch, were given border protection duties. In addition to a fixed livelihood, they were given a piece of land in Charburjak in fief, a portion of land or its produce for a livelihood or pension, in exchange for providing cavalry.[43] Nowadays, no state-owned farms or fields may be seen in this area, and both the tilled and untilled lands are in the possession of the khans.

The crops in this area are wheat, a lesser amount of barley, lentils, vetch, and *maak* (a kind of bean). As for garden produce, only onions and squash are grown there. Other kinds of vegetables cannot be grown because in the early summer the canal water is already cut off by silt and sand. Although they could alleviate this difficulty by means of water pumps, the landowners of this area are not yet aware of this.

Fruit trees are rare in Afghan Sistan. In a few parts of this area the occasional little vineyard may be seen, but because of the lack of water vineyards do not yield much, and their insignificant produce is no more than the khans consume. Of all the vine fruits, only two kinds of melon are common, and their harvest does not last for more than a month. Because of the heat, melons do not last more than three to four weeks after they are picked. In Herat and a few other places, pumpkin seeds are roasted, but the people of Sistan roast watermelon seeds and in the fall and winter use them as a dried fruit.

Five factors are discernable in the distribution of agricultural produce in most of the country: the land, water, livestock, seed, and the workforce. In the vicinity of the lower Helmand River and Afghan Sistan, other factors are also at work: one *pagao* of land takes up sixty to eighty *jeribs*, and in a good year the harvest amounts to 1,200 *man*, which is distributed as shown in Table 3.3.

Table 3.3
Distribution of the Annual Harvest of *Pagao* Lands
(Assuming 1200 *Man*)

Receiving Party	Amount of Share	Amount of Harvest Remaining
Of total harvest		
1. *Mushrif* (inspector)	20 *man*	1200-20 = 1180 *man*
2. Magistrate	20 *man*	1180-20 = 1160 *man*
3. Blacksmith	20 *man*	1160-20 = 1140 man
4. Carpenter	20 *man*	1140-20 = 1120 *man*
5. Barber	10 *man*	1120-10 = 1110 *man*
6. *Mirab* (controller of water)	20 *man*	1110-20 = 1090 *man*
7. Land tax	300 *man* (1/4 harvest)	1090-300 = 790 *man*
8. Plow-animal hire	120 *man* (3 *man*/day)	790-120 = 670 *man*
9. Landowner	335 *man* (1/2 remainder)	670-335 = 335 *man*
Per farmer		
10. Each of six farmers taking equal shares	(335/6 =)	55.9 *man* each farmer
11. Each farmer gives clergy 1 *man* in every 10	5 *man*	55.9-5 = 50.9 *man* each farmer

In the province of Nimruz, and especially in Charburjak and the environs of the Qala-i Fath Canal, the landlord takes one quarter of the crop as land tax. The land tax in Afghanistan from the time of Amir Amanullah Khan has changed from goods to cash and is paid over annually to the government by the landlords. But in this area, the landlords still exact wheat as tax from the farmers at harvest time. The price of wheat has gone up about ten times since tax was changed from goods to money, but the amount of tax paid to the government by the landlords did not increase until recently.[44] The landlords took no notice of the change of value, and they took the same one quarter of the wheat harvest from the farmers as had been established in the past. In fact, the farmers who were charged with half of the tax at that time were now giving ten times as much value to the landlords as before, though the landlords' tax burden was unchanged.

Chapter 3: Agricultural and Pastoral Production

Figure 3.6. The granary storage pits of Hajji Nafaz Khan, and several of his farmers delivering grain, beside the "Glass Mound" (Shishagi Ghundi), Khwaja 'Ali Sehyaka, Helmand Province, 1975. Photo by Robert K. Vincent, Jr. © Helmand Sistan Project.

The transporting of the wheat from the threshing floor to the landlord's house was also the responsibility of the farmer (Fig. 3.6). In the event that the farmers were unable to carry it, for every *kharvar* they had to pay 2.5 *sir* for transport, and in that case the landlord carried the agreed amount with his own animal.

The mullah, *mushrif* (controls and certifies harvest for landlord), *kutwal* (foreman for canal cleaning), blacksmith, carpenter, and superintendent of water also share with the farmers in the harvest, their shares being shown in the Table 3.3.

In the Sasanian administrative structure, continued also after the Arab conquest of Sistan, the *mushrif* had the duty of an inspector.[45] Nowadays, in addition the *mushrif* has responsibility for controlling the harvest for the landlord. After the grain has been threshed and winnowed, it is always inspected and certified (by marking) by the *mushrif*, and in his absence the farmers do not have the right to touch the markings on their own.

The control of the dam and the river is the responsibility of the superintendent of water (*mirab*), and in times of danger he warns the farmers. At the request of the landlord, usually one person from the county is employed to take charge of the canal cleaning operations necessitated every year by the silting-up and by the 120-day winds. This man is called the *kutal*, and his duty is to act as the overseer or foreman of the entire cleaning operation. In other areas they pay the mullah, the barber, and the superintendent of water, but it is not common in the other parts of the country that the shares of the *kutal*, the *mushrif*, and the landlord's quarter of the harvest be taken from the communal harvest as taxes.

It is common in most parts of the country that the blacksmith and the carpenter, who spend the year making and repairing iron and wooden agricultural implements for the community, take their wages out of the harvest. But in the *pagao* system of farming, the farm implements belong to the landlord, but the wages of those who make and repair them are taken from the communal harvest. In addition to this, the landlord takes the share of each of the above-mentioned people directly from the farmers (amounting to 20 *sir* from a *pagao*), and he himself settles accounts with all the craftsmen who are to receive shares of the harvest.

The barber and the mullah/imam of the village also have a share of the harvest. In a few villages in the country, the barber tends the hair and beards of the men once a week all year, and his wages are taken from the crop at harvest time. In Sistan, he is given one *kisheh* of unthreshed wheat and ten *man* of threshed grain from each *pagao*. In addition, at weddings when he trims the hair and beard of the bridegroom, he receives money and other goods from the bridegroom. The imam of the mosque in some

Figure 3.7. Hajji Nafaz Khan supervising the division of wheat at harvest time, near Khwaja 'Ali Sehyaka, Helmand Province, 1976.

Chapter 3: Agricultural and Pastoral Production

areas is given as "God's right" one *man* in ten, and in other areas one *man* in twenty, from the farmers' portion of the harvest.[46]

The cost of hiring plow animals belonging to the landlord is three *man* per day (in the lower reaches of the Helmand from Darwishan to Rudbar and Galudand, a *man* is ten pounds and a *kharvar* is eighty *man*), amounting to a total of about 120 *man* per agricultural year. It is paid to the landlord from the communal harvest. Since the land, seed, and water all belong to the landlord, after the payment of the above amounts, the remaining harvest is divided into two equal parts, half going to the landlord and half to the farmers (Fig.3.7).[47]

Craftsmen also receive a percentage in the other farming systems. The carpenter takes one *sir* per *kharvar* of the harvest in *galgir* and *mamateh* farming. In the area of Palalak, Landi, Rudbar and Khalmuq, the carpenter is paid eight *man* per *pagao*, but at harvest time the carpenter takes one *kisheh* of unthreshed wheat from each *pagao*, from which he can probably obtain about ten *man* of grain. In addition, he takes one bag of threshed grain and straw, from which he obtains about four *man* of grain.

This method of the distribution of the harvest was common in Sistan during 1282–1283/1904–1905[48] and today it is still current in most parts of Nimruz province, especially in the areas adjoining the Qala-i Fath Canal.[49]

The distribution of the harvest in *kashtmandi* farming is as follows: the entire harvest is divided into four; two and half of the portions are divided equally between the landlord and the *kashtmand*; half of one portion goes to the hired farmers; and the last portion is used to pay the carpenter, blacksmith, superintendent of water, for the hire of plow animals, and other costs. In times of scarcity, the fourth portion is made up from the portions of the *kashtmand* and the farmers, and if there is an excess, it goes to the *kashtmand*. The *mamateh* harvest is divided evenly between the landlord and the farmers, but the landlord has no right to the straw, the *mamateh* farmer tithes eight *man* from his own portion. Up to now, the buying and selling of straw has not been common from Landi to Charburjak. In times of need, the landlords give straw free to the farmers, but in the areas of Charburjak, Chakhansur, and elsewhere, straw is sold. In the autumn of 1354/1976 in Zaranj one bag of straw weighing about four *sir* sold for 35 afghanis.

Formerly, a quarter of the *galgir* harvest was given to the landlord, but later he took half of it and the *galgir* farmer was freed from having to dig ditches. Nowadays in Rudbar the landlord takes half the harvest, and in addition he requires from the farmer three days of ditch digging for each ten *man* of seed. From the *bagri* harvest, one third goes as tax to the landowner, and the farmer tithes from the remainder.

In the environs of Helmand province, from Hazar Joft to Rudbar, the usual method of distribution of the harvest is somewhat different. In these areas, after paying the blacksmith, carpenter, superintendent of water, *mushrif,* and mullah twenty *man* each, and the hire of the plow animals at the rate of 90 *man* per 30 days of work, and two *man* per *kharvar* for the threshing of the grain, the remainder of the produce of one season is divided into six equal parts. Two of these portions go to the landlord, two to the *kashtmand,* and two to the farmers. The white straw is divided into five equal portions, two being given to the landlord, two to the *kashtmand,* and one to the farmers.

Of the above methods, it can be seen that in all of the lower Helmand region sharing of the harvest is common in agriculture and that the share of the peasants in the produce is negligible, so that they cannot assure themselves of even the lowest standard of living, as the peasant is always considered superfluous by the landlord.

Domestic Animals and Animal Husbandry

Because much of this area has a semi-arid desert climate, livestock is bred of a type to survive in these conditions. The livestock can be divided into two types: domestic and wild. They use three kinds of domestic animals: first, those used as draft animals and transporters of goods; second, those whose milk, meat, and wool is used; and last, those used in hunting and guarding. Donkeys and horses are of the first group, cows, goats and sheep form the second, and camels belong to both these groups. *Tazis* (Afghan hounds) are used for hunting and ordinary dogs for guarding.[50]

According to 1346/1968 statistics, in the whole province of Nimruz there are 23,372 head of ordinary sheep, 1,000 head of karakul sheep, and 83,800 goats. In the province of Helmand there are 399,080 sheep and 78,820 goats.[51]

Most of the khans of the area have from 200 to 400 sheep and goats, for the care of which they hire a shepherd. The wages paid to the shepherd in one year are as follows:

1. for each three sheep and goats, 0.5 *sir* of wheat and 0.5 *sir* of barley
2. one in ten sheep's fleece
3. one lamb in ten

Chapter 3: Agricultural and Pastoral Production

Figure 3.8. Muhammad Bahram Borahudi (Brahui), a shepherd with the camel-hair cap and felt boots he had made. He was one of our employees at Khwaja 'Ali Sehyaka, Helmand Province, 1975.

4. an amount of money for the purchase of clothes

5. money (called *chuti*) for the purchase of shoes

Because the price of clothing and shoes varies, the amount of money given to the shepherd for this purpose is also not fixed, and is tied to the going rate. Cowherds receive a monthly cash stipend of 50 afghanis per animal. In addition, the cowherd's food is the responsibility of the stockowner.[52]

The shepherd stays with the flock night and day and grazes it wherever there is pasture. In Rudbar they usually drive the flocks at night from the valley of the Helmand towards the Gaud-i Zirreh plain and at dawn take them back to the river.[53] In the plains, there grows a kind of shrub called *taratkeh* that the shepherds believe fattens the sheep.[54] In this area, a farmer who is unable to buy a milch cow will do his best to procure one or two milch sheep or goats. The sheep of this region are widely famous as "Helmand sheep," smaller than the sheep of other areas of Afghanistan. A Helmand sheep averages two *sir* of meat and fat, while a Badghisi sheep averages three *sir*.

Male sheep and goats are raised for meat. Animals that are being raised for meat are usually gelded. Many animals die during gelding because an unclean razor or other sharp instrument is used to make the incision to remove the testicles. The wound is then sewn up with a needle and thread. Usually, the razor used for this operation is germ-infested and causes infection of the wound. As a result, 15 percent of the animals sicken and die. In the area of the Hamun-i Puzak Basin, Chakhansur, Kanak, Khwabgah, etc., the method of gelding is as described.

In a number of other places they use a different method. In this technique the animal's testicles are squeezed between two pieces of wood (*shekanjeh*) so that they completely lose their form and function and the

Figure 3.9. Milch cows on the *ashkin* around the Hamun-i Puzak, Nimruz Province, 1974.

animal is neutered.[55] In both cases, the animals lose the desire to eat for two to three days, and signs of discomfort are noticeable for at least ten days. Sheep are gelded at the age of six months, and cattle at one year.

In the Helmand Valley and the reed beds surrounding the Hamun-i Puzak, the herds of milch cows are also worthy of note. In the whole of Helmand province there are 61,240 head of cattle and 220 water buffalo, and in Nimruz there are 30,760 head of cattle.[56] Because of the lack of veterinary facilities, various illnesses may be seen, and the cattle owners suffer heavy losses. In the area of the Hamun-i Puzak, the cattle suffer most from liver-worms and die.[57] The people believe that the feet of the

Chapter 3: Agricultural and Pastoral Production

cows become infected with the organism called *marak* when the animals are walking in the lake. Because they are in the water, they do not notice the effects of the organism, but upon leaving the water, the areas of their bodies which had been submerged begin to itch. This itching is pleasant at first, then burning. The more they scratch the more painful it becomes. The animal does nothing but lick its legs from the time of leaving the water until it reenters it, and in order to lessen the pain it licks itself vigorously. This rubbing increases the infection, and gradually the animal loses its appetite. The worm eventually attacks the liver, which has swollen beyond normal size. The result is the death of the animal. This sickness alone kills up to 10,000 cattle, sheep and so forth each year in the coastal waters of the Hamun-i Puzak, Kanak, and Chakhansur.[58] *Marak* also attacks people, and its poison causes itching in the area of the bite. As a result of scratching the affected area, eruptions occur, causing great difficulties. If a person can overcome the itching the bite does not have serious effects.[59]

Another disease which affects cattle is known in this region is *tupaki*.[60] This sickness is very serious and kills the animal within one or two hours. In the Pashto language, *tupak* means gun. Since the effects of the disease are like a gunshot wound, it is called *tupaki*. This disease is contagious. An animal affected with it trembles violently. The flesh of afflicted

Figure 3.10. Long, reed-roofed mud animal shelters at the village of Asak on the shore of the Hamun-i Puzak, 1974, and some milch cows.

animals is tasteless and unpalatable. The last outbreak of this disease was in 1976 in Panjdeh near the *ashkin*; many cattle died.

Another kind of disease, which in the opinion of the people generally appears in cattle in the fall after they have eaten melon rinds, is known as *mahghau*.[61] In this disease the mouth of the animal becomes swollen, and it salivates profusely. This disease is also contagious, but it is not as fatal as *tupaki*.

Although the weather in Sistan is usually temperate and mild in the winter, occasionally a cold and violent storm causes a radical change in the weather, and the animals in this vicinity suffer heavy losses through lack of shelter and food (Fig.3.10). As mentioned in chapter 2, the inhabitants of the basin area call it the "one in five cow killer." Sir Henry McMahon reported it thus: towards the end of March 1905 (1283) blizzards, or in the local slang "Black Winds," lasted for four days. This storm killed 100 camels at a stroke and 200 in the course of the four days, while in a two and a half year period, 4,900 camels died from various causes.[62]

Figure 3.11. Transport camels loaded with wheat in the Helmand Valley, 1976.

In the province of Nimruz there are 12,520 camels, and in Helmand, 12,230.[63] Since the greater part of this region is semi-arid desert lacking water, camels are the only animals that can easily transport heavy loads (Fig.3.11). Camels can go without water for seven days if their grazing is fresh and five days if it is dry straw.[64] This animal cannot swim, since the rear portion of its body weighs more than the front.[65] In swimming, its head becomes submerged and causes the animal to drown. They can only cross large bodies of water if someone rides on their backs and establishes equilibrium.[66]

Chapter 3: Agricultural and Pastoral Production

In Afghan Sistan there are several kinds of camels. *Badi* or *mari* camels, which are also called "riding camels," are swifter than the others. The easy running action of this camel enables it to cover seven or eight kilometers in an hour at its normal pace, but they are not much used for carrying loads.

Mayeh camels are the second group of camels in Afghan Sistan. They are famed for load-bearing. *Mayeh* camels have stronger bodies than all other camels, and they have much wool. The wool on their throats and necks is abundant, with very long hairs that can reach 20 cm in length. The usual load of a *mayeh* camel is 44 *sir*, and when necessary they can carry 50 or 55 *sir*. The female usually carries a load of 35 *sir*. A male and female *mayeh* camel cannot produce a good colt. The result of their mating is called by the locals a "jackal," a term usually used to denote any inferior specimen of an animal.[67] Compared with regular camels, this offspring carries a smaller load and is usually deformed.

The regular camel (*lidau*) is another type that is also used in the transportation of goods. The average load of a male *lidau* camel is 30 *sir*, while that of the female is 25 *sir*, and a "jackal" of their mating cannot carry more than 20 *sir*.

Numerous diseases are fatal to camels. *Bughameh* can be taken as an example. This disease manifests itself in the liver and lungs of the animal, and the symptoms are the eruption of pustules and trembling of the limbs. When the ill beast lies down, it rolls onto its side instead of lying on its chest. Because of the lack of veterinary clinic facilities, camel owners treat the animals themselves with traditional remedies. For *bughameh* they dissolve a walnut-sized lump of ammonia salts in water and pour it down the animal's gullet. Sometimes they lance the animal near the eye above the nose and let it bleed for a bit, but this kind of treatment does not have much effect. Roughly 70 percent of the afflicted animals die. In 1287/1909, as the result of an outbreak of influenza in the course of one week, between 800 and 900 camels died at a Boundary Commission camp.[68]

Another disease frequently fatal to camels is called *marghak*. A camel afflicted with this disease sweats and cannot raise its head and neck but rests them on the ground. This disease can kill a camel within a day, and a camel that survives it is sick for four to five days and eats no food. As a remedy for this disease, camel owners make the camel drink warm kid's blood. A camel also becomes sick and dies through lack of water. If a camel is deprived of water for about a month, it dies.

Branding with a sickle is used as a remedy for lameness and a few other more common diseases. This is done by experienced individuals who brand the animals on various parts of their bodies. The usual food of camels is thorns,[69] but the camel owners of Sistan believe that eating thorns in the springtime makes camels ill. At this time the thorn bushes exude a milky sap. When they see this sap, camel owners prevent their animals from eating the thorns. In addition to the thorns, camels eat *reshkeh*, clover, wheat straw, the leaves of any kind of tree, and any other kind of forage.

During the winter, a number of camels rut for a period of one month to 40 days. During this time they eat less and their sexual drive increases. An untethered rutting animal will wander away and not return. Also, if its tail is not tied, it can injure its testicles by drumming its tail against them. *Mayeh* camels are more strongly affected by this condition than any others, and if confronted with other camels, they fall to fighting and competition. Since they are eating less, they lose weight.

The price of a camel, depending on its qualities, varies from 15,000 to 30,000 afghanis. A group of people in Sistan are known as *kirakesh*, camel drivers. They own on average two or three camels, and their income is derived from hiring them out. But some camel owners and landlords have 200 to 300 camels, and they hire camelmen (*sarbans*) to tend them. The camelman (Baluchi *begjet*) takes the camels to pasture and looks after them. The compensation a camelman receives annually for his services is based on the following:

1. A camelman is responsible for 30 camels. In special circumstances, he may be given a few more or a few less, but the normal number is 30.
2. The camelman receives 5 *man* of wheat for each camel (Baluchi *arti*).
3. He is also given a quantity of wool to make a felt rug (*teppor*).
4. A kind of footwear (*chut*) is given to the camelman by the owner.

The camel owner usually gives the camelman the camels that he keeps for selling or breeding, not to hire. The camelman goes with the herd to pasture (*chur*), and usually he can use the milk the camel produces. Camelmen take flour with them, and bake their bread in the sand. Camelmen help each other out, and will take over a friend's duties for two or three days while the friend visits his family.

Another animal which is used for carrying loads is the donkey. The donkey is used only for load-bearing.[70] In the province of Nimruz, there are 31,640 of these animals, and in Helmand 36,070.[71] Most of the *kashtmands* and some of the farmers have donkeys, according to their needs.

Chapter 3: Agricultural and Pastoral Production

Figure 3.12. Cowherds, a portion of a *tavileh* (trough), and two donkeys at the village of Asak on the shores of the Hamun-i Puzak, Nimruz Province, 1974.

The landlords usually have two or three donkeys (Fig.3.12). The usual load for a donkey is 16 *sir*, and the animal can carry this load easily for five to eight km. If the animal has to travel further, the farmer lightens its load.

Horses are kept both for riding and for carrying loads.[72] In the province of Nimruz in the years 1350–1352 (1972–1974), there were 1,340 horses, and in Helmand there were 790,[73] but the figure for Nimruz is exaggerated because, as can be observed in many parts of the province, the number of these animals is much less than the above figure.[74]

There is a kind of horsefly in Sistan that bites the animals.[75] As soon as it bites, blood flows from the wound, and the horse suffers greatly. This fly is particularly harmful to horses. To protect them from the flies, they cover them with a blanket or horsecloth, and even when they are being ridden the horses wear "pajamas." Despite this, many horses die of the disease these flies infect them with, and it is for this reason that the people in this area are not interested in keeping so many horses. For the animals included in the above figures, there are 1,272,900 *jeribs* of pasture in the province of Nimruz and 579,600 *jeribs* in Helmand.

Hunters breed a kind of hunting dog in this region for the hunting of waterfowl and quail. When the quarry falls in the water of the *hamun* or Helmand River, the dogs find and retrieve it.[76] Also, in spring and autumn,

71

during the quail season, the dogs find the birds by their scent, and hunters catch them in nets. Gazelles also are hunted with *tazi*, known outside Afghanistan as "Afghan hounds," the fastest dogs in the country. As soon as the hunter sees the gazelle he sets the hound after it. This swift animal, which can run as fast as the gazelle, has greater stamina than its prey, and soon engages the gazelle and brings it down, holding it until the hunter arrives to take it. The Afghan hound is also used for hunting foxes. There are not many Afghan hounds now in Afghanistan, and they are seldom found in Sistan. Because of the strong sun in the summer and the cold in winter in Sistan, Afghan hounds are dressed in "pajamas," except when they are hunting,[77] a practice that is at present accepted as normal. Ordinary dogs are generally kept for guarding purposes. Shepherds who look after flocks of goats and sheep have these dogs. The dogs protect the flocks from thieves and the depredations of wolves. Some people also keep these dogs to guard their homes.

Wild Animals

Of the wild animals in Sistan, the first category is gazelles, which the khans of Sistan very much like to hunt. Since there are no game limits, they hunt as much and as often as they wish and are able. By their own admission, the number of gazelles decreases every day.[78] They also hunt gazelles from motor vehicles.[79] They chase the gazelles in vehicles across the plains and knock them down with the vehicles. It is even easier to hunt gazelles on a motorcycle.[80] Usually two people pursue the gazelle, one having a gun and the other driving the motorcycle. When they approach the gazelle, the one with the gun fires at the animal until he brings it down.

Foxes are also among the wild animals. During the course of archaeological excavations at Shahr-i Gholghola, a fox came to the camp every night and sometimes caused a shambles among the foodstuffs in the cook's tent. This animal is hunted in various ways for its skin. During the 1353/1975 excavation season, Mullah 'Abd al-Hamid, one of the excavation workers, caught a fox in a very simple trap that he himself had set in the ground near the workers' kitchen.[81] Another night one of the drivers (Khan Zaman) caught a fox near the camp without a trap. That night the cook and his assistant distracted the fox's attention by throwing food and calling "pu pu." The driver crouched down and sneaked up on the fox from behind the water barrels. While the fox was busy eating, the driver grabbed it by the tail and, so that it could not bite him, held it by the tail

Chapter 3: Agricultural and Pastoral Production

for a while and then let it go. This story may astonish a few people. In most parts of Afghanistan, the fox flees from people and even from other animals, and will not approach closer than one kilometer. In Sistan, perhaps because they see fewer people, foxes do not fear humans. On the other hand, extreme hunger and the presence of food may have deranged the fox and removed all fear from its mind.[82]

Another wild animal found in these parts is the boar. This animal traditionally lurks among the reed breaks and tamarisk trees of the *ashkin* region. It is now found only in the reed breaks around the basin. Since they cause damage to the fields by night, people kill them every time they find them, regardless of their usefulness. For this reason, the numbers of wild boar decrease daily, and they will probably soon be extinct in this area.[83]

Wild wolves are also sometimes found in this region. This rapacious animal attacks mostly goats and sheep. In times of extreme hunger it will attack and eat donkeys, cattle, other animals, and even people.[84]

Dairy Products

In Sistan, as in other areas, milch animals are milked by hand. Before milking, the young of the animal is set to suckle for a few minutes. When the animal lets down its milk, the young is taken away, and they milk the animal into a vessel previously prepared for the purpose. The large landowners hire several milkers to milk their flocks of goats and sheep and herds of cows. Milking is done almost exclusively by the women. Newly calved cows are milked three times a day, morning, noon and evening, and goats and sheep are milked twice, morning and evening. Cows that have calved more than seven months previously are also milked twice a day. Except for the camel herder on the plains, no one else uses camel milk.

In Sistani conditions, if milk is exposed to the weather for more than a day, it ferments and sours. For this reason people try to make it into yoghurt as soon as possible. They boil the milk then cool it, and when it is lukewarm, they mix one soup spoonful of yoghurt culture with two spoonsful of water and add this to half a *sir* of milk. They stir the liquid until it is well mixed, and in five hours it becomes yoghurt.

Yoghurt, too, does not last long in this climate. After three or four days it becomes sour and unusable, but before it sours they make it into *dugh* (buttermilk). For this they pour equal amounts of yoghurt and water into a leather sack called a *mushk*. The *mushk* is tied on the back of a camel, which they drive out to pasture. The camel's movement turns the yoghurt into *dugh* and separates off the fat.[85] When they pour the *dugh* from the *mushk* into containers, the fat is on the top. They skim it off and melt it. This is called "yellow" or "cow's fat" and is famous in the area, commanding twice the price of vegetable oil. *Dugh* is used for noon and evening meals for these people. In addition to this they make curds from *dugh*. They boil it until all the water has evaporated, and then pour it into a canvas bag and leave it to drain.[86] They mix the residue with a specific amount of salt and make it into balls the size of an apple or pear. These they leave to dry in the open air.

Rakhmi is something else made from the liquid separated from *dugh*. They boil it until it thickens, then they clarify it and dry the sticky solid residue. *Rakhmi* is sour tasting and can be eaten by itself or with water.

They also make cheese from milk, but the variety of cheeses found in other countries is not to be seen in this region. Here only two kinds of cheese are made—"raw" and "cooked." Raw cheese is made with rennet and unboiled milk. The rennet is made from the seeds of a kind of bush called *khameh khuri*. Several seeds the size of large peas are wrapped in muslin and put in the lukewarm milk. After a few seconds the seeds in the muslin bag are squeezed so that their essence mixes into the milk. After four or five hours, the raw cheese is ready.

Cooked cheese is made from yoghurt and milk. One part yoghurt is mixed with two parts milk until the mixture separates. The solid residue is cooked cheese. Cooked cheese is made into balls weighing approximately one kg each. This cheese is seasonal; its season is spring, and in most parts of the country it is eaten with raisins. In places where raisins are expensive and scarce, it is eaten with sugar or brown sugar.

The fleeces and skins of animals present another source of income for the flock owners of the region. Sheep are sheared twice a year, in spring and autumn. Animals who die of their own accord or are slaughtered are skinned, and the skins are sold as needed.

Chapter 3: Agricultural and Pastoral Production

Notes

1. Original source not provided. WBT
2. In the century before the invasions of Hephthalites. WBT
3. "Feudalism," in one of its many forms, certainly had long existed in Afghanistan. With the coming of Islam it may have been reorganized along new lines, but it had long been present. WBT
4. For all practical purposes, the time frame meant here extends from after the Arab conquest until the rise of local dynasties with regional authority, such as the Saffarids in the tenth century AD. WBT
5. Ghobar, *Afghanistan in the Course of History*, 1346/1968, pp. 143, 145, 146, 149, 246, 277. GRA
6. Lambton, (trans., Minuchihr Amiri), *Landlord and Peasant in Persia*, Tehran, Translation and Publication Foundation, 1339/1961, pp. 121, 122, 134, 135. GRA
7. Chiefly the area occupied by Paktia Province. WBT
8. It is unknown to the editors what these objects are. MA
9. Scarcely exaggerated. Normally they were fed, and at times small sums were paid in the form of grain, a partial tax relief. WBT
10. For a full account of the economics and politics of Afghanistan in the late nineteenth and early twentieth centuries, see Gregorian (1969) and Kakar (1975). WBT
11. A. A. Poliyak, *The Economic Organisation of Afghanistan*, Soviet Academy of Science, Institute of World Economics and International Relations, 1964, pp. 39–41. GRA
12. Reference is made to the many foreign or partly alien conquests: Kushan, Sasanian, Hephthalite, Ghaznavid, Mongol, Iranian, the latter ephemeral, to be sure. WBT
13. Certainly a reflection of the poverty of the region and the greater need here for the regulation and control of water resources. WBT
14. The construction of a *band* (dam) and the canals its reservoir feeds is a highly complex undertaking requiring much skilled labor and calculation. Our illustrations here are all taken from the *band* at Malakhan, beyond which water is drawn off to feed the Khwaja 'Ali Canal. The purpose of the *band* is not to stop the flow of water in the river, but merely to elevate it sufficiently to reach the mouth of the canal. One might ask why the canal is not dug sufficiently deep so that the level of the river would not need to be raised to enter it. By having the bed of the canal one to two meters above the normal level of the river, the flow of water in the canal is more easily regulated, and sudden rises in the level of the river will be more easily controlled within the canal, whereas slow drops result only in the impoundment of more water in the pool behind the *band* so that in either case—excepting extreme flooding—the reservoir level remains constant, and the supply to the canal regular. WBT
15. The construction of canals is generally a cooperative effort, the work arranged among the khans whose lands will be served by the main canal and its branches. WBT

16 From the spot on the river bank where the water is to be drawn off into the proposed canal, these stakes are driven into the river bed, at an angle pointing upstream, for perhaps half a mile. These will be used to form a channel parallel to the main stream, one in which the flow of the river will be gradually regulated by raising its bed so that when the water is finally diverted into the cut canal, it has already been slowed (or increased, in the dry season) to the desired flow for the canal, a speed which will neither erode the canal bank by its swiftness nor by its slowness permit the deposit of silt. Above this "horse," the dam is turned perpendicular to the river banks and is constructed across to the far side. The leading, or upstream, face of the dam is constructed of poles or stout branches available in the region. These are driven into the river bed, and a loose matting of tamarisk bark bound against the upstream side. Behind this line of piers and matting, hundreds of loosely woven tamarisk bags filled with rocks are dropped onto the river bed until they reach the height of the posts. This construction is not intended to obstruct the flow of the river, but to impede it sufficiently to raise a pool of water behind the *band* high enough to feed the canal, i.e., perhaps only one to two meters in height. Water circulates freely over and among the stones of the *band*, and the fish thus trapped among the stones are collected twice a day. If, after a sudden rainstorm, the river level rises several inches, then more water flows over the *band*. Only the spring floods may breach such *bands* and sweep away portions of the front screen and carry stones downstream, but *bands* are easily repaired. On the canal side of the river, water is drawn downstream between the river bank and the "horse" section of the *band*, which is constructed in the same fashion as the *band* and leaks as badly. The flow in this channel is slower than that of the river as it reforms in its bed below the *band*, and the "horse" channel drops less precipitously. When it reaches the canal opening, it is turned obliquely into the excavated canal, and this action further slows its flow. The canals may be ten to fifteen miles long and are so constructed that a consistent flow of water is maintained. When droughts are severe, the *band* is unable to hold sufficient water to feed the canal; in times of flood, when *bands* may be broken, canals also will be without water until repairs are made. Normally these periods are short, and the villages fed by the canals have wells. The water table in the valley was normally about four meters below the surface during the years we worked along the Helmand. In drought years, such as 1970 and 1971, hand dug wells had to be deepened. Once a year, normally in the autumn when the river is low and the canals are not needed yet for irrigating the winter agricultural fields, the canals are blocked at the river bank, and the khans responsible for the maintenance of the water systems assign crews, in accordance with the population of the villages using a particular canal, to clean out the accumulated silt of the preceding year together with the sand that may have blown into it. The men are paid very small wages and work away from home. The cleaning work, depending on the length and depth of the canal and the terrain through which it passes, generally requires four to six weeks to complete. This work, in Sistan, is normally performed in October and November. WBT

Chapter 3: Agricultural and Pastoral Production

17 Tate, *The Frontiers of Baluchistan*, 1909, p. 54. GRA. It was, of course, *bands* of this sort that Timur destroyed. Since they are easily rebuilt, this destruction could hardly have occasioned the abandonment of Sistan, as has so often been maintained. WBT
18 So long as the population of the Helmand Valley remains as small as it is today, no more sophisticated system is required. By the time the canal reaches the region to be irrigated it has, by dropping less precipitously than the valley, been brought to the surface, so that by gravity it may be let into the fields. Irrigation is normally done by the flooding technique, since the dry soils are slow to absorb water. The water is drawn from field to field until all of it is absorbed, or the excess is drained off into drainage ditches that either deliver it to unsuitable land or route it back to the river. It is in many respects a system both more complex from the standpoint of engineering and more suited to the land than the modern irrigation systems constructed by the USAID mission in the Lashkar Gah region in the 1960s and 1970s, most of which placed too much water on the land, drew salts upward through capillary action, and provided either no, or at best inadequate, drainage. WBT
19 Where canals run perpendicular to the constant wind direction, they can be clogged by blowing sand in a very short while. WBT
20 Military Topographic Section of the United States of America, 1957, 1970. GRA
21 The khan of Sabzgozi refused, or was unable, to send men for the cleaning of his portion of the canal. According to stories current among our workmen (who were largely from Hauz, Qala-i Fath, and Jui Nao), the khan of Sabzgozi was unpopular with his villagers. It is alleged that some short while before our coming to this region to work in 1972 he had executed a young man and girl for fornication, and that as a result of this act his villagers left him and moved to Iran. Whether or not the tale is true, it suggests the degree of independence villagers felt toward their khans by the early seventies. WBT
22 An indication of the great decline of population in the Helmand and Sistan region subsequent to the rise in prosperity in Iran. WBT
23 Farmers with such large sums of money had doubtless worked in Iran, or had had members of their families in Iran sending money back. It is obvious that the infusion of this money from Iran was contributing to the breakdown in the traditional relationship between the khans and their farmers. In most cases, the khans lacked the absolute authority to command men to work, but they did not miss the opportunity to impose fines. In 1975, 3,000 afghanis equaled $53.57, a large sum of money for a farmer working within an essentially barter economy. WBT
24 Tate, *Seistan (A Memoir on the History, Topography, Ruins and People of the Country)*, 1910-1912, pp. 326–8. GRA
25 We were told that the men worked between eight and ten hours daily; when working for the Helmand-Sistan Project, they worked a seven hour day (with half an hour food break), a length fixed by the government. During Ramazan the work day was reduced to six hours. WBT

26 Baluch shepherds and travelers commonly cook their bread in this fashion since the normal subterranean bread oven required two days to construct. WBT
27 In contrast our Project workmen, provided with ample amounts of water, washed their clothing often. WBT
28 The reports of the Helmand Valley Authority with responsibility for the administration of the vast and frequently faltering irrigation systems of the Helmand Valley around Lashkar Gah show little evidence that such consequences for agriculture in the lower Helmand Valley and Basin were considered in either the planning or operation of the system. WBT
29 Where the foreign-advised Afghan Fertilizer Company maintains an office. Fertilizer was introduced largely to improve yields on the lands of the Helmand Valley Authority, and little effort was made to promote its use elsewhere. WBT
30 Another practice is commonly followed. The khan determines where on his lands a village will be located. Every four or five years he may cause the village to be moved some distance off to fallow land, the nitrogen enriched soil where the village stood then being converted into fields. We noted this practice in the region of Malakhan especially. The simple construction of the Baluch hut makes it possible for an entire village to be dismantled, moved, and reconstructed in a single day, if the distance is not far. WBT
31 Few khans are sufficiently wealthy to own tractors, and in any event they may more likely be used for hauling than for plowing. There is no gas pump between Lashkar Gah and Zaranj. Hence gasoline for motorcycles, tractors, and, increasingly, pick-up trucks used in the flourishing smuggling trade, has to be brought long distances. Increasingly during the seventies, Iranian gasoline in four-gallon tins was brought into the Helmand Valley from Zahedan in Iran since the pick-up traffic normally plied this route. At places along established smuggling routes, underground fuel dumps were maintained. WBT
32 The plows are wood, with a metal conical point. Some heavier, more advanced steel plow designs are seen; the harrower is constructed locally of wood. WBT
33 But these are subject to possible yearly flooding with the spread of the *hamuns*. The land is so flat, the lakes so shallow, that a rise in the lake level of two or three feet can inundate much of this land. The villagers at Asak, a small cluster of huts made from the dried lake reeds on the eastern shore of the Hamun-i Puzak, complained that they had attempted to grow their own wheat but had been prevented from doing so by a khan at Chakhansur from whom they would otherwise be obliged to purchase it. Their main activity was raising cattle that roamed through the shallow waters of the *hamun*, grazing upon the tender shoots of the new rushes. In the autumn, villages around the *hamuns* normally burn off the dried reeds, which become extremely dense, so that their cattle may be able to reach the fresh sprouts in the early spring. This practice has gone on for a long time; a photograph taken by the Perso-Afghan Arbitration Commission (1903–1905) shows a vast column of smoke rising above a *hamun*. WBT

Chapter 3: Agricultural and Pastoral Production

34 Oxen trample the wheat on circular platforms of hardened earth, knocking the grain ears off the stems. WBT
35 This process is similar throughout rural Afghanistan. WBT
36 It amounts to a more efficient plow. WBT
37 On the shaft, above the spade, is a wooden crosspiece, or projection, on one side only. This is the foot brace required by bare feet. WBT
38 Demographic Research Project, The Prime Minister's Central Statistical Office, *Atlas of Villages, With an Explanation of Local Administrative Districts,* Vol. 3, 1975, p. 119. GRA
39 *Statistical Data on Afghanistan (1350–1352),* p.125. GRA
40 Demographic Research Project, p.119. GRA
41 *Statistical Data on Afghanistan (1350–1352),* p.125. GRA
42 *Statistical Data on Afghanistan, (1350–1352),* pp. 123, 139, 142, 143
43 Kakar, *Afghanistan in the Reign of Amir 'Abd al-Rahman Khan,* 1975, p.131. GRA
44 After the establishment of the Republic in Afghanistan in July 1973, land taxes came under investigation, and in 1976 progressive taxes were imposed. GRA
45 C. H. Bosworth, *Sistan under the Arabs,* 1968, p. 26. GRA
46 Even from this small amount remaining to the farmer, some must be paid to the miller. In Khwaja 'Ali Sehyaka, a diesel mill was operated by the khan, who took an additional percentage of grain ground. WBT
47 The division of the harvest is conducted on a hand threshing platform, and normally the khan is present. The khan's portion, and all those portions he receives for future distribution as wages to entitled community members, is then loaded onto camels and delivered to his residence, where it is placed in large, but shallow pits dug into the ground. At Khwaja 'Ali Sehyaka these are close to the base of the sandstone mound upon which the archaeological site rested. The broad opening of the pits was simply covered over with tamarisk mats and sand. It is hard to imagine that mice and rats, which abound in the region, do not exact a considerable toll on the harvest thus stored. The individual farmers were able to carry their shares away on the backs of none-too-heavily laden donkeys. We attended this division at Khwaja 'Ali Sehyaka in November 1975. WBT
48 Tate, *Seistan (A Memoir on the History, Topography, Ruins and People of the Country),* 1910–1912, p. 329. GRA
49 It is common throughout the lower Helmand Valley and Afghan Sistan so far as we could determine. WBT
50 Anyone who has travelled in rural Afghanistan knows that these extraordinary mastiffs are not ordinary dogs. With a thick muscular neck, powerful jaws and forequarters, and clipped-off ears, their brutish and ferocious charge greets the visitor to almost any camp or house. Motion more than strangeness motivates them to some extraordinary acts of violence and self-destruction. I have seen these dogs run at a gallop into moving vehicles. Yet, it is perfectly true that if one stands stationary before their charge, or even sits or lies down,

they will cease charging and, at most, approach in puzzlement to sniff one out. One's natural sense of preservation renders this last course of activity both tense and difficult, but it works. It has been demonstrated that it works as well with attacking wolves. WBT

51 *Statistical Data on Afghanistan (Years 1350–1352)*, p. 127. GRA

52 It is not uncommon for such employees of khans to pass long periods without being paid. Frequently recruited from small towns or farms outside the district, they are lured by the khan's men, his personal servants and bodyguards. We encountered instances where these men had been purchased as boys in Pakistan. They perform a variety of tasks for the khan. If a farmer is behind on something he owes to the khan, one of these men may act as an enforcer and is empowered to inflict physical pain or break an arm or a leg of the victim. They tend to wear dressier clothes, carry rifles, and wear crossed bandoliers of shells. They do no manual labor. Some may wear an earring, but these seemed to be simpler servants in charge of the khan's womenfolk. These "bully boys" may journey to neighboring towns to swagger about, spend money, and boast about how liberal the khan is who employs them. Lashkar Gah is a favored town for their operations. In this fashion they have little difficulty in recruiting the special servants the khan requires: a mechanic/driver for his truck or jeep, a cowherd. The promised salary is handsome, but when the naïve young man arrives in the village, the khan, using one excuse or another, puts off payment of the salary. Instead, he lends the worker a smaller amount at interest. The employee is soon trapped by debt, and repeated supplication only succeeds in obtaining additional small loans. Without money the young man cannot leave Sistan. Usually, he does not know precisely where he is, or how far he has been brought. He cannot carry sufficient water to make the journey back on foot, even supposing he knows the direction to travel. If he walks along the valley, he must pass through villages. There he may be detained by any khan who knows he is attempting to escape from his employer, perhaps owing money against the salary never paid, or perhaps having committed a theft. He will be sent back to his khan, who at the least will berate him for his ingratitude. In the course of several years we met several such young men. All of them were open, naïve, and friendly, the type the khan's agents seek out. They seemed to bear their lot with quiet desperation, if not resignation, and they show neither fear nor shame in telling their stories. I do not know what eventually happens to these young men. Many must escape somehow, perhaps when the khan tires of their bothersome presence. WBT

53 The flock may stay out for two or even three days before returning to the valley for water. In the spring when there are still shallow ponds of fresh water deep inside the *dasht*, shepherds may stay out with their flocks until these have dried up with the approaching hot weather. The shepherd's food consists of flour made into a dough with sheep's milk he collects in a small aluminum bowl, and he bakes it in the sand. WBT

54 This bush is virtually invisible to the naked eye, being very small and growing low to the ground. Even to a practiced observer, the *dasht* upon which these

Chapter 3: Agricultural and Pastoral Production

flocks graze contains a few dead camel thorn bushes, no living plant for as far as the eye can see. WBT

55 In this case, I wonder if it is not sticks bound tightly together above the testicles, closing the spermatic cord and its artery so that the testicles below lose sensation and can be cut away without bleeding and with diminished chance of infection. Simply crushing the testicles, besides causing the animal wild discomfort, would precipitate rupture, internal infection, and death. In either case, I have not observed the operation. WBT

56 *Statistical Data on Afghanistan (Years 1350–1352)*, p. 127. GRA

57 Since their pasture is in the shallow waters of the *hamun* where they may browse for eight or more hours a day, I wonder if this is not the liver fluke common to the Nile and Tigris-Euphrates deltas. The Helmand was some years ago reported on no unimpeachable authority to be the only major river between the Tigris and the Indus free of the schistosome, but this must be doubted. The evidence of the cattle supports its presence. WBT

58 Sistani, *"Lake Zareh," Aryana,* Joint Issue 258, Hamal-Saur 1343/1965, pp.176–7. GRA

59 Though debilitating, and perhaps eventually a contributing cause of mortality, schistosomiasis is slow in development and seemingly not always fatal in itself. WBT

60 Unidentified. WBT

61 Unidentified. WBT

62 McMahon, "Recent Survey and Exploration in Seistan," 1906, p. 336. GRA. This is a paraphrase of McMahon's description. MA

63 *Statistical Data on Afghanistan (Years 1350–1352)*, p. 129. GRA

64 Local opinions varied vociferously on this point, since a camel is a valuable possession. When in 1974 we attempted to organize a caravan to reach with greater ease remote areas difficult for motor cars, we could find hardly a camel owner/driver who did not insist his camel had to have water every third day and special watery gruel (to be packed) as food once a day. Since this matter could not be resolved, the journey was made by vehicle and on foot. WBT

65 And has more buoyancy. WBT

66 Or keeps their heads up using reins. WBT

67 I have heard men refer to other men's daughters as "jackals" in the presence of others where it was received as a jest. In private, I do not believe it would be so received. WBT

68 Tate, *The Frontiers of Baluchistan*, 1909, p.171. GRA

69 The "camel thorn" bush. WBT

70 But also as an inferior form of riding animal. WBT

71 *Statistical Data on Afghanistan (Years 1350–1352)*, p.129. GRA

72 But only by the khans. WBT

73 *Statistical Data on Afghanistan (Years 1350–1352)*, p.128. GRA

74 Horses are, in fact, rare, and seldom seen out of their stables. My guess is that in 1971, in the Helmand Valley below Kuh-i Khan Neshin, there might not have been more than a couple dozen horses. The largest stable I saw was

that of Lal Muhammad Khan at Deshu with six horses. In upper Helmand Province they are more numerous, but the figure given here is surely inflated, as the author asserts. The climate of Nimruz Province is still more unsuited to horses. The only horses I ever saw in Nimruz were kept by the military at their forlorn post at Qala-i Fath, but I assume there are several others in the province. WBT

75 This horsefly is especially common near the lakes. The horses of the Perso-Afghan Arbitration Commission, 1903–1905, suffered great mortality from this pest. WBT
76 This is not the *tazi*, or Afghan hound, which is a land chase dog. WBT
77 The *tazi* of Sistan is a short-haired variety. In the summer it wears a padded quilt of rags on its back to prevent the intense sun and heat from cracking its skin. In the winter a similar garment is worn for warmth. WBT
78 While probably not near to extinction, their numbers are severely depleted, and we did not spot one more often than once a year. WBT
79 This practice was introduced by foreigners from the various diplomatic and aid missions. Actually, very few khans possess motor vehicles capable of pursuing gazelles. WBT
80 This is the method favored by the khans and their sons. WBT
81 The fox was ransomed and set free. WBT
82 Since we were deliberately attempting to tame the fox, this playful treachery was more easily achieved. WBT
83 The Afghans do not, of course, eat boar. While their number may be declining in the reed beds of the *hamuns*, they are greatly increasing in the irrigated lands around Lashkar Gah. Abandoned agricultural settlements, disused canals clogged with reeds, flooded fallow fields have greatly enlarged the wild boar's habitats in this region, and they were considered to be great sport among foreign diplomatic and aid mission personnel stationed at Kabul and Lashkar Gah. WBT
84 Jackals abound; the presence of wolves we could not verify. WBT
85 The action is also achieved by jostling and swinging a leather bag suspended between upright poles. WBT
86 Dripping through the porous cloth, more than evaporation, achieves the effect. WBT

Chapter 4
Crafts, Trade, and Travel

The Population

It has been intended that this research should shed light on one individual and geographically small area with regard to people and human resources, which are considered some of the major factors in progress and the understanding of society. People can make great use of resources and treasures to make for themselves favorable and effective grounds for the propagation of economic activities. The results are increased production and a rise in the standard of living. From an economic standpoint, this area is now backward, with a standard of living lower than the Asian average. In Sistan overpopulation and its attendant problems are not a cause for concern. Instead, population decline is worthy of close inspection, for fluctuations in the population here have long historical antecedents. From our study of the archaeological ruins of the region, it is possible to calculate that before the invasion of Tamerlane towards the end of the fourteenth century its population numbered around 250,000.[1] By the time of the Boundary Commission in 1281–82/1903–04, it was figured that the inhabitants numbered roughly 161,000, on the basis of each farm family consisting of 4.3 individuals. This was better than in 1250/1872, following a fifty-year period of anarchy and bloodshed in Sistan, when Sir Frederic Goldsmid reckoned the population of the region to be only 45,000.[2]

A survey of 25 workers who in 1352/1974 were employed in our excavations revealed that farm families averaged 4.8 members. Inquiries among 27 workers the following year revealed an average of 4.6 members per family. While the average of the two above figures is 4.7, a survey of 678 families in Kabul showed each family averaged 7.5 members.[3] In a 1970 study, Professor Dupree calculated that the average number of members per family in various areas of Afghanistan to be from 7.0 to 7.7.[4]

Table 4.1

Number of Families in Various Villages along the Qala-i Fath Canal

Village	Farmers	Shepherds, Animal Hirers, Shopkeepers	Khans	Clergy	Carpenters	Blacksmiths	Barbers	Canal Keepers
1. Mehrabad	120	28	4	2	1	1	1	
2. Baluchan	55	23	3	2	1	1	1	
3. Baghak Pa'in	10	9		2		1		
4. Baghak Boland	16	7		2	1			
5. Mateh Jat, Shuri	12	3		1				
6. Na 'Ilaj	9	2		1				
7. Shahr	10	4	1	1				
8. Tao Shakh	66	35	3	3	2	2	1	
9. Modi	44	23	2	2	1	1	1	
10. Malakhan	16	2		1				
11. Delanguk	54	25	1	1	1	1	1	
12. Hauz	54	25	2	2	1	1		
13. Zandak	20	8		2				
14. Godri	42	23	2	2	1	1	1	
15. Shuri Pa'in	45	8	1	1	1	1	1	2
16. Shuri Bala	15	4		1				1
17. Shahr-i Nao	45	7		1			1	6
18. Sabzgozi	60	40		2	1	1		9
Total	693	276	19	29	11	11	8	18

A comparison of the above figures suggests that Sistan's population is very small relative to the rest of the country. The figures in Table 4.1 were taken from my 1352/1974 investigation in the areas adjoining the Qala-i Fath Canal.

By reckoning that each family has on average 4.7 members, one can place the total population of this area at 4,991. Not taking the uninhabitable sandy region into account, the above population lives in an area 35 km (22 miles) long by 10 km (6 miles) wide on average. This region, then, is about 350 square km (135 square miles) with a population density of slightly over 14 individuals per square km. United Nations statistics estimated the population of the rest of Afghanistan to be 28 person per square km.[5] By comparison with the rest of Afghanistan, therefore, the population density is less than average. But even with the limited population subsisting in a vast land area, the standard of living is extremely low.

In the villages along the Qala-I Fath Canal, Qala-i Fath has 24,000 *jeribs* of agricultural land, Jui Nao, 12,000, and Sabzgozi, 6,000, for a grand total of 42,000 *jeribs*.[6] All of this land belongs to 18 khans and 18 village owners, or 3.5 percent of the region's inhabitants.

Population decline in the lower reaches of the Helmand and Afghan Sistan has many causes. A few of the factors which have great influence and create change in this statistic are as follows:

1. With regard to public health in the province of Nimruz and those portions of the province of Helmand that we have been investigating, health standards are very low. As a result of inaction by the health services, dropsy and related deaths are rife, especially among children, and certain diseases—such as defluxion (or alopecia) of the chest,[7] pneumonia, measles, smallpox and the like, for which there exist in the cities of the world adequate treatments and medication—are in this area a major cause of death.

2. Only a few people in Afghan Sistan are addicted to the smoking or ingesting of opium, in contrast to G.P. Tate's contention that 80 percent of the population was so addicted.[8] In my observations, not more than 10 percent of the inhabitants of Afghan Sistan may be addicts.[9] For example, of the 25 excavation workers, representing various parts of this region, employed by us in 1351/1973, only one was an opium addict. Similarly, in 1352/1974 no one was addicted, while in 1353/1975 two out of 27 were addicts.[10] Because opium addiction is deemed a vice and a crime,[11] its perpetrators try their utmost to hide it. For this reason, it would be impossible to gather accurate statistics on the problem without actually living with those being observed. Instead of approximately 4 percent that my observations suggest, their estimate is closer to 10 percent. Tate's statement that the problem of addiction impacted the birth rate in this area may have been made because during Tate's own lifetime,

a higher percentage of the populace were indeed dependent upon opium, thus coloring his opinions. Now, however, one may assume that the effects of this habit are not great on the birth rate. The problems connected with opium have far less effect on birth rate than do other problems in the region: lack of modern medical services, poverty, propagandization of the people with regard to material needs, physical afflictions, exhaustion from day-to-day physical labor, lack of energy, and poor nutrition.

In any event, as a result of factors discussed above, the average number of members per farm family in Sistan is probably about 4.6, of whom two replace each parent, so a mere six-tenths of a person remains to increase the population.

3. In comparison with most regions of the country, the costs of getting married are greater in relation to income. The purchase price of the gift and other general wedding costs are insupportable. Some young people, either permanently or temporarily, are unable to afford a wedding. The postponement in life of one's wedding plans certainly has an effect on the birth rate.[12]

   In addition, the overwhelming majority of women in this region breast feed their children, normally for a period of two years. When the mother herself receives inadequate nourishment, this method of child rearing both weakens the mother and shortens her life span and endangers the life of the child. Furthermore, this two-year lactation period prevents the parents from conceiving another child for a while after one birth. These two factors have an effect on both the birth rate and the general decline in population.

4. The existence of a very large land area for work and the fact that discrepancies exist in wages paid from one place to the next do not escape people's notice, in particular the young. Working outside this area repays a person. In 1351/1973 the disparity between wages paid in this region and those paid in a neighboring region was a factor of two;[13] in 1353/1975, the difference was a factor of three to four times, so that we did not succeed in hiring anyone to work for our archaeological project for less than 70 afghanis per day.[14] During the same year, however, on the archaeological excavation project in Hadeh in the province of Nangarhar under the auspices of the General Excavation Authority, the daily wage per worker was 35 afghanis, with which the people were content but could not all be employed by the project.

Chapter 4: Crafts, Trade, and Travel

Now most of the region's youths spend from three to six months annually working in other regions and return home with considerable sums of money. The existence of wide possibilities for work and the means of securing a livelihood beyond this region has caught the notice of people here to the point that they travel to likely areas whenever the opportunity arises.

5. In 1352/1974 the government of Iran built a dam in the Kuhak area in a channel of the Helmand with the help of American engineers. This dam brought the Helmand under control in the direction of the Sabiri Basin. The adequacy of the water level in the portion of the basin belonging to Iran is no longer threatening to them. Whenever the Iranians have no need for additional water and there is an excess in the Sabiri Basin, they cut the flow of water to Iran through the Kuhak Dam and force the flow entirely into the Nad-i 'Ali Rud on the Afghan side of the border and into the Puzak Basin. As a result, every year since 1330/1952 during periods of high water, a great proportion of the former agricultural lands surrounding the Puzak Basin is submerged and removed from crop production. On the other hand, at the first sign of drought, when this water might be useful on the Afghan side of the border, the gates of the Kuhak Dam are thrown open to their maximum extent, sending an increased amount of water in the direction of Iran.[15]

In this way, lands that received water and were cultivated before the building of the Kuhak Dam now suffer from lack of water. In order to circumvent this problem, landlords and farmers decamped to other areas. With respect to this situation, 'Abd al-Hamid Nahif Zahri wrote thus:

> Especially from 1330 H.S. or 1952 onward, that Our Iranian brothers have constructed a baked brick dam[16] in the vicinity of Kuhak near the frontier above the Helmand towards the Sabiri Basin, bringing the flow of water under control. As a consequence most of the agricultural lands in the center of Chakhansur and much of the county of Chakhansur have been inundated, while other areas have been drained and left dry. As a result, many of this region's inhabitants have been obliged to move to other provinces so that the population diminishes daily, such that in 1303/1925 which is to say 32 years ago, the population under local government jurisdiction in Chakhansur and

Charburjak numbered 72,000 individuals; now although the county of Lash and Juwain, the county of Deshu, and the area of Khash Rud who at that time together numbered fewer than 30,000 people and that, according to the formula for population growth, should now number roughly 350,000. Yet according to the statistics of the Ministry of Education, during the month of May 1345/1967 they in fact numbered 111,994 people.[17]

Although the population of Iranian Sistan has increased during the past few years by 200,000 people, its entire population is now estimated at 700,000, which is still underpopulated in comparison with other areas of Iran.[18]

6. Another factor which limits the agricultural land while increasing the amount of unworked land is the encroaching sand. The Helmand River carries sand and silt from the mountains and the lands through which it traverses to the Sistan Basin. This has been happening for many centuries and has now almost filled up the low-lying areas of Sistan. During the summer when the water in the Basin is low, sands which have been exposed by the 120-day winds are blown by the same agency over the agricultural lands to the southeast of the Basin as far as the Helmand. In addition, in some areas of Sistan where the layer of topsoil has been removed by wind erosion, there is exposed a layer of sand that was laid as an alluvial deposit in the past during the period when the Helmand Basin covered a greater area. The depth of this sand layer decreases with distance from the Basin. This layer of sand is another source of the sand that is now deposited over some areas by the wind.[19]

The unfortunate thing is that sands from that portion of the basin belonging to Iran that have been carried by these winds continue to drift southeast into Baluchistan. Mountains such as the Kuh-i Malik Siyah along the border near Robat and Malik Dokand form a barrier, changing the wind direction and sand movements from southeast to east or even northeast. It is for this reason that the left bank of the Helmand as far as the vicinity of Kandahar is covered with this sand—thus the name of Registan.[20] According to some sources, the amount of sand in the Registan of Afghan Sistan is greater than in the past.[21] Areas that were formerly populated and cultivated are now covered in sand, as is shown by the hundreds of ancient ruins and the signs of life and agriculture up through

Chapter 4: Crafts, Trade, and Travel

the time of the Timurids in the site of Shahr-i Gholghola, in the surrounding Sar-o-Tar region, and over a vast area to the north, stretching to the Dasht-i Amiran.[22] In addition, if one compares the photographs taken by Hackin, the French archaeologist, who visited the historical ruins of Sistan in 1315/1936, with the present conditions, an increase in the sand is evident even in the short space of 38 years.[23] It is clear that the incursion of the sand has gradually diminished the agricultural land and forced the people who lived off this land to leave.[24]

7. Another factor leading to the decrease in agricultural land in the lower reaches of the Helmand River and Afghan Sistan is the devastation of the irrigation system in that region. The factors listed below have recently had an effect on the irrigation system of the area.

   a) At the end of the two consecutive dry years 1349–1350/1971–1972, the water level had fallen along the lower Helmand, resulting in some canals drying up completely and several others running very short of water.[25]

   b) With the deforestation of Sistan, the 120-day winds became stronger and more prolonged, so that Gholam Khan (an old man of the region) now calls them 'the 320-day winds.' As a result of the deforestation and the increased wind, the amount of sand deposited in the irrigation canals is greater and the task of cleaning them is more onerous.[26]

   c) As has been mentioned, with the building of the Kajaki Dam on the lower Helmand the water has become clearer and swifter and deepened its bed more rapidly. As a result, the agricultural lands and the irrigation canals are now higher than the river, and the flow of water to them has been cut off.

For these reasons the irrigation systems in the lower reaches of the Helmand and Afghan Sistan now face paralysis, and the amount of water delivered to the agricultural lands is gradually diminishing. As a result of the decrease in agricultural lands and their products, the people who obtain their livelihood from them have slowly been obliged to leave and go elsewhere. Because of the decrease in population and in the number of agricultural workers, wages for those picking cotton in Darwishan, Laki, and Safar rose from two afghanis per *man* in 1353/1975 to more than ten afghanis per *man* in 1354/1976. Even at those higher wages, sufficient workers could not be found.[27]

These factors are all causes of the downward trend in the population graph of this region. With fewer people engaged in the effort, the struggle against the depredations of nature, chiefly wind and sand, is gradually becoming weaker in Sistan. Perhaps in the future the remaining people will succumb, and the entire area will be taken over by the wind and the dust.

Housing

In the lower Helmand and Afghan Sistan region not only does the agricultural land belong to a 3 or 4 percent minority of the population, but this minority also considers the uncultivated land to be its own and does not allow anyone else to work it or to live on it. The farmers of this region are not only barred from having their own land, they also do not own their homes. The landowners of the region are not willing to sell their land to the landless who want to build a cottage on it. If a homeless person wishes to build a cottage beyond the agricultural lands along the edges of the desert or in the sandy, waterless areas among the *dashts*, far from the means of a livelihood, without any records of land ownership, the landlords can still block their efforts simply by proclaiming that all of the agricultural lands of the Helmand Valley and the uncultivated *dashts* on both sides of the valley belong to them. This claim of the khans is generally accepted, and the people of the area believe the khans own all the agricultural and non-agricultural lands of the valley, the sandy plains, the mountains, and the hills.

Because of the general need for housing among the people, the landlords can squeeze as much profit as they want from the peasants and workers. For example, if a farmer chooses to take a job other than farming in which he will not be under the landlord's control, or if a neighbor or worker defies the landlord, the landlord will threaten to expel him from his land. The movement of peasants from one area to another is not an easy thing. In addition to the fact that they have no means of transport, moving from the property of one khan to that of another interrupts their work for several days. Moreover, the second landlord often finds it difficult to fit the newcomer into his own economic structure.[28]

Under these conditions, the farmers, workers, and others may, with the permission of the landlord at places designated by him, build themselves simple temporary shelters. They set about building wattle and daub huts from local materials. In some areas of the Helmand Valley indigenous trees grow, such as the tamarisk, and the people use tamarisk branches

Chapter 4: Crafts, Trade, and Travel

Figure 4.1. Framing of a Baluch dwelling, formed of bound scrub tamarisk boughs, at Khwaja 'Ali Sehyaka, Helmand Province, 1976.

Figure 4.2. Baluch dwelling with tamarisk framing (left), woven reed mats placed over the tamarisk framing (rear right). At rear center the mats have been partly mud-plastered. Khwaja 'Ali Sehyaka, Helmand Province, 1975.

regularly in the construction of their dwellings. Cut tamarisk branches are woven into a mat (Baluchi *chapar*), and the longer twigs are tied together in groups of five. The thick ends of the bunches are stuck into the ground at specific intervals. The basic shape of the house is created with a series of these bunches (Baluchi *kori*), including the door.

The first stage in a house is to make an oval structure, bend the top

Figure 4.3. A completed Baluch dwelling, the reed mats covered with mud plaster. A portion of the ceiling is left unplastered for the escape of smoke. Khwaja 'Ali Sehyaka, Helmand Province, 1975.

Figure 4.4. The size of the entry to a Baluch dwelling is illustrated by the farmer 'Abd ar-Rahim and his son standing by his house. Near Hauz, Nimruz Province, 1974.

Chapter 4: Crafts, Trade, and Travel

inwards, and tie the opposite bunches together (Fig. 4.1). On the outside over the skeleton they affix mats made of closely-woven tamarisk branches, and cover the house with these mats (Fig. 4.2).[29] Because the walls of the house are upright, bowed toward the center, and the ceiling is not level, you bang your head on the wall when walking upright around the house. The outer surface of the mats is covered with daub (Fig. 4.3). The houses have only one narrow entryway, usually 120 by 60 cm (47 by 23 in) (Fig. 4.4).[30] This doorway admits little light, and the house has no windows. An entirely daubed house would be completely dark, so on one side of the house an area of the matting is left undaubed so that light may filter through and light the house (Fig. 4.5). Sometimes these undaubed patches have various geometric and decorative shapes, rounded, triangular, and the like. These serve to admit light into the house and to provide exterior and interior decoration. In winter these bare patches are daubed over to make the house warmer. In the summer, they remove a large section of daub on the northwest (windward) side of the house and attach thorn twigs to the mat or to the frame. Alternately, they tie together bunches of thorn with string and secure them to a wooden structure erected 1.5 m (5 ft) from the house wall, and attach the top of this to the roof of the house. In some places, they attach the matting to that part of the house also. Some villagers pull the skirt of the matting away from the house frame and store milk and other perishable foodstuffs in the resulting space, which is the coolest place in the house. The thorns are kept wet throughout the day so movement of the wind brings moist, cool air into the house. In this way the air inside the house is 10°C to 15°C cooler than the outer air. At night the occupants usually sleep on a *maneh*, a large wooden and reed platform that most Baluch families attach to their houses (Fig 4.6).[31]

Figure 4.5. Light-admitting panels on the sides of Baluch dwellings are frequently executed in decorative designs. Khwaja 'Ali Sehyaka, Helmand Province, 1975.

The Helmand Baluch

Figure 4.6. A Baluch dwelling in summer. The mud plaster has been knocked off; woven woolen *qilims* have been placed over the top as sun shades. The outside platform is for the storage of food away from the reach of animals and provides a sleeping platform for the family. Khwaja 'Ali Sehyaka, Helmand Province, 1975.

These houses have no surrounding enclosures. A full 50 percent of Baluch families live tedious and monotonous lives in rustic houses such as this, shared between all the family members, usually numbering between four and five, along with their hens, roosters, and sheep. They have no lavatories, but make use of the wide surrounding areas of land to relieve themselves. The *tashnab* (an area for washing) is also located outside the dwelling. There is another washing area within the house, at one end. This end of the house is set aside for this purpose and is curtained off. Sometimes they seclude this area with piles of rugs, bedding, and quilts. During the day when the men are away at work, the women are obliged to wash here, whereas the men wash in the open air in the canal or in the Helmand River. Their animals are usually tethered outside near the house. Sometimes they keep sickly or newborn animals inside with them. The wheat that is the peasant's portion at harvest time is kept outside the house inside reed mats that have been rolled and stuck firmly in the ground and covered with daub (Baluchi *jilt*). These resemble stumps of mud pillars. Sometimes they dig a hole (*kram*) and bury the wheat inside it. On top of this they spread a layer of white straw and daub, covered with earth or sand. In any case, mice and other rodents dig their way in and take their share.

The wheat bread that forms the normal diet of the farmers of the area is cooked by the women in ovens built outside the houses. Each family has its own oven. Occasionally, two or three families use a single oven cooperatively. To enable family members to enjoy more warm bread, they bake it twice a day.[32] Sometimes if they cook food such as soup, *pyava*, or curds in the oven or on an iron tripod in a part of the house interior set aside for the purpose. In the cold weather this area is also used for warming the house. If a family member becomes ill and it is necessary to nurse him at night, they keep a fire burning in this same place because they can nurse him better by the light of the fire, since some of the farm families can't afford oil and oil burners. These typical Baluch houses in the Helmand Valley are uncommon elsewhere in the country.

These houses can be built very quickly and cheaply. Usually a single person can build such a house in one or two days. It takes one person only about five hours to dismantle it. The owners can easily transport the used branches and mats elsewhere and build another house with them (Fig. 4.7). The people of the region cut tamarisk branches in their spare time and store them up so that they may use them to build themselves new houses at various times of the year. Since the stored branches dry out and lose their natural elasticity, builders soak them in water for two or three days before they use them to restore their flexibility. Stores of tamarisk branches can be seen near Baluchi houses (Fig. 4.8).[33]

The houses and fortresses of the khans and the wealthy are very different from the simple villager huts. Their homes are usually built of sun

Figure 4.7. The Baluch house is easily dismantled and the structural parts easily moved to a new location for cleaner ground, to be closer to new fields, for recently arrived relatives, or for other reasons. A house may be dismantled, moved, and re-erected in a single day. Khwaja 'Ali Sehyaka, Helmand Province, 1975.

Figure 4.8. Tamarisk branches of the sort used in the construction of Baluch houses are also used to fence private yards while drying for fuel. Khwaja 'Ali Sehyaka, Helmand Province, 1975.

dried mudbrick. The mountains are far from this region, and transporting stone is difficult due to the sandy plains. So houses do not contain stone in their foundation or construction. Some of the ancient buildings we studied were built of baked brick, but modern fortresses do not use it. In the living quarters of these buildings air shafts are constructed to ventilate the house. House walls are thick, their ceilings domed and very high. Ventilators are built through the walls to the outside in such a way that the houses remain cool. Even though the rooms are cold in the winter, this

Figure 4.9. Compound and house of 'Abdal-'Aziz Khan, one of the landowners of Hauz, Nimruz Province, 1974. The flat-roofed, concrete, mud brick, and plastered houses are considered more fashionable.

Chapter 4: Crafts, Trade, and Travel

cold is insignificant compared with the heat of the summer. The ventilators are built in the walls in such a way that the mouths face away from the direction of the wind, to avoid debris being blown into the house during periods of high winds. Ventilators are also occasionally installed in the domes of houses, where they also serve as decorations (Fig. 4.9).[34]

In some buildings one can also see *iwans* (vaulted halls open on one side) decorated with tall porticoes. These houses are built according to the wind direction, and the main entrance is in the leeward of the building (i.e., the southeast). In front of the house there is usually a dais where the khan meets the people.[35]

The construction of these houses depends upon the free labor of the farmers and artisans, and they are built at very little cost to the khans. For this very reason, such houses do not hold much importance for them, and sometimes when a khan's house needs to be repaired, it is abandoned instead and a new one built.

The shepherds of Sistan generally live like nomads in tents (Figs. 4.10, 4.11).[36] Cattlemen around the Basin build houses of the reeds that grow there (Fig. 4.12).[37] These houses are not geometrically designed and in many ways resemble the twig houses of the Baluch. These houses are also great fire hazards, and in the space of a few hours, or even minutes, an entire village can be burned down. It has to be said that the houses of the city of Zaranj, the capital of the present-day province of Nimruz,[38] are similar to those in other parts of Afghanistan.

Figure 4.10. A *palas* or goat hair tent belonging to a Baluch *kirakesh* (camel transporter) near the village of Hauz, Nimruz Province, 1974. These men camp on the edges of villages awaiting chance employment.

Figure 4.11. The *palas* of another *kirakesh*, to which a mudbrick outbuilding has been attached. Near Hauz, Nimruz Province, 1974.

Figure 4.12. Two Baluch, with the dwellings of Asak constructed of rushes and mud in the background. On the shores of the Hamun-i Puzak, Nimruz Province, 1974.

A group of wattle and daub hovels make up a village.[39] The villages of this region are, like the tamarisk houses, impermanent. By comparison with villages in other parts of the country, the villages in the lower Helmand valley have a shorter life span for several reasons:

1. The houses that usually make up these villages are built of perishable materials and quickly deteriorate due to natural and human causes. With the disappearance of the houses, the village naturally disappears—and probably springs up somewhere else.[40]

2. As mentioned above, the use of fertilizer is still not common in this region. Farmers prepare the semi-fertile ground for crops with animal and human manure. After a while when the soil around a village has become enriched, the khan orders the inhabitants of the village to move their homes elsewhere where fertilizer is needed.

3. The wide agricultural lands controlled by a khan are cultivated either every year or every other year. Sometimes, the village is a long way from the farmers' fields, forcing the farmers to live in temporary shelters near the fields to be worked that year. In such instances, the khan decides that the villagers should move closer to land being cultivated.

For these reasons, few villages in the area under discussion have proper names; most are known by the name of the local khan. Sometimes it happens that several villages in the territory of a khan are known by the same name. When a khan dies, his villages are renamed after his successor. Because the villages are in a constant state of flux, the inhabitants use the easiest form of nomenclature, that being the naming of things after the local khan. In addition, basic and enduring religious structures such as mosques and shrines, which are found in other parts of the country, are not to be seen here.[41] Some of the villages do have names other than the name of the khan, for example Shirak, Lop, and Lat in the area of Rudbar.[42]

Travel and Communication

The feudal economy is reflected in transport and in the use of beasts of burden. Of all such animals in Afghan Sistan, the camel excels the most in its ability to carry. Those responsible for transport of goods are known as *kirakesh*, their duties being to look after the camels and to carry freight. Their income is drawn from fees charged for the movement of goods.

Motorcycles are the best form of motorized transport, since much of the area is sandy and does not easily lend itself to road building. The sand dunes in this region are constantly being shifted by wind action, covering the roads that do exist. The extension of roads into areas not yet covered by sand is not practical, as there is always the danger that the sands may soon cover them. A few of the khans of this area also own motor vehicles,[43] but most of them use motorcycles for their personal comings and goings. Unencumbered by baggage, the motorcycle is well suited to the terrain. There is now daily passenger service between Lashkar Gah and Khan

Neshin on the right bank, and from Girishk to Zaranj, also along the right bank. Between Kandahar and Zaranj there is service three times a week. From Zaranj to Charburjak (approximately 70 km by unpaved motor track) until 1352/1974 there was an open Russian truck for public use. In 1354/1976 there was a twice-weekly service, the price of the trip being 100 afghanis, very expensive considering local income levels.

A limited number of trucks have routes from Lashkar Gah to Deshu, Khwaja ʿAli, and various other fixed stops along the right bank of the Helmand, carrying passengers and their belongings. There are small boats for use in carrying passengers and their belongings across to the left bank in times of high water. In addition, there are a few small boats belonging to the khans, these boats being made up of empty oil barrels lashed together.[44] In times of need barrels are put to many uses, and restored afterward. When the water level falls low, passengers cross the river on camels or other animals, or swim across. But when the water level is high, they cross by means of these boats. In addition, provision has been made by the government for a water gate keeper, Muhammad Amin, who lives near the water gate at Girishk. It is incumbent upon him to provide boats and crews whenever the need arises, to serve the routes on the Helmand in the provinces of Helmand and Nimruz. At present, he has arranged for two boats, one in Charburjak and another in the area of Deshu. When the waters are high, especially in the spring, his boats are put into operation in these places.

The boat which is moored at Deshu near Malakhan above the river can carry three people. It is attached to a line suspended between points on either side of the river and is moved by means of a winch. This boat, however, cannot carry heavy loads.

When the water is low and people can cross the river with animals or by swimming, boat service is suspended. Transportation of necessary government goods, such as dressed wood for building, telephone poles and the like, thrown into the water upstream, is also the responsibility of Muhammad Amin, who has to take them out of the water at prearranged points. Motor traffic along the left bank of the river from Banader to Malakhan is made very difficult because of the sand and rugged terrain around Kuh-i Khan Neshin—although some trucks can navigate it with difficulty by passing far to the south of Kuh-i Khan Neshin to reach Deshu, Khwaja ʿAli, and even Bandar-i Kamal Khan. Because of the difficulty, owners of these vehicles will only send them in this direction when absolutely necessary.[45] Owners of motor vehicles can generally only be persuaded to dispatch their vehicles along that side of the river or to the border regions when they see a very great necessity. Even so, they try if possible to avoid travelling on the left bank in several areas between Deshu and Khwaja 'Ali Sehyaka.

For this reason, most travel on the left bank from Darwishan to Charburjak and Bandar-i Kamal Khan is carried out by riding animals or on foot. To cross from the left bank of the river to reach the provinces and towns on the right bank is difficult, as there is no bridge crossing the river beyond Darwishan. In addition, with the exception of Lashkar Gah and Zaranj, the capitals of the Helmand and Nimruz provinces, there is no place where supplies such as gasoline and oil are available. In a few places in this region gasoline and other petroleum supplies are brought in from Zahedan.

Recently, planning of a major highway has been undertaken between Yakhchal, Deshu, and the Iranian border to open up of this region. This highway will begin at Lashkar Gah and continue to Border Post No. 22 on the Iranian border. The road will be 10 m wide and 464 km (288 miles) long and will be built of asphalt. Its total cost will be in the neighborhood of $80 million. The survey to plan the road was conducted in 1355/1977. With the completion of this project, another bridge will span the Helmand, in the vicinity of Deshu.[46]

Another road is now being built between Dilaram and Zaranj, from the northeast to the province of Nimruz. This will further diminish the area's isolation. This 416 km (259 miles) road will cost 35 million afghanis. It will connect Dilaram and Zaranj, the capital of Nimruz. Construction work began in 1349/1971, and as of 1353/1975 roughly 78 km (48 miles) of the road had been completed, another 53 km had a foundation, and the paving was scheduled to have been completed in 1355/1977; it is now finished.[47]

Adjacent to the present city of Zaranj there is an airport boasting a runway 1,000 m long and 30 m wide, able to support 2.5 kg of weight per square cm (35.5 psi), and unpaved. Until 1349/1971 the Bakhtar Afghan Airlines had regularly scheduled flights, but then the service was suspended. Now, an occasional flight takes place when officials perceive a need for it and allow it.[48]

Telephone connection in the province of Helmand reaches the county of Khan Neshin, and in the province of Nimruz reaches the county of Charburjak.[49] The area on the left bank of the Helmand between Charburjak and Darwishan has no telephones. From Lashkar Gah to Hazar Joft and Khan Neshin there is a set tariff for calls, so that a 3-minute call between Lashkar Gah and Hazar Joft costs 18 afghanis and from Lashkar Gah to Khan Neshin costs 30 afghanis. There is a post office in Lashkar Gah and another in Zaranj. From Lashkar Gah to Khan Neshin and the county of

Hazar Joft, and similarly from Zaranj to the county of Charburjak, the post is carried by contract vehicles. This service will also carry passengers. To reach other localities, there are contracted individuals who deliver the mail, and those who wish may return personal mail by the same route.

The government printing office of the province of Helmand issues twice weekly the Pashto language newspaper *Helmand*. This paper publishes primarily local and regional news and other news of importance. The greater part of the local news consists of stories and reportage concerning the province.[50] In addition to the newspaper, on feast days and festivals, ennobling sentiments are broadcast to the public by loudspeaker.[51] During holidays, there are films and cultural exhibitions, but these activities are limited to the towns and their immediate vicinity.[52]

The general populace in Afghan Sistan does not benefit from these activities; all of their news of the country comes from battery-operated radios, and items of importance are generally broadcast by the Baluchi service of Radio Kabul.

In the province of Nimruz, representatives of the Bakhtar News Agency disseminate the news. Because the lines of telephonic communication in Nimruz are not a channel system, the representatives of the Bakhtar Agency give news relating to Nimruz to agents of the Farah Agency to transmit to the capital. News in this province is concerned mainly with the projects of the seven-year plan; some of it is news of smuggling. A survey of news broadcast in 1334/1956 up to the month of December shows more than fifty news items. Newsworthy items in this province are printed in the newspaper *Sistan*, published in the province of Farah.

Crafts and Manual Arts

The disordered economy and unfavorable material conditions have turned the attention of the people of this region more towards the acquisition of everyday necessities and hindered the development of fine arts and crafts. As a result, such crafts have never developed or have remained in a very primitive state. What is surprising is that even the pottery industry, which in times past flourished enormously in this region, as attested by the prolific ceramic remains found in ruins and historical sites, is now nonexistent in the lower reaches of the Helmand and its environs. In spite of the fact that the people have plenty of good clay for making pots and ample fuel for firing them, they still get their clay vessels from Lashkar Gah and Kandahar.[53]

Chapter 4: Crafts, Trade, and Travel

Figure 4.13. Muhammad Anwar, carpenter, sawing a rough plank into thinner boards. Khwaja 'Ali Sehyaka, Helmand Province, 1975. Photo by Robert K. Vincent, Jr. © Helmand Sistan Project.

Carpentry

Carpentry and woodworking have also not been greatly developed among the Baluch. The usual occupation of a carpenter is the making and repair of agricultural equipment (Fig. 4.13). Most commonly made agricultural equipment are the yoke, the wooden fork, and the *mangasheh* (pitchfork), plus several other kinds of implements, such as the spade, the sickle, and the mattock, which are made of iron but have wooden handles (Fig. 4.14). In addition to agricultural implements, other things made of wood by the carpenters of the region include the cradle (Fig. 4.15); the spindle; the wooden frame for keeping the bedding off newborn infants; the *kalu*, or measure with a capacity of one *man* of wheat that is used as the standard measure; the *jugan* or mortar to pulverize various types of food; and decorated doors and windows for houses (Fig. 4.16). The carpenter's expertise in this region does not go beyond the making and repairing of these implements and necessities. The materials are provided by the customer. *Archeh* (douglas fir) wood is considered more suitable than the woods found in this area. Fir trees grow in the southern and eastern mountains of the country, and the wood is transported to other areas, though Sistan is far

Figure 4.14. Muhammad Anwar, carpenter, and the objects he had made: *mangasha* (pitchfork), *kamunūk* (child's playpen), *jaunat* (cradle), *jilak* (spindle). Khwaja 'Ali Sehyaka, Helmand Province, 1975. Photo by Robert K. Vincent, Jr. © Helmand Sistan Project.

Figure 4.15. *Jaunat* (cradle) made by a village carpenter. Khwaja 'Ali Sehyaka, Helmand Province, 1975. Photo by Robert K. Vincent, Jr. © Helmand Sistan Project.

Chapter 4: Crafts, Trade, and Travel

Figure 4.16. Doors of Baluch houses are often elaborately carved with geometric and floral patterns. Adam Khan by the door to his parents' house, Khwaja 'Ali Sehyaka, Helmand Province, 1975. Photo by Robert K. Vincent, Jr. © Helmand Sistan Project.

from the source and transportation is difficult because of the lack of roads. The wooden implements are also often made of tamarisk and any other kind of wood locally available. Another cause of the backwardness of carpentry in the region is the lack of basic materials, which has kept carpentry at a mediaeval level.

Masonry also has remained in a primitive state in Afghan Sistan. Unlike the khans, peasants, workers, and farmers, who make up the vast majority of the population, do not own houses or permanent dwellings because the land on which their houses stand does not belong to them. They themselves, therefore, do not know permanent home ownership. They build their temporary houses very simply from tamarisk mats free from any excess of design and in which no modern technical or artistic skill is visible. The dwellings of the khans, which are scarce in this area, are an exception in size but not in architectural quality or amenities.

Figure 4.17. Nur Muhammad, blacksmith, with apprentice, at his smithy. Khwaja 'Ali Sehyaka, Helmand Province, 1975. Photo by Robert K. Vincent, Jr. © Helmand Sistan Project.

Iron Working

Blacksmithing is also a necessary profession (Fig. 4.17). It, too, is limited to the making and repairing of basic agricultural implements. Every year the blacksmith gives free to each farmer and *kashtmand* one knife, an iron tripod upon which pans and other cooking vessels are placed, a packing needle, and a sickle.[54] For the making of other agricultural implements— such as spades, axes, and scythes—if the iron belongs to the buyer, the smith takes half the price, but if the smith himself provides the metal, he keeps the whole price. In making these implements of iron, the smiths use used machine and equipment parts that are brought into Afghanistan from abroad, such as used automobile suspensions, axles, and gears. The smiths of this region get used parts for their work from Kandahar and other places. They change the shape of the used parts by heating them and make the parts and implements that are needed. Although iron ore is available in this area, the smelting and extraction of the metal by the smiths is not usual.[55]

Chapter 4: Crafts, Trade, and Travel

Figure 4.18. Baluch woman spinning woolen thread with a *jilak* (spindle). Khwaja 'Ali Sehyaka, Helmand Province, 1975.

Weaving

Of the handicrafts of this region weaving of woolen textiles is worthy of notice. This craft is predominantly the preserve of the Baluch women, and progress and development of the craft are due to the skill and worthiness of these women (Fig. 4.18–23). The men help the women in the preparation and dyeing of the wool. The woolen textiles produced here include carpets, qilims, bags, saddle blankets, and hats. The carpets are woven in ancient designs. Innovation is rare in their construction or design. Designs

Figure 4.19. Wooden handled shears, *do-kirch*, used for shearing carpet knap. Khwaja 'Ali Sehyaka, Helmand Province, 1975. Photo by Robert K. Vincent, Jr. © Helmand Sistan Project.

Figure 4.20. Weaver beginning a *qilim* on a narrow ground loom. Khwaja 'Ali Sehyaka, Helmand Province, 1975. Photo by Robert K. Vincent, Jr. © Helmand Sistan Project.

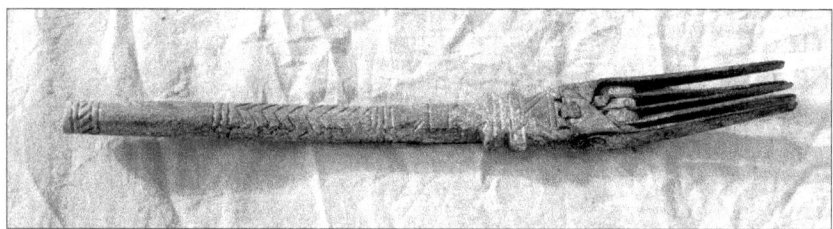

Figure 4.21. *Daup* (or *dūp*) resembling a comb, used in beating back woof in *qilim* weaving. The handle is carved wood, the tines iron. Khwaja 'Ali Sehyaka, Helmand Province, 1975. Photo by Robert K. Vincent, Jr. © Helmand Sistan Project.

of flowers and leaves, natural scenes, depictions of animals and birds or household implements do not exist in the carpets. There is no standard length or width in the making of carpets; dimensions vary according to the availability of materials, the needs of the household, and the enthusiasm or lack of it of the weaver. These carpets are not commissioned often enough that the sizes are standardized.[56]

There is also no consistency in the sorting of the wool quality and texture. Wool from different parts of the sheep, from different breeds of sheep, and even spring and autumn fleeces, which ought to be kept separate, are all mixed together in the carpet industry which can cause wrinkles in the carpet. Because the summer fleeces grow during the winter time and in the spring rains, they collect enough moisture to enable them to stretch, and wrinkles do not appear in them. But the autumn fleeces, which grow

Chapter 4: Crafts, Trade, and Travel

Figure 4.22. Baluch *qilim* with typical local design on purplish brown ground. Khwaja 'Ali Sehyaka, Helmand Province, 1976.

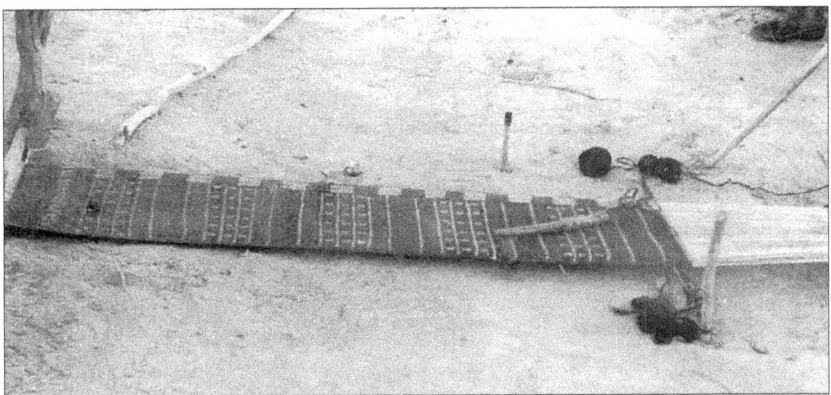

Figure 4.23. Portion of a *qilim* being woven on flat loom. Khwaja 'Ali Sehyaka, Helmand Province, 1975.

throughout the summer when the air is dry, develop many wrinkles when they get moist. This wrinkling lowers the quality of the carpet and shortens its life. Therefore, the autumn wool absolutely should not be used for the warp and weft, but only for the filling.

In the dyeing of carpets, vegetable dyes are available in some areas. From boiling a kind of shrub called *rudang* (an indigenous plant) they get the color brown, from willow leaves they get green, from pomegranate skin yellow, and by mixing these compounds with other colors they get red and bright orange. They also use walnut shells, an indigenous yellow spring flower called *zelir,* and *ushlan,* another plant, in carpet dyes. These plants are boiled until the color appears, then the wool is placed in the dye until it takes on a good color. Camel-colored, black, and white are obtained by using the natural fleeces in these colors.

With the introduction of chemical dyes, craftsmen gradually abandoned natural dyes in favor of chemical ones, since natural dyes are difficult to procure and mix and take longer to produce. But older carpets show that vegetable dyes had greater durability and do not change color very much. Domestic and foreign markets have shown a greater desire for vegetable dyes, and craftsmen have therefore shown an interest in a return to their use. Despite this, some places still use chemical dyes; the predominant color in their carpets is blue.

Rug weaving is a very difficult and extremely tedious occupation. One weaver might with difficulty weave one inch of a five-foot wide rug in a day. The work areas for rug weaving in Baluch villages are usually horizontal, and the loom is placed on the ground in such a way that the weaver is obliged to lean over to weave, sitting on the loom. There is great strain on the feet, shoulders, back, and neck. In addition, the eyes of the weaver are severely tried. But the product is very precious.

In a vertical working area, usually in houses with higher ceilings in the larger villages and towns, the loom is attached to a wall, and the weaver can sit more comfortably on a wooden stool or bench, is spared much bending over, and does not suffer as much strain. The problem with the vertical system of carpet weaving is this: the slackness of the web causes the pattern to be repeated or run together. To alleviate this problem, it is best that a pit be dug beneath the loom in the ground, so that the loom rests in it. The weaver can easily see the completed portion of the rug. In this way, stretching, crooked edges, and irregularity in the pattern can be avoided, and yet the weaver does not sacrifice any comfort.

Among the Baluch, the Madadkhani, Rokhshani Lajehyi, and Sanjrani tribes are known for their carpet weaving. The most famous Baluch carpets are those of the Madadkhani, which are usually brown-colored and, like the Maur carpets of Herat, have less soft hair.

A common problem in carpet weaving is that the warp threads of the web are wrapped at both ends around rollers. The threads at the ends are pulled together during weaving, while the threads in the middle stay apart. As a result, the carpet is made wider in the middle than at the ends, will not lie flat, and is usually puckered.[57]

In addition to carpets, Baluch women also make a kind of woolen bag called a *dozdan* in which they keep their possessions. Every Baluch girl is given one of these bags decorated with hoopoe feathers and shell-work as a dowry at her wedding. Since these textiles are decorative and highly prized, Baluch women sometimes use these bags arranged at one side of the room in decorating their houses. A *wadan* is a woven woolen bag used to hold salt.

Baluch hats are woven from camel hair in such a way that they cover the whole head except the eyes and neck. This style of hat is suited to the climatic conditions of Sistan, especially during high winds when they prevent sand and dust from entering the ears, nose, and mouth. In cold weather, they keep the head warm.

The qilims of the Baluch can be distinguished from those of other parts of the country by looking at the backs, especially regarding the method of weaving. The best kind of Baluch qilim is called a *spikar*, which means "white border." The borders of these qilims are white, and the centers are decorated with various designs and colors.

Tanning

Leather tanning is also practiced among the Baluch. The raw hides are treated in various ways. The hides of sheep and goats that are to be used for domestic purposes are usually made into *sinach*. In this method the hide is removed in the shape of a bag, with only the neck area being torn. The holes that remain where the animal's legs were are closed up. *Sinach* is prepared in a special way. First the *sinach* is filled with sand in order to remove the wrinkles. Then it is emptied, and a red substance called *chanak* is put in it. *Chanak* is a kind of shrub that grows in Sistan. It is boiled until it turns red. It tastes sour. This substance remains in the *sinach* for one week and then is replaced with another liquid that is obtained from the boiling of thorns and is a yellowish color. This substance remains in the *sinach* for four or five days. This last process is repeated several times until the skin is ready and soft. At the end of these processes, the raw hide has been transformed into dressed leather, and the *sinach* is henceforth called a *mashk*. The *mashk* is used for carrying water and making *dugh*. If people wish to use the *mashk* for storing prepared oil, they fill it with melon juice that has been boiled until it becomes sticky and leave it for ten to fifteen days. The Sistanis believe that the melon juice affects the *mashk* so that the oil will not spoil, even if it is kept for a long time. The *mashk* that is prepared for storing oil is called a *hak*.

In some areas, skins are prepared in a different way. In this method, they make some barley flour into a paste and leave it until it ferments (Fig. 4.24). They mix another quantity of barley flour with specific proportions of water, salt, and the fermented paste and put the skin in this concoction for a while. The length of time for which the skin is left changes with the season. During the warmer months, it remains for ten to twelve days, and

Figure 4.24. Large wooden tub in which paste for tanning hides is prepared. Khwaja 'Ali Sehyaka, Helmand Province, 1976.

in the colder months, from fifteen to twenty days. During this stage, the skin is taken out every day and stretched in all four directions to open the pores in the skin so that the mixture can penetrate well. At the end of this period, the skin is removed from the mixture, a portion of which is mixed with an amount of salt and flour and is rubbed into the skin, and the skin is left exposed to the sun to dry. It is next cleaned of all residue; if fragments of meat still adhere to the skin, they are removed with a special knife (Fig. 4.25). Finally, they moisten powdered pomegranate skins with warm water and rub this on the hide. After it dries, they again dampen it and scrape it. They repeat this operation twice and finally knead the

Chapter 4: Crafts, Trade, and Travel

Figure 4.25. Tanner scraping a hide with metal scraper. Photo location unknown, possibly Lashkar Gah. 1976.

Figure 4.26. A treated sheep hide upon which rests the metal scraper. Photo location unknown. 1976.

skin until it becomes soft. This completes the dressing of the skin. Hides tanned in this way are used in the making of leather coats and jackets, thongs for tying up agricultural equipment such as bundles of branches, leather goods, saddle straps, yokes, and harnesses (Fig. 4.26).

Embroidery

Hand embroidering is another valuable craft at which Baluch women are skilled. Some of the pleasing and valuable pieces that demonstrate this skill and accomplishment can be seen in Afghan Sistan. This craft reaches its apogee among the Baluch people in the men's hats and women's skull-caps (Fig. 27).[58]

Figure 4.27. A *qurs*, disc lozenge hat, belonging to Sultan Muhammad, one of our workmen. 1975.

Jewelry

Another craft which now is almost unknown in this area is goldsmithing. Because of poverty and the lack of basic necessities, Baluch women pay little heed to luxuries. In this entire area only one or two goldsmiths are to be found, and even they do not make enough to live on. Gold as an ornament for women is scarcely known in this region. Women's ornaments are generally made of tin mixed with a little silver.[59] Since the ornaments are made of alloys, whenever they tarnish it is felt that polishing is required. A greater portion of the goldsmith's time is therefore taken up in polishing these ornaments than in making or repairing them. The goldsmith's source of materials for these ornaments is from the people themselves. The Baluch women generally give their old and broken ornaments to the goldsmith. Part of this goes to the smith as wages, and of the remainder he is commissioned to make an ornament of the owner's choosing.

The usual kinds of ornament in this region include *tatik*, a triangular metal plate from one side of which a number of baubles hang. Baluch women hang these from their skullcaps (Fig. 4.28). A *poluk* is a star-shaped piece of metal worn in a hole in one side of the nose. A *pizvan*, a decorated metal semi-circle that is worn suspended from the center of the nose above the lip, *sangvar* (bracelets), and earrings make up most of the rest of the ornaments used by Baluch women. The goldsmith in Sistan is itinerant. Because of the way the people of the region are scattered,

Chapter 4: Crafts, Trade, and Travel

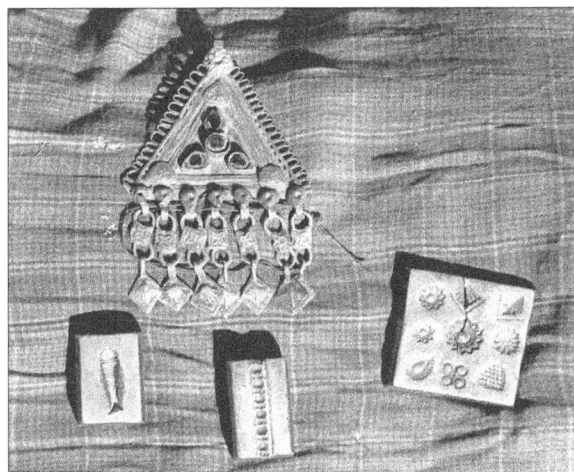

Figure 4.28. Brass molds and low quality jewelry made by silversmith Muhammad Isma'il, at Lop, Rudbar, Nimruz Province, 1975. Photo by Robert K. Vincent, Jr. © Helmand Sistan Project.

Figure 4.29. Smith Muhammad Isma'il fashioning jewelry on his *tayyak* (anvil), at Lop, Rudbar, Nimruz Province, 1975. Photo by Robert K. Vincent, Jr. © Helmand Sistan Project.

there is not enough work for him in any one locality. Since the tools of his trade are simple, he can easily travel from one village to another in the Helmand Valley, filling the needs of the Baluch women with regard to the making, repairing, and polishing of their ornaments. For example, in 1353/1975 I spoke with the goldsmith Muhammad Isma'il in the village of Lop, Rudbar (Fig. 4.29). He was originally from Khwaja 'Ali and had come there four days earlier to find work.

The art of weaving thread is in decline now in Afghan Sistan. It was known formerly that there were weavers in Kanak, Karim Koshteh, Chakhansur, and in the vicinity of the basin, and that they made some of the clothing of the local people. Now, in this entire region not a single meter of woven material is to be found, and the importation of foreign cloth, especially synthetic fabrics, has had a deleterious effect on the craft.[60]

Commerce

As a result of the backward system of production that has led to stagnation and lack of development in trade, the people of Sistan do little selling. Usually, their small transactions take the form of bartering things of equivalent value, such as a chicken for a few *man* of wheat or a pair of shoes for a few loads of firewood. In the whole area there is not a single large enclosed market.[61] There is usually a small shop in each village providing some of the basic necessities for the inhabitants.[62] The things found in these shops include tea, candy, matches, tobacco, soap, thread, needles, eggs, oil, and foreign cloth. In some of the shops a few basic medicines are also available, such as calamine, aspirin, and novalgin. These are brought from abroad and used without a doctor's instructions. The people procure most of these things in exchange for grain, though certainly some things are also sold for cash. Although moneylending is not common in Sistan, and there is no one who earns his entire living that way, some of the shopkeepers do in certain circumstances lend money at interest. The interest which they earn on their money is less than in other places. For example, on 1,000 afghanis they earn about 200 afghanis per year. This interest, moreover, is calculated only if they know that the borrower cannot pay off the debt in a short time.[63] If the borrower is a local village man and can be trusted not to default, no cash interest payment is required of him. Nevertheless, the lender will once or twice during the period of the loan ask for a couple of chickens and some milk or yoghurt and curds from the borrower at no charge.

Because of the dominance of the tribal system and the lack of capital and trade routes, trade in this region has made no notable progress, and no great merchants have appeared. There is no covered market in the entire area, and the necessary mechanisms for trading excess agricultural produce have still not been established. There is no grain chandler to deal

Chapter 4: Crafts, Trade, and Travel

with excess wheat and send it to the population centers where it would command a better price. This function is fulfilled by people from outside the region who come from Lashkar Gah and Kandahar. They come in the spring and give money in advance to those who need it, taking in exchange low-priced wheat at harvest time.[64] After the harvest they collect their wheat and leave. In a year of relatively little water, they take wheat from the left bank of the river near Lower Khwaja 'Ali and transport it eastwards by camel to Malakhan and to the motor stops on the right bank of the river opposite Deshu, Upper Khwaja 'Ali, and Khwaja 'Ali Sehyaka. Similarly, they take wheat of the left bank of the river from Lower Khwaja 'Ali westwards to Bandar-i Kamal Khan and Charburjak, where the motor stops for Zaranj are located, and from there by motor to Zaranj and Lashkar Gah. Another amount of surplus wheat is taken by the nomads who roam the border areas between Afghanistan and Baluchistan.[65] Since they are engaged in herding, they sell sheep, goats, and other livestock to the people of the Helmand Valley, and with that money they purchase wheat (Fig. 4.30). The nomads of the borders of the sandy deserts collect the needles of a certain kind of pine tree called *barek* and take them by camel to Lashkar Gah and Kandahar. Skinners and tanners buy these needles and use them in tanning. In Lashkar Gah in 1354/1976 the price of a single *man* of needles was 22 afghanis.

Fiugure 4.30. Migratory Baluch at Khwaja 'Ali Sehyaka, Helmand Province, 1975.

The buying and selling of animal skins is also not a specialized trade. To preserve the skins of camels and cattle the people treat them with ash while they are still fresh and treat sheep and goat skins with salt. Once or twice a year, buyers come from Kandahar or Herat and buy the skins. Skins are sold according to weight. In 1354/1976 camel skins were valued at 50 to 70 afghanis per *man*. A skin normally weighs from two to three *man*. A cow hide was valued at 100 to 120 afghanis per *man*, each hide weighing from half a *man* to two *man*. Goat skins were worth 50 afghanis and sheepskins as much as 120 afghanis each.

Another animal product that is sent to Kandahar or Herat is dried curds.

Ancient relics like seals and coins that the people of this area find in their wanderings through historical ruins and sites are collected and sold to the antique dealers who come once or twice a year from Kandahar or Lashkar Gah.[66]

Wool and animal fat are collected by some people of the region and exported. These products are sold piecemeal in small quantities by the herdsmen. As a result, the price of a *man* of wool in Sistan has risen to 400 afghanis by 1976. The price and the selling of the wool outside of the area is a severe threat to the carpet and weaving industries in Afghan Sistan. At present, throughout the region only a small number of people make carpets and qilims for sale.[67] In addition, the people of Afghanistan believe that clarified butter is better for one's health than is vegetable oil. For this reason, in Afghan Sistan the price of one *man* of clarified butter is 600 afghanis, whereas a *man* of vegetable oil costs 350 afghanis in 1976.

Animal products such as camels, cattle, sheep, animal fat, wool, chickens, and even eggs are exported from Sistan.[68] Such items as *bashur* and *shari* (fabrics for making clothes), shawls, plastic shoes, watches, radios, tape recorders, blankets, ceramic tiles, gasoline and other motor oils, tires, tubes, brown sugar, and even gold are imported. Transfer of merchandise in this region does not depend on local transactions alone, but also includes transit trade.[69] Because the region is sand-covered desert over much of its area, some foreign goods are also transferred through to other regions. The roads crossing this area are constantly changing due to the moving sands. Camels and other draft animals cross the trackless areas carrying goods. There are also several motor roads. In every vehicle there are one or two people who know the route. They scrutinize the sides of the road and guide the vehicles in the desert. They are ready for defense at any moment. The number of guards varies with the size and value of the load being carried. Whenever they are faced with an obstacle they leave the road and make a detour, and if they are obliged to stop, they try to remove the obstacle. Usually two or three vehicles travel at various distances from each other. The first vehicle carries the least valuable load and acts as a vanguard. The occupants leave signs for their comrades in the following vehicles concerning dangers so that the latter can prepare to remove the obstacle or to circumvent it. So that their comrades do not encounter the same difficulties, they leave signs along the road to warn them to change their direction. For example, on our return from Jali Robat on 16 November 1354/1976 along the northeast edge of the Gaud-i Zirreh basin, our guide spotted a thin raised line of sand at the side of the road giving warning of a roadblock, either by hijackers or police. To make the sign stand out more, several round stones had been added to the line of earth. Since we did not know the meaning of these road signs, the guide who had been hired for the expedition explained it. It is an indication to proceed with extreme caution, or alter one's route if need be.

Transport across the desert is frequent. For example, on 13 November 1354/1976, during the space of fifteen hours we saw 27 motor vehicles in the distance carrying goods or passengers between Khwaja 'Ali Sehyaka and Char Gumbad in the Shela Rud. On 16 November, during the space of seven hours of travel the mission saw 8 motor vehicles. In this year, the amount of water in the Helmand Basin had increased, and the runoff in the Shela Rud channel reached as far as the Gaud-i Zirreh. As a result of the water in the Shela Rud channel, the regular road was cut off to the west of Gaud-i Zirreh. During the brief time the mission was observing the area, the water dried up and the regular road was opened again. But a large number of drivers had not yet been informed of this, and they took a new route to the east of Gaud-i Zirreh, of which we were previously unaware.

Notes

1 While there is no way of making firm estimates of the population at this time, this figure would not seem unreasonable. At the height of the Timurid Renaissance in the area, ca. 1420–1480, the population may have been still larger. It was evidently greater yet in Parthian times if one may judge from the numerous ruins belonging to this age, and the dense cover of potsherds belonging to this period. WBT

2   Tate, *The Frontiers of Baluchistan*, 1909, pp. 223–4. GRA
3   Anne T. Sweetster, "Family Formation Attitudes among High School Girls in Kabul, Afghanistan," 1974 (Unpublished research), p. 6. GRA. While the unpublished version of this study was the one available to Amiri at the time of his writing, it was eventually published as Occasional Paper 9 by the Asia Society Afghanistan Council (New York) under the same title in 1976 and is listed such in the References. MA
4   Louis Dupree, "Population Review 1970, Afghanistan," Southeast Asia Series, *Asia*, Vol.XV No.1, 1971, p. 10. GRA
5   *Statistical Year Book, 1973*, New York, UN Publishing Service, p. 70. GRA
6   On the basis of local knowledge. GRA
7   Obviously alopecia is only symptomatic of a more serious disease. WBT
8   Tate, *Seistan (A Memoir on the History, Topography, Ruins and People of the Country)*, 1910–1912, p. 329. GRA
9   Addiction, or even use, appears to be very low indeed, and to be restricted primarily to the landowner class. Inexpensive as opium is, it is certainly still beyond the financial capability of peasant families to indulge. However, most men take *naswar*, a mixture of powdered green tobacco leaf and lime paste, which appears to be an extremely inexpensive addictive stimulant. People unused to it may be made dizzy, unsteady, and nauseous by taking a small quantity only, which is held under the tongue for maximum results. But those accustomed to it, as those accustomed to the betel nut, seem to require it perhaps a dozen times a day. WBT
10 While it might have been possible in 1975 for workers to hide opium addiction from us, their employer, because we were working in their villages, our camps in the sand dune fields of the Sar-o-Tar basin in 1973 and in 1974 for many weeks, would have made it impossible to hide regular use or to make regular purchases of opium without notice. MA
11 I do not believe the consumption of opium is considered to be a crime. That it may be considered a vice may reflect attitudes toward the khan class that uses it and is generally considered by the farmers to be wanton or dissolute in other ways as well. Hence, whatever stigma may be attached to the consumption comes in part from the class that uses it, and probably only secondarily from the clergy. The use of opium by a khan is seen by all to make him indecisive, detached from his community responsibilities, and given over to the kind of pleasures that, because it is a type unknown to the average man, may more readily be perceived as vice. WBT
12 The bride price for a young woman is well beyond the ability of the average farm boy to ever pay. Accumulation of money to buy a wife is a leading cause of young men leaving the area for places where a better wage may be gained for unskilled labor. Though some Sistanis express a desire to leave the area for other reasons—general poverty, health, oppression—most do return, or hope to return, to Sistan. Because the price of a bride is so high, compromise relations have developed. Young men may marry widows still of child-bearing age for a much lower fee. One of our workmen at Rudbar (one of the youngest) was about to marry a widow. Boys may be contracted to marry very small

Chapter 4: Crafts, Trade, and Travel

girls at a reduced fee since it cannot be certain the girl will grow into a beauty. Finally, a man who has many daughters can be persuaded to part with the less handsome ones at lower prices, especially if the possibility seems to exist that her hand may not be sought at all. Men may speak disparagingly of homely daughters in order to drive down the price, or pay relatively little for a woman who is known, or believed, not to be a virgin. Still, it seems the average farm boy lives in abject poverty all his life, first to pay for a wife, and then to make the pilgrimage to Mecca. One cannot help but wonder how much easier their lives might be were these two cultural obligations ever to be lifted. WBT. See chapter 6 for more on marriage customs. MA

13 Iran is meant. However, at least one young man from Hauz drove a tractor in the north of the country near Mazar-i Sharif at least part of the year, returning to work for us at distinctly lower wages. WBT

14 In 1971 our workmen received 40 afghanis ($.50) per day; in 1972 they received 50 afghanis ($.625) per day; in 1973 they received 50 afghanis ($.90) per day, raised to 55 afghanis ($.99) toward the end of the season; in 1974 they received 55 afghanis ($1.06) per day; in 1975, in a different locality, workmen at first demanded 240 afghanis ($5.58) per day, but one of the younger khans of the village convinced them we could not pay Iranian wages, and they settled grudgingly for 70 afghanis ($1.63) per day, but generally did not work well at this wage. In all seasons but one, because the workmen could not live at home, work proceeded seven days a week, and double wages were paid for Friday. The seeming discrepancies between the afghani wage and its dollar equivalent are the result of the increasing strength of the afghani throughout the years of our work. WBT. See the Editors' Foreword for afghani-dollar exchange rates during these years. MA

15 However, by strictly regulating the flow of the Helmand River into Iran, flood years have altered the main channel of the Helmand, which now flows into the Hamun-i Puzak on the Afghan side. While it is true that the Hamun-i Puzak is now first of the terminal *hamuns* to fill, when it reaches a certain depth, water pours into the Hamun-i Sabari in Iran and then into the Hamun-i Helmand further south, both entirely within Iran. If sufficient water comes, it flows from the Hamun-i Helmand southeast through the Shela Rud into the Gaud-i Zirreh, and back into Afghanistan. Hence, while Afghanistan is first to receive flood waters, the degree of flooding is determinable by the flow of the flood waters back into Iran, and eventually back into the dead, uninhabited depression of the Gaud-i Zirreh. The water will have circulated a full 180 degrees to flow back into Afghanistan far to the south of the Hamun-i Puzak. The flooding problem for Afghanistan is only a matter of degrees more serious since building the Kuhak Dam than before. In flood season the Hamun-i Puzak fills anyway, but the Hamun-i Sabari in Iran is flooded first. More serious than flooding is the shortage of water in droughts, when it appears to be possible for Iran, by means of the Kuhak Dam, to capture the scarce water in the lower Helmand. But if, as seems apparent, the main channel is moving to the east because of regulation at Kuhak, then Iran should soon have difficulty in capturing water even in drought years. WBT

16 A figure of speech; it is concrete. WBT
17 Zahri, *Famous People of Ancient Sistan*. GRA. Formulas for population growth in Afghanistan have always been unrealistic, and the government claimed in 1975 a population double that suggested by a demographic study group after five years of intensive study. Burgeoning populations entitle countries to larger United Nations contributions and large aid packages. The population of Nimruz Province in 1974 could not have been more than a third the official estimate. We guessed the Nimruz province contained hardly more than 30,000 people. WBT
18 Joe Alex Morris, Jr. *Los Angeles Times*, 1977. GRA. The population figures for Iran are equally groundless. WBT. Attempts were made to identify the specific article referred to by Amiri, but without success. Joe Alex Morris, Jr., a Middle East reporter for the *Los Angeles Times*, was the only western journalist killed during the fighting during the Iranian Revolution of 1979. MA
19 This problem is too complex to be dealt with here. It is more fully explored in the geological monograph by John Whitney (2006) and archaeological reports still in process. Ostensibly, the more land covered with water, the less sand to be blown. The present sanding problems have nothing to do with the present use of the Helmand waters by Iran and Afghanistan. It is a much older problem. The sand blowing across Afghan Sistan comes exclusively from the Hamun-i Puzak and deeper deposits laid down tens of thousands of years ago over a larger area; the sand desert of the Registan to the south of Kandahar likewise comes from the Hamun-i Helmand in Iran, down the Shela Rud into the Gaud-i Zirreh, and to the east beyond. There is no accurate estimate of the depth of the sediments in the Sistan Basin, and whether they constitute exclusively sand and silt strata. WBT. Our excavations at Qala 169 in Sar-o-Tar in 1974, which we date to about 1000 BCE, determined that the perimeter walls of the qala were seated in a layer of sand. MA
20 There is no natural injustice in this since all of the sand and silt delivered to Iran by the Helmand River came from Afghanistan in the first place. Satellite photographs reveal, however, that far from the Baluchistan mountains deflecting eastward all the Iranian sands into the Registan south of Kandahar, much sand passes over and through these mountains and continues to move southward into Pakistani Baluchistan. WBT
21 The dunes of the Registan appear to be fairly stabilized. The fact that they are oxidized to a reddish color indicates their great age. It would be difficult to say the amount of sand in the Registan has greatly increased in the last several thousand years. During the spring there are many water pools formed there, and for a short while there is good grass in many places. The nomads avail themselves yearly of the bounty, and the maps show many scattered "ruins" that are much more likely to be sheep corrals. WBT. Recent satellite surveys of the Registan by David Thomas and Fiona Kidd (2017) have identified many human-made structures in the Registan, but there is as yet little opportunity to ground truth them for age or function. MA

Chapter 4: Crafts, Trade, and Travel

22 The sands of Sar-o-Tar are geologically recent, but they represent a cyclical phenomenon. With the right hydrological conditions, they will disappear again. WBT

23 An effort was made to repeat all the Délégation archéologique française en Afghanistan photographs of 1936, as well as those of the Perso-Afghan Arbitration Commission, primarily to study the rate of erosion in the ruins. While on the whole, this series of photographs seems to show the presence of a greater accumulation of sand in recent times, this may be more apparent than real, and would have no real meaning for the long run anyway. WBT. We plan a future article comparing the photos of these locales at three moments over the first 75 years of the twentieth century. MA

24 The people who were forced off the Sar-o-Tar tract were done so five hundred years ago at the end of the Timurid period. Nor was it for the first time in history. The same may have occurred about 800 BC and again about AD 350-450. The sanding of the Sar-o-Tar tract comes and goes. Without fresh supplies, the region could probably blow itself clear in fifty to seventy-five years. And a Hamun-i Puzak full of water to its maximum spread is one of the most important ways of preventing the Wind of 120 Days from transporting its dry bed to the south southeast into the Sar-o-Tar tract. WBT

25 The scouring of the Helmand channel following the construction of the Arghandab and Kajaki dams is in part responsible for the gradual failure of the hand dug canals along the lower Helmand. WBT

26 While there can be little doubt that there are fewer trees now in Sistan than at several times in the past, "deforestation" implies to a degree the unnatural cutting of trees. As recently as a hundred years ago, groves of dead mulberry trees were still to be seen. And while Gholam Khan can remember from his youth thicker stands of *jangal* along the banks of the Helmand (see note 1 of the Preface concerning our interview with Gholam Khan), the modest increase in vegetation certainly had no effect on the strength of the winds in the region, nor the periodic droughts from which we may assume the region has always suffered. Today, irrigation canals exist on a small scale only in the river valley. Five centuries ago when the vast Sar-o-Tar and Dasht-i Amiran tracts were sand free and irrigated, the humidity of the area was elevated, the water table higher, and doubtless many more trees flourished along the banks of the hundreds of miles of canals. Great stands of rushes also grew along the canals and in lower drainage areas. None of this vegetation was natural; all of it was there because of human efforts to till the soil. None of it could survive without human's constant efforts at maintaining the irrigation systems and planted fields. The arrival of the sand and/or the flagging of the political and economic will to maintain this difficult balance caused its reversion to desert. It would be wrong to imply that "deforestation" was ever a major cause in the desiccation of this region. The causes are more complex and will be dealt with in subsequent reports. The result, however, is the same—a drier, hotter, dustier, and increasingly inhospitable land. WBT

27 But again, the greater prosperity in Iran at this time was chiefly responsible, for in normal circumstances quadrupling a wage in one year could not have failed to produce a surplus of workers had there not been a place to earn even more money. WBT

28 And yet, the Baluch peasant does not necessarily feel oppression lifted if he manages to escape from his khan. Most return. As a vassal of the khan his life is difficult but secure. There will be seed for planting, land for his crops, someone from whom to borrow money. Never mind that he is not free in the Western sense; he is integrated into a protective society. Some have left for Kandahar or even Kabul. There are few Baluch in these cities. He will have no friends, there will be no one to offer him a job, lend him money, excuse him from labor if he is ill. There will be no one to marry. He will be lonely and frustrated. He will be an outcast in cities where other tribes predominate. He will return to his homeland if he possibly can. WBT

29 The author is describing the simplest, most rudimentary type of house. Frequently, the area inside the upright "beam staves" is plastered so that the floor may be kept clean and insects kept out. Around the sides a curb will be raised a few inches about the beam staves, to strengthen them and to seal the crack between floor and wall. All have one or two shallow, curbed areas marked off toward one end into which grain to be used that day may be poured without risk of its being scattered about the floor. Each also has a central, or nearly central, shallow fire pit. Fire inside the house is for warmth and minor cooking. The large bread oven, or *tandur*, is close by outside the house. A small area of plastering may be left off the roof above the fire pit to help the smoke escape. But since it does not draw well through the matting in any case, the roof is sometimes fully plastered. The interior fire is kept small, not only to reduce smoke, but because it is quite sufficient to warm these structures that normally are about two meters wide and four meters long. Of course, both smaller and larger houses are built. A single residence may consist of two or three similarly constructed huts arranged to form two or three sides of a square compound. The doorway is never in the center of one of the long sides, but near one end. The largest house of this construction I saw belonged to a khan at Rudbar. The structure rested upon a mud platform raised a meter above the ground. The "beam staves" were fully a foot in diameter at the base, where they were sunk into a raised mud curbing. They were formed of hundreds of scrub tamarisk branches twisted together and bound round stoutly at intervals. The mud covered matting over these was much the same as any other such structure. The building was perhaps 3.5 meters wide and 10 meters long, and the ceiling was correspondingly high. It was clearly not a residence, but served as the khan's reception room. I had called upon him since. In the progress of our 1971 survey, we had just entered his territory, though we had thought we were closer to his residence. In fact, we had camped half an hour's drive up the valley. "It is far," he said, and I explained that the error was unintentional. "Would you like one guard or two?" he asked laconically over tea. "Whatever you feel may be best advised," was my diplomatic answer. I had

Chapter 4: Crafts, Trade, and Travel

not come to request guards for I had not felt any were needed. I was simply paying a courtesy call upon a khan whose territory we had entered without advance warning, because there is no way to send advance warning in this region. Across the river some miles to the west was the Charburjak telephone terminus, seldom in working order. Many miles further to the east northeast was the other telephone terminus at Khan Neshin, again across the river. "I will send two men," the khan said. In consequence we passed a restless night sleeping under the stars, stared at by two bored guards, crossed bandoliers and rifles slung over their shoulders.

The Baluch hut can be very snug indeed on cold winter nights, but if there is a rain storm accompanied by high winds, the Baluch declare they get no sleep all night for the shaking of the structure. Dust and bits of mud plaster fall upon them, and of course water drips through the many cracks naturally formed in the mud outer coating. WBT

30 Formerly the doors, and occasional windows, were elaborately carved, but the practice is declining. The fact that the narrow doors are doubled is probably less from a sense of elegance than the absence of wide pieces of wood. WBT

31 The platform, for obvious reasons, cannot be on the roof of the house, which in other parts of the country is used for sleeping on summer nights when it is excessively hot. The platform is elevated primarily to catch the wind and to be above the dust that blows along the ground. It also protects them from the attentions of animals in the night, be these their own dogs or the various poisonous scorpions and snakes that live in the area. WBT

32 The flat oblong loaves generally weigh approximately a pound. A working man will eat two of these a day. Some old people eat only one. WBT

33 They are heaped like brush fences and usually serve to enclose a small courtyard. Some of the dry twigs are used to fire the bread ovens outside the house. WBT

34 Domes are common because of the shortage of timber for roof beams, though not unobtainable. One of the khans of Hauz has a flat roofed house. WBT

35 Amiri is describing the house of the principal khan at Khwaja 'Ali Sehyaka in which the mission lived for several weeks, having been encouraged by the villagers to do so upon their mistaken advice that the khan had moved away. One day he returned on camel back, having driven on the *dasht* along the north bank of the Helmand, and then having crossed the valley and forded the stream by camel. Under the circumstances he was the soul of hospitality in his greetings to us in his own house, and he insisted that we remain where we were until our work was completed. He moved into a small, ordinary Baluchi hut outside the walls of his compound, visited us daily, and extended every kindness which we have come to associate with the Baluch. Certainly, it is hard for us to recall that they were described as bands of marauding robbers and cutthroats a century ago. WBT

36 Except when wandering in the desolate *dasht* with their flocks, in which case they simply lie upon the ground at night to sleep, using the end of their turban as a thin cushion for the head. WBT

37 Animal shelters take the same form as the houses, but tend to have outdoor reed enclosures. In either case, the reeds are not plaited in any way, but are simply tied in loose bunches and leaned against each other. They are clearly not capable of withstanding high winds, and built close to the lake shores, they are regularly flooded out. WBT

38 The new town of Zaranj was constructed in 1966. It is laid out on a grid plan, the one-story vaulted structures built of poorly-fired soft baked brick. The capital of the province was moved here from Kang at this time because Kang had been isolated by shifts in the Helmand channel following the construction of the dam at Kuhak in Iran. Zaranj was for some years simply known as Shahr-i Nao (new town), and is perhaps still more commonly known by this name among local inhabitants. It was laid out on a rather ambitious plan, and though only two or three main streets were paved to the edge of town, it contains a petrol station, hotel, school, telephone switchboard (seldom operable), several streets of bazaar containing many empty shops, a dirt landing strip where small planes may at risk land when the dust is not up, and Governor's residence, which resembles in architectural form an element detached from an art deco ocean liner. The roofs bristle with radio antennas, since the telephone is rarely operational. The "all weather" approach road across the playa beyond the town, impassable when wet, was in 1966 made entirely of whole and fragmentary one- to two-thousand year old baked bricks pulled from nearby ruins and was certainly among the worst roads in the world. WBT

39 Small villages outside Zaranj are built of mud brick with vaulted ceilings. The inhabitants are mixed Pashto, Baluchi, and Dari speakers. WBT

40 There is much drifting sand to the east and south of Zaranj, and the most common cause for the abandonment of a village is its being overwhelmed by moving sand dunes. WBT

41 With the exception of the Ziarat-i Amiran isolated in the Dasht-i Amiran, of which more will be said below. WBT

42 These villages are named for the small geographical parcels of land on which they are constructed. Rudbar is the general name for a stretch of territory along the south bank of the Helmand. Where the principal khan lives will normally be called Rudbar. The districts of Lat, Lop, Shirak, and Demarda are all small districts of Rudbar. A village within one of these districts may be called either by the district name or by that of the khan. Khel-i Bibarg Khan is the village controlled by Bibarg Khan in Lat, Rudbar. But it may also be called Lat. The district name gives way to the khan's name especially when there are two villages within the same district. Khwaja 'Ali is another name defining a stretch of river course farther upstream. It is divided into three districts: Khwaja 'Ali Bala (Upper), Khwaja 'Ali Sehyaka (One-third), and Khwaja 'Ali Pa'in, or Sufla (Lower). Within each area, small villages will bear the names of further geographic subdivisions as well as that of the khan. WBT

43 Four-wheel-drive Russian or American jeeps in various states of dilapidation. WBT

Chapter 4: Crafts, Trade, and Travel

44 I am unaware of the existence of any boats, unless Amiri refers to the barge operated by the military at Charburjak and Bandar-i Kamal Khan or another kept far up the river near Girishk. WBT

45 This left bank traffic with any truck larger than a four-wheel-drive pickup is extremely difficult and requires expert drivers. I have seen only three larger trucks brought over this route downstream, but I have not heard of them making the return trip. They were purchased by khans for local use. WBT

46 Report of the Authority Coordinating Foreign Projects, Directorate of Road Maintenance of the Ministry of Public Works. 1977 GRA. The ground survey for this road was conducted by an Italian firm in the summer of 1975. The Eritrean engineer and his Afghan assistant completed the work as quickly as possible, owing to the heat of the summer. They were back again in the autumn of 1975 because their calculations had been faulty. The road, as it was described to us, was to be a "super highway" between Lashkar Gah (itself serviced by only a "washboard" gravel road) and the Iranian border, with no access provided to the villages along the way. It entailed the construction of several bridges, one more than a mile long. It seems unlikely that this road is yet beyond the planning stage, there no longer being any reason for such a road to Iran. Iran was to complete a straight highway between Boundary Post 22 and Bandar Abbas on the Persian Gulf in an effort to capture Afghanistan's foreign trade, which then passed through Pakistan except when the countries were quarrelling, or otherwise through Russia. This same Italian firm was in 1976 engaged in building a road straight between Birjand and Mashhad in eastern Iran. And straight it was, up hill and down dale, over them rather than through or around them, without apparent regard for the steepness of slopes. In the light of events since 1978, it seems unlikely that this unpromising project was completed. WBT

47 *Statistical Data on Afghanistan (1351–1353)*, p.58. GRA This road, presenting few engineering difficulties, was completed but remained unpaved in the early 1980s. WBT

48 The flights were suspended partly owing to the frequent poor visibility at Zaranj, partly because it was a convenience largely for the governor, and partly because Bakhtar crashed itself out of existence. The airline has been reformed, but the weather at Zaranj has not improved. WBT

49 On no occasion in the 1970s were we able to reach Kabul on the Nimruz line, whether from Qala-i Fath or from Zaranj. WBT

50 A weekly newspaper item, and a daily Radio Afghanistan item, reported the constant absence of the Deshu representative from Parliament. WBT

51 In Lashkar Gah only. WBT

52 In fact, exclusively to Lashkar Gah. WBT

53 To the best of my knowledge, no pottery is made in Lashkar Gah. What is sold there is of uniformly poor quality and came from Kandahar. While some pottery may be made at Farah, Herat is the only center of ceramic manufacture in western Afghanistan. With the exception of Kandahar, then, pottery is no longer made anywhere in southern Afghanistan. WBT

54 That is, long curved iron needles used in stitching up camel or donkey pack bags. WBT
55 Iron ore is present in Afghanistan, but to my knowledge it is not present in Helmand and Nimruz Provinces, except possibly in economically non-viable quantities. Copper, lead, and possibly silver smelting, common in this region for thousands of years, is no longer undertaken. WBT
56 While qilims of reasonably fine quality are still produced for local consumption, knotted carpets are of infrequent manufacture and are of decidedly inferior quality. WBT
57 Amiri's description might be derived from Tate *Frontiers of Baluchistan*, 1909, p. 234, but is presented somewhat differently here. WBT
58 The embroidery of these hats can be very fine indeed, the patterns intricate and of considerable beauty. Commonly threads of many colors are used, and gold and silver threads are especially popular. In most instances now, the metallic threads are substitutes for the precious metals, but the effects are the same. It can take two to three weeks for a cap to be completed. Mothers normally make an especially rich and beautiful hat for a son on the occasion of his marriage. The Baluch are extremely proud of these caps. Nowadays, heavily embroidered men's caps are produced in Pakistan cheaply with the use of sewing machines, but these are easily distinguished and not highly prized. WBT
59 The quality of metal used in the manufacture of personal adornments has greatly declined everywhere in the country. While more gold and silver exists in Kabul than elsewhere, jewelry is now made of what is commonly called "pot metal," with little or no silver content. The craftsmanship is accordingly poor. If the value and quantity of a woman's jewelry were formerly taken to reflect on her wealth and status within her tribal group or clan, then there are few women of wealth and position left in Afghanistan. WBT
60 While Japanese and Indian machine-produced fabrics predominate in Kabul, the textiles in the Helmand Valley and Sistan Basin come exclusively from Iran. They form a part of the smuggling trade. In spite of their unsuitability to the climate of the area, being colder to wear in the winter and warmer in the summer, synthetic fabrics are the most esteemed, possibly because of the wider range of colors in which they are produced. WBT
61 Apart from the bazaar at Zaranj, which could hardly be described as flourishing, only Charburjak has a single street of shops one block long. The range of products available is extremely limited. Cloth, cigarettes, *naswar* (a tobacco-based stimulant), tea, Russian matches, a few canned goods accidentally acquired, some ironmongery. Often no fresh food of any sort is available. This is the only "bazaar" between Darwishan and Zaranj on the Helmand. WBT
62 These shops have no signs and are indistinguishable from the other houses of the village. This is the common practice in small villages throughout the Middle East and Central Asia. WBT
63 That is, the full amount of the interest must be paid even if the loan is repaid before it is due. WBT

Chapter 4: Crafts, Trade, and Travel

64 That is, they lend money at a time when it is most needed, and collect the sum owed after the harvest in undervalued wheat. This system is inevitable so long as the local people lack the means to transport their own overproduction to the more lucrative city markets. WBT

65 The pastoralists live in the region between the Helmand Valley and the mountains beyond the Pakistan border to the south. In the spring, they pasture as well in the Registan, and more rarely in small areas of the Dasht-i Margo, where pools of rain water may last a few weeks. These nomads do not belong to a single linguistic or cultural group. They are Pashtun, Baluch, and Brahui. WBT

66 The people of the Helmand Valley visit the ruins in the Sar-o-Tar tract on a fairly regular basis, especially after the winter rains, to search for coins, stone seals, and beads that may have been exposed by erosion. This is by no means an activity of recent times. It is called *dagal gardi*, which means simply "searching the ground." The practice was well established at the time of the Perso-Afghan Arbitration Commission's residence in Sistan 1903-1905 (Tate 1909, p. 107). To judge from the objects purchased by members of the Commission, coins and seals constituted the majority of the finds. Sir A. H. McMahon presented his collection of coins to the British Museum (Codrington 1911). G. P. Tate, the most serious antiquary affiliated with the commission, appears to have collected scarcely more coins in spite of the length of his residence and his personal *dagal gardi* in the Sar-o-Tar tract (Tate 1904; Codrington 1904 and 1905; Rapson 1904). Although coins of considerable rarity were obtained, most were in poor condition. The lead coins collected by McMahon have since disintegrated in the British Museum owing to contact with wood vapors. The objects collected by the *dagal gardi* are not exclusively for sale. Coins and seals may be kept as talismans or converted into jewelry. In some cases, villages sell objects for small sums to the khans. During my visit to Sistan in July 1966, I was on more than one occasion shown small collections by khans who seemed to appreciate the objects for their antiquity since they consisted mainly of fragmentary steatite and travertine vessels, colorful bits of ceramic, and a few seals and coins. I am inclined to believe that objects of great artistic value have rarely, if ever, been found during the last century. A son of one of the khans of Hauz recounted the discovery several years before of several graves in which some gold jewelry was found. But he could neither identify the locality, nor was he able to describe the exact nature of the finds. While it is not impossible that pre-Islamic graves containing treasures might occasionally be found, the likelihood of discovery and looting of many pre-Islamic burials during the centuries of Islamic occupation of the Sar-o-Tar tract is strong. Some were probably plundered even earlier, shortly after the burials occurred in the pre-Islamic periods. WBT

67 Two women will generally work in their spare time on a carpet. They will complete perhaps only two a year. A son will take the carpet to Kandahar or even to Kabul for sale. The practice is now rare because the carpets are of inferior quality. Qilims are produced for local consumption and are used for floor

coverings. Some of the patterns are unique to the area. As with the carpets, the qilims now being made rarely equal in quality those of even twenty years ago. For a general introduction to comtemporary Baluch textiles, weaving, and tools from Iran, Afghanistan, and Pakistan, see Konieczny (1979).

68 In the 1970s the wealth of Iran and the scarcity of all products in rapidly growing towns such as Zahedan created a great demand for the products of Afghan Sistan that formerly had been largely consumed locally. In consequence, there was great scarcity in Afghan Sistan as more was exported to Iran than the area could easily afford to lose. By 1975, a single chicken egg in Afghan Sistan (when it could be found) sold for four afghanis, whereas it might fetch three to four times this sum across the border. More serious was the export of chickens and large flocks of sheep to Iran. With the inadequate resources at its command, and a long essentially open border, the Afghan government was virtually powerless to interfere with this trade. Corruption among the government officials and police did not improve matters. Trucks were occasionally conspicuously seized in the Zaranj area, but the payment of a fine was sufficient to assure their return to their owners so that business might be resumed. Smuggling in certain commodities was conducted openly. Trucks laden with Indian tea destined for Iran were frequently seen on the streets of Zaranj. WBT

69 In fact, few of the imports arriving from Iran were for local consumption, but were forwarded to Kandahar and Herat. One extraordinary commodity imported from Iran was the romance novel, a type of literature banned in Afghanistan. Though hardly prurient by Western standards, they are nonetheless found agreeable to at least certain of the few literate Afghans. Zaranj appeared to be especially well stocked and they seemed to be openly sold. The market is, of course, primarily a masculine one, since the percentage of literate women in Afghanistan is very small. WBT

Chapter 5
Labor and Family Relationships

Landlord and Farmer

Between the farmers and the khans there is a very great class difference, and neither side is aware that it has a mutually dependent relationship in the vital business of agricultural production, and that co-operative effort is necessary between landlord and farmer. With very few exceptions, the khans and the farmers distrust each other. The khan despises the farmer and thinks that his only function is to provide profit for the landowner. If the khan treats him other than harshly, then the farmer will slyly and deceitfully trample on the landowner's privileges.[1] The landlords as a whole believe that if they take one unnecessary step towards the well-being of the farmers, the farmers will consider this a sign of weakness in the landlords and will not support the landlords' interest. With the exception of a few enlightened landlords they do not believe that education, health care, and better housing are necessary for the farmers. On the other hand, the farmer himself is also a great traditionalist and remains very backward. Whenever he is confronted by an attempt to change his ancient ways and customs, he remains intransigent, even when this change might improve his way of life or his agricultural techniques. It is for this reason that the great majority of people in this region work hard both to feed and please the few khans and overlords. The local phrase is that they "give the khans both bread and greetings" (Fig. 5.1).

In years past the khans themselves had their own prisons. Insubordinate farmers were put in the stocks or subjected to *lakehtab*. The stocks were made of two pieces of wood about twenty inches long and two and a half inches in diameter with places cut out at fixed intervals to hold the feet. When in use, the two pieces of wood were nailed together so close to each other that the victim could only with difficulty make small movements. For *lakehtab,* the accused was suspended for a time by his feet.

The Helmand Baluch

Figure 5.1. Abi Borkhan, known as "Bibarg Khan," and several of his farmers at Lat, Rudbar, Nimruz Province, 1975.

During the course of the fifth season of excavations in 1975 at Rudbar, I spoke with Muhammad 'Umar, a farmer, about the treatment by khan in the area. Gholam Dastigir, a farmer, who was listening to our conversation, suddenly broke in and said, in dialect "Sir, you don't know this khan. One day he told me to go call the carpenter; I was delayed a little as I was busy irrigating. He sent someone else after the carpenter and called me too. As soon as I arrived he ordered *lakehtab* for me, which lasted a whole day. When it was over, I felt that my heart and liver were in my throat." The speaker had suffered *lakehtab* at the hands of a khan who was no longer there.[2] A large number of the khans nowadays have armed bodyguards, in the face of whom the farmers are not likely to consider insubordination (Fig. 5.2).[3]

In addition, the khans maintain friendly relations with government officials. When these khans go to Lashkar Gah or Kabul for business or pleasure, they return with exaggerated stories of the welcoming kindness of the government officers. The farmers also, judging from their historical experience of the connections between the khans and government functionaries and their united front in protecting the class structure, are not inclined to disbelieve them. And whenever a competent official, in the course of his duty or for some other purpose, visits the lower Helmand Valley and Afghan Sistan, he stops for supper or to spend the night with one of these khans.[4] In the whole of this region there are no hotels, markets, or other facilities for travelers except for the primitive guest-houses owned by the khans. These visits serve merely to confirm the farmers more strongly in their belief in the collusion between the landlords and government officials.

Chapter 5: Labor and Family Relationships

Figure 5.2. Hajji Nafaz Khan (second from left) with his bodyguard Muhammad 'Osman (left) and members of the Helmand-Sistan Project, at Kona Qala II, Nimruz Province, 1975. Americans left to right: M. Allen, W. Trousdale, J. Whitney, J. Knudstad, and R. Vincent, Jr.. Far right is Niaz Muhammad, camp mechanic, guide, diplomat, and manager.

The khans of Afghan Sistan have a superior position also with regard to economic conditions. They have very strong influence in politics. In parliamentary elections, candidates from other classes cannot get more votes than they, and for this reason no one except them presents himself as a candidate.[5] Their relations with the clergy are good. The clergy try to put a religious face on the privileges of the powerful men, and they encourage the people to acquiesce in the wretchedness of their lives. For their part, the khans try to help the clergy financially on the one hand, and they urge the populace to support them on the other hand. They spread stories and tales of a miraculous nature to bolster the position of the clergy.[6]

Border Control by the Khans

Since in this region the Baluch people live on both sides of the border with Pakistan and the links between them are strong, the khans in the area also have great influence in the border region from the fortress of Jali Robat on Kuh-i Malik Siyah (Fig.5.3) to Nal-i Ab to the east, which includes ten fortresses.[7, 8]

Several khans of Sistan have been charged with the security of a portion of the border. To Sardar Ghulam Dustigir Khan, who lives in Charburjak, has been assigned that part of the border extending from Jali Robat in the Kuh-i Malik Siyah to Thaneh-i Jaliljal in the east,[9] a distance requiring a journey of about six hours by car or two nights and three days by camel.[10] The khan has transferred the burden of overseeing his stretch

Figure 5.3. Hajji Nafaz and bodyguards at boundary pillar near Jali Robat. Afghanistan is in foreground, Pakistan in background. 1975.

of border to the shoulders of Hajji Muhammad 'Isah, who, with his relatives, occupies twelve houses and lives in Jali Robat.

Three other people, Vakil Muhammad Ibrahim Khan living in lower Khwaja 'Ali (leader of the group), Sardar Taj Muhammad Khan of upper Khwaja 'Ali, and 'Ali Mardan Khan, a resident of Bagat, are charged with the security of the 330 km border extending eastward from Thaneh-i Jaliljal. Along this stretch of border there are nine border posts as follows: Thaneh-i Jaliljal, Robat, Mamu, Biramchah, Bulu, Mahiyan, Shah 'Isma'il, Karvan-Rah, and Tel-Ab.

Table 5.1

Distances along the Afghan-Pakistani Border Guarded by Sistan Khans

From	To	Distance (in km)
Thaneh-i Jaliljal	Robat	40
Robat	Mamu	40
Mamu	Biramchah	60
Biramchah	Bulu	30
Bulu	Mahiyan	40
Mahiyan	Shah 'Isma'il	50
Shah 'Isma'il	Karvan-Rah	40
Karvan-Rah	Tel-Ab	30

Chapter 5: Labor and Family Relationships

Of all the posts listed, only four—Jaliljal, Biramchah, Mamu, and Shah 'Isma'il—are constructed of baked brick, while at the remaining five the defenders are still living in tents.

A total of 63 defenders man these nine border posts, this number not being assigned equally to the various posts, but distributed more or less according to perceived need. Each of these defenders is provided by the government with a monthly wage of 178 afghanis in 1976, while their three leaders each receive 600 afghanis. In 1976 this latter figure was raised to 1,000 afghanis. The wages of the border defenders, according to Vakil Muhammad Ibrahim Khan, are by no means sufficient, although the khans also provide them with material support.[11]

There are camels for the border defenders to ride on during their patrols, with the khans providing sixty camels in the name of the government during each five-year period.[12] The border guards themselves are chosen by the khans on the basis of the number of inhabitants of each locality, the service being a means by which landless Baluch and Sistan Afghans may be excused from military duty. Their weapons consist of English, German, Russian, and other firearms and are provided by the landowners.[13]

From the fortress of Nal-i Ab to the east lies the area of Mangalistan; most of the inhabitants are Brahuis. Tate has said the following with regard to these people: another tribe lives in Sistan, who call themselves Zughar. Zughar is probably derived from Zughad, a place near Samarkand which was later called Sogdiana. Another legend is that they possibly came from Managar, an ancient town in Sind.[14]

East from Tel-Ab there are three more border posts, at Kafi, Purtus, and Ayshi. These posts are assigned to Sardar Govarom Khan and Sardar Qadir Bakhsh Birahudi, who live in Mangalistan and have responsibility for that section. East from Thaneh-i Ayshi is the area of Shurawak, where the government assumes responsibility for the border.[15]

Notable Sistan Khans

In the Helmand valley, from Darwishan to where the river flows into the Sistan Basin there are many khans. Table 5.2 lists the most notable khans of the area.

Table 5.2

Some of the More Prominent Khans Living in the Helmand Valley between Darwishan and the Sistan Hamuns

	Place of Residence	Khans' Names	Khans' Ethnicity	Villagers' Ethnicity
1.	Upper Darwishan	Wakil Muhammad Khan, Hajji 'Abdu's-Samad Khan	Pashtun	mostly Pashtun, some Baluch
2.	Lower Darwishan	Ri'u Khan, Khodai-i Nazar Khan, Hajji Faqir Muhammad Khan	Pashtun	mostly Pashtun, some Baluch
3.	Kashti or Miyan Pushtu	Hajji Muhammad Na'im Khan, La'l Muhammad Khan	Pashtun	mostly Pashtun, some Baluch
4.	Laki	Muhammad 'Umar Khan, Ni'mat-ullah Khan	Pashtun	mostly Pashtun, some Baluch
5.	Safar	Shir Muhammad Khan, Dust Muhammad Khan, Zaman Khan	Pashtun	mostly Pashtun, some Baluch
6.	Upper Banadar	Muhammad Hashim Khan, Umanu'llah, Khan, Hajji Gauhar Khan, Shah Wali Khan	Pashtun	mostly Baluch, some Pashtun
7.	Lower Banadar	Yar Muhammad Khan, Muhammad Zahir Khan, Shah Nazar Khan, Ri'u Khan	Pashtun	roughly half Baluch, half Pashtun
8.	Upper Bagat	Hajji 'Ali Mardan Khan, Mirza Rahmatu'llah Khan	Baluch	mostly Brahui
9.	Lower Bagat	Zaqum Khan	Baluch	mostly Brahui
10.	Landi	Bi Bur Khan	Pashtun	mostly Baluch, some Pashtun
11.	Diwalak	Wakil Shingal Khan	Pashtun	mostly Pashtun, some Baluch
12.	Khan Neshin	Khan Zaman Khan	Pashtun	mostly Baluch, some Pashtun
13.	Qala-i Nao	Muhammad 'Umar Khan Kalan, Muhammad 'Umar Khan Khward, 'Abdu'r-Rashid Khan	Pashtun	most definitely Baluch, some certainly Pashtun
14.	Khairabad	Muhammad 'Umar Khan, Nek Muhammad Khan	Pashtun	most definitely Baluch, some certainly Pashtun
15.	Taghaz	Muhammad Hanif Khan	Pashtun	most definitely Baluch
16.	Malakhan	Hajji Muhammad 'Umar Khan	Pashtun	most definitely Baluch

Chapter 5: Labor and Family Relationships

	Place of Residence	Khans' Names	Khans' Ethnicity	Villagers' Ethnicity
17.	Deshu	'Abdu'r-Rahman Khan, La'l Muhammad Khan, Hajji Muhammad Anwar Khan, Muhammad Ya'qub Khan	Pashtun	most definitely Baluch, some certainly Pashtun
18.	Upper Khwaja 'Ali	Sardar Taj Muhammad Khan, Khodai-i Nazar Khan, Darwizeh Khan	Baluch (Brahui)	roughly 95% Baluch
19.	Khwaja 'Ali Sehyaka	Hajji Nur Ahmad 'Ali Khan, Muhammad 'Ali Khan, Mehrabu'd-Din Khan, Sultan Ahmad Khan (brothers)	Baluch	roughly 95% Baluch
20.	Lower Khwaja 'Ali	Sardar Muhammad Sharif Khan, Wakil Muhammad Ibrahim Khan, Khan-Muhammad Khan, Muhammad 'Ali Khan (foster brothers of the khans of Sehyak)	Baluch	roughly 95% Baluch
21.	Palalak	Hajji Bi Bur Khan, 'Abdu'r-Rashid Khan	Baluch	roughly 95% Baluch
22.	Landi Sehyaka	Hajji 'Abdu'r-Rashid Khan, Muhammad Sarwar Khan, Shawali Khan, Din Muhammad Khan	Pashtun	roughly 95% Baluch
23.	Landi Watan	Muhammad Naoruz Khan, Ghulam Muhammad Khan, Muhammad Islam Khan	Pashtun	roughly 95% Baluch
24.	Upper Rudbar	Sardar Bi Bur Khan	Baluch	roughly 95% Baluch
25.	Lower Rudbar	Mir Hamzeh Khan, Muhammad Da'ud Khan	Baluch	roughly 95% Baluch
26.	Khajau	Muhammad Karim Khan	Baluch	roughly 95% Baluch
27.	Guludand	no khan (Until the channel went dry the land belonged to Sardar Ghulam Dastigir Khan, (Charburjak), but in 1975 the government cleared the channel and distributed the land to the Baluch people at a rate of twenty *jeribs* per family.)	Baluch	roughly 95% Baluch
28.	Ishkanak	Muhammad Amin Khan, 'Abdu'l-Habib Khan	Baluch	roughly 95% Baluch
29.	Charburjak	Ghulam Dastigir Khan, Khodai-i Nazar Khan, Muhammad Amin Khan, 'Abdu's-Samad Khan	Baluch ('Ayduzi)	mostly Baluch
30.	Deh	Sardar Shir Muhammad Khan, Yar Muhammad Khan (brothers)	Baluch ('Ayduzi)	roughly 95% Baluch

The Helmand Baluch

	Place of Residence	Khans' Names	Khans' Ethnicity	Villagers' Ethnicity
31.	Bandar-i Kamal Khan	Hajji Muhammad 'Umar Khan, Wakil 'Abdu'r-Rahman Khan, Sha-Pasand Khan	Baluch ('Ayduzi)	roughly 95% Baluch
32.	Mehrabad	Muhammad Akbar Khan, Gol Aqa Khan, Shir Aqa Khan, Muhammad Hashim Khan	Pashtun	mostly Baluch
33.	Baluchan/ Maluchan	Muhammad Anwar Khan, Muhammad Sarwar Khan, Ghulam Nabi-Khan	Gargaj	mostly Baluch, some Pashtun and Farsivan
34.	Qala-i Fath	'Abdu'l-Ghafur Khan, La'l Muhammad Khan, 'Ali Ahmad Khan, Muhammad Nadir Khan, 'Abdu'r-Rahman Khan	—	mostly Baluch
35.	Hauz	Ghulam Haidar Khan, 'Abdu'l-'Aziz Khan, 'Abdu'l-Qadus Khan	Baluch	Baluch ('Ayduzi)
36.	Godri	Muhammad Karim Khan, 'Abdu'r-Rahim Khan, 'Abdu'llah Khan, Ahmad Khan	—	Baluch ('Ayduzi)
37.	Jui Nao	Muhammad 'Alam Khan, Hajji Muhammad Khan, Ghulam Rasul Khan, Muhammad 'Umar Khan, Muhiu'd-Din Khan, 'Abdu'l-Hamid Khan, Hajji Aqa Khan, Hajji Muhammad Sarwar Khan	—	Baluch ('Ayduzi)
38.	Sabzgozi	Sardar Paradin Khan, Hajji Halim Khan, Hajji Mir Khan, Muhammad Khan, Muhammad 'Umar Khan, Shirin Khan, Muhammad Anwar Khan, Rostam Khan	Baluch	Baluch ('Ayduzi)
39.	Shoru	Muhammad Alim Khan	Pashtun	Baluch ('Ayduzi)
40.	Nad-i 'Ali	Muhammad Hashim Khan	Pashtun	mostly Baluch, minority are Pashtun and Farsivan
41.	Kanak	Hajji Malanak, Muhammad 'Azim Khan, Faqir Muhammad Khan	—	mostly Baluch
42.	Chakhansur	Muhammad 'Ashur Khan, Muhammad Hasan Khan, Khodai-i Nazar Khan, Muhammad Islam Khan, Ghulam Muhiu'd-Din Khan, Amanu'llah Khan	Baluch	mostly Baluch

Chapter 5: Labor and Family Relationships

Corvée or Gratis Labor

The new laws promulgated after the establishment of the Republic in Afghanistan in 1973 prohibited corvée labor. Clause 8 of the new constitution stated in this regard, "The abolition of exploitation in whatever form it takes." In addition, clause 43 also stated that "the imposing of compulsory labor, even if it is for the state, is illegal." [16] The enforcement of these laws in the far-flung corners of the country requires the concerted efforts of people of vision and progressive ideas and the wholesale education of the masses of farmers and peasants. Despite this, the burden of corvée labor, which is one of the principal factors in feudal oppression, is still laid by the landlords on the shoulders of the peasants.

In Afghan Sistan there are several types of corvée labor performed by the farmers. In addition to cleaning canals (discussed earlier) and repairing buildings for the landlord, the farmer has to take the landlord's share of the grain from the threshing floor to the landlord's house or to storage. The farmer, though he lacks the means of transporting the landlord's grain, has to pay for its transportation. The maintenance of the wattle and daub roof and walls of the landlord's house, which are damaged each year due to climatic conditions, also devolves on the farmers. Tending vines and building and repairing garden walls are also among the duties incumbent upon the farmers. Running messages and dunning for debts is another office that the khans expect the farmers to perform. It is normal for a farmer to be sent to fetch someone with whom the khan has business. The wood usually used as fuel by the khans is collected by the farmers and brought to the khan's house by camel or donkey, or sometimes in the khan's own motor vehicle. From time to time, the khan has to travel to the capital or to other cities, such as Kandahar or Lashkar Gah. In the same way, he sometimes travels to the deserts, to the standing water of the basin, or to the Helmand River to hunt or fish. During these trips the khan takes with him one or two of the villagers or his own servants, according to his needs.

The care of the khan's flocks and herds and the tending of sick animals is also the responsibility of the farmers. The building and repair of tracks leading to the khan's lands and the construction of the bridges that the khan decides he wants built is done by the farmers. The farmers also maintain the telephone poles, which in the areas where they exist consist of mud pillars about 1.5 meters tall, above which is affixed a wooden fork roughly 1 meter high. Because the telephone wires in some cases are less than 2.5 meters above the ground, they are frequently brought down by passing pack camels or motor vehicles. Sometimes the bases are also knocked down. When this happens repairs are required of the area landlords who have telephones, but the landowners always assign the farmers to execute the repairs.

It is not only the men whose services are commandeered by the khans. The women, too, have to perform gratis or poorly-paid labor for him. Every khan has his own bread baker chosen from among the village women near or far. The baker has to bake bread to fill the needs of the khan's family and guests. Because the khans' families are extensive and their guests are many, the baker's day is taken up with making dough and baking. The wheat set aside for the khan's personal use is also cleaned by these women. Nowadays there are a few diesel-run flour mills in Sistan. A few years previously, when wind-powered mills had fallen into disuse and diesel-run mills were not yet operating, flour for the khans' use was hand-ground by these women. It is also usually their duty to milk the khan's cows. The khan's clothing is also washed once a week or every other week with the help of these women or by these women themselves.

The duties described above are extracted from the farmers and their women without payment. Of course, they are sometimes rewarded with some trivial sum, some old clothes or shoes or some other tip from the khan. In this way it can be said that corvée labor is part of the payment for the use of the piece of land granted to the farmer by the landlord. But it must be said that recently the prohibiting of corvée labor in the constitution, the existence of wide tracts of workable land in neighboring areas, the raising of the wages of the people there, and the lack of farmers in Afghan Sistan have greatly contributed to the diminishing of corvée labor in this region.[17]

Family Organization and Relationships

Family ties among the Baluch, as among the other peoples of Afghanistan, go beyond the limits of a man, his wife, and their children. After marriage, sons usually live with their parents and siblings, forming what sociologists call an extended family. Family and tribal ties are stronger than any other social ties. All the members of a family share cooperatively in production, and usually the most senior member of the household makes the decisions. The livelihood is shared between all members until the death of the most senior member. The head of the family makes the decisions in family matters and arranges all outside matters for each member of the household. The home is indeed the center of education, instruction, and labor, and a place of safety for the family members. Since one of the most common characteristics of tribal structure is that the members of a family work more for the sake of the family than for individual goals, there is little scope for the development of individuality within the family.[18] The unworthiness of one member of a family affects the others with his bad reputation and shame.

Sons work with their fathers, and their relationship is friendly. The father exacts obedience and respect from his children, and in return he protects and provides for them. Every Baluch man may marry up to four wives, a greater number of wives in the family giving the appearance of wealth.[19]

Women have a lower status in Baluch Sistan. The birth of a daughter is regarded as unfortunate. This state of affairs has a very demoralizing effect on the women of the area and makes them feel inferior, as they must obey even brothers younger than themselves. After the age of eleven, girls are secluded and their formerly circumscribed lives become even more restricted. In wealthy families, girls of this age are confined to the house and cannot go out without permission. Whenever they want to visit friends or relatives they must wear a *chador* (veil). Lower-class women do not wear *chadors* and participate as much as possible with their husbands in duties outside the house. But in general they too have limited freedom and are firmly controlled by their menfolk. Baluch men in this region consider women unintelligent, weak-willed, and incapable of performing fine or difficult work.[20]

In this region there are no factories where women can find employment, and the majority of women are home-makers. If work is available for the women, their wages are less than half those of the men. For this reason, much use is made of village women. The foremen prefer single women and young girls, and so avoid nursing mothers feeding their babies every few minutes.

The women of this region obey the commands of their husbands without exception and have no chance to rebel. Women's property rights are also very limited. Their share of an inheritance is half that of a man.

A Baluch woman does not have the right to seek a divorce. Whenever a woman wants to do anything against her husband's wishes, she is liable to be repudiated by her husband. A man has the right to beat his wife, as long as he does not injure her body parts. Whenever one of the woman's body parts is injured, the man is questioned by his wife's relatives. If they are dissatisfied with his answers, the family can take their complaint to the local khan, whose judgement in the matter is considered final. The

Baluch have a saying about this: "The flesh of a woman belongs to the husband and her bones belong to her parents."

Girls do not have the right to choose their own husbands. No importance is attached to their wishes in the matter of marriage. A match is proposed by the head of the household in the boy's family and finalized with the approval of the girl's family. It is considered wrong to consult the girl's wishes regarding the choice of a husband.

Wedding ceremonies begin with the consultations and agreements between the heads of the two families. The boy's family takes the first step and sounds out the girl's family. In the course of these discussions, the conditions of the bride price and the dowry are also fixed. Meanwhile the girl's family seeks the opinion of their close relatives. Since the khans of Sistan have jurisdiction over everything that happens, the heads of the families of both the boy and the girl seek the counsel of the local khan, too. If the khan agrees to the proposal, they set about organizing the wedding. In the past most people sought the khan's opinion, but now this custom has weakened and forty or fifty percent of the people do not adhere to it.

In any case, after the public announcement by the girl's family, a group of elders, young men, even children of the village, and the bridegroom (contrary to the custom in other parts of the country) take a suitable opportunity—usually after the evening meal—to go to the house of the girl's family, where they demand sweets for the agreement of the wedding. The girl's family give them sweets, usually *nuql* (frosted almonds). To some of the elders and respected men of the village, a handkerchief is given in addition to the sweets. The kerchiefs have previously been left with them by the boy's family. At the end of the ceremony, shots are fired into the air, the purpose of which is to communicate the fact to one and all.

Most Baluch girls are betrothed in childhood between the ages of two and ten years. Sometimes two pregnant women will decide that if one of them should bear a daughter and the other a son that the boy and the girl will be betrothed to each other. In this way, children can be betrothed before they are born. Sometimes a girl is betrothed at no more than three days old. An uncle or some other relative of the child brings an item of clothing to the girl and seeks the betrothal on behalf of their son. If the parents agree, the newborn girl becomes betrothed to the son of whomever sought the engagement. This practice has recently become less common, and in about 85 or 90 percent of solicitations of this kind, the answer is negative.

Chapter 5: Labor and Family Relationships

The people of this region do not consider the age of a girl at marriage to be important. What is important is the amount of the bride price, which is exorbitant compared to most people's financial status and income. In 1976, the bride price generally ranged between 20,000 and 100,000 afghanis, depending on the beauty of the girl and the social and financial status of her family. A third of the sum is paid in cash and the rest is made up of goods and livestock. Since most young men are unable to pay the whole bride price at once, a young fiancé contracts to pay it in installments as he grows up, as they do not consider marriage with a young girl to be wrong. Part of the cash portion of the bride price is used to buy clothes for the bride and groom and part to furnish their home. During the Eid holidays the groom's family usually sends one or two sets of clothing and some sweetmeats to the family of the girl.

If the girl dies during the period of betrothal, the portion of the bride price which the groom has paid is returned to him as long as he has not been extravagant[21] in using engagement privileges. After the paying of the bride price, preparations for the wedding ceremonies begin. The bridegroom provides food for one meal for the family and the neighbors of the girl and delivers it to his prospective father-in-law. He must also provide food for his own family and relatives. In cases where the bride and groom come from the same village, their families agree to entertain the guests together in one place. If the bridegroom is financially able, he also hires a group of musicians, and most of the guests liven up the proceedings by dancing (Fig. 5.4). At the end of the ceremonies, the

Figure 5.4. Baluch workmen dancing during a night celebration at archaeological site named Qala 169, Sar-o-Tar, Nimruz Province, 1974.

marriage vow is taken. To represent the girl, her father, uncle, or failing them, one of the elders is chosen. This person is fully empowered to accept or refuse the groom's suit on behalf of the girl. The mullah calls two men or four women to serve as witness to this proxy. As witnesses, two women are the equivalent of one man, but it is not common for women to serve as witnesses. When the witnesses have authenticated the girl's proxy, the designated representative is empowered to hand over the girl herself to her suitor.

The khan is also involved in the marriage vows. The bridegroom must previously have given the khan either a sheep or a lamb for roasting, otherwise the officiating mullah will not be given permission by the khan to take the vows. According to my interviewees, marriage contracts were not common until about 1346/1968, and people were married with the permission of the khan.[22] Nowadays, along with the khan's permission, there is also the marriage contract, which sets forth the rights and marriage portion of the girl.

At the end of the wedding ceremony, the groom is carried to the bride's house (contrary to the practice in the rest of the country, where the bride is taken to the groom's house), where he remains for three days. After that, some of the groom's relatives come and take the couple to the groom's house amid great ceremony.

In some areas of the region such as Rudbar, Khwaja 'Ali, Landi, and Palalak, at the end of the wedding ceremony, a tent is raised for the bride and groom near the bride's house, and the couple lives there for three days and nights. Then they are taken to the house of the bride's father, where they remain for a further one or two months. Afterwards, the bride and her mother go with the groom to his house, and the mother remains for one or two months. This completes the wedding ceremonies, and the next stage in the couple's life begins.

Despite all the drawbacks of this kind of wedding, it has some points worthy of attention. The exorbitant and crippling expense of a wedding precludes many multiple marriages, especially among the middle and lower classes, and the rate of divorce has been kept very low. Furthermore, since a Baluch boy and girl do not plan their own wedding, marital problems arising later fall on the shoulders of the people who arranged the marriage, and they settle the disputes.

After the household has been established, the responsibility for the internal running of the home rests with the woman. Baluch women have varied duties in their daily lives. They are occupied with the cleaning of the home, with the arranging of household affairs, and with cooking. Most of the women also gather firewood when it is available near the house. The care and feeding of livestock is another of the women's responsibilities. They have to sew and wash the family clothes; they also tend the children. Feeding and breeding the hens and turkeys is also their task. When wool is available, they weave *dastarkwan* (cloth),[23] qilims, and occasionally rugs according to the family needs. In addition to all this, they help their husbands as much as possible in the fields.

In washing clothes, they use an anise bush instead of soap. This bush grows in the region and is about 75 cm (30 in) tall. The flowers of this bush are pink, and the leaves are green. The women collect the flowers and leaves and store them under straw in a clay pot for two to four weeks until they rot and turn black. While it is still damp they form the anise by hand into little balls, each weighing about 150 gm (0.33 lbs). They put each of these balls into about ten liters of water, thus turning the water yellow. They wash their clothes with this water. Some women also use this concoction for washing their faces and heads.

During the hiatus between the use of wind-powered and diesel-powered mills, the women ground grain for the family's needs by hand. They sometimes called in other women to help them in this task, which is known in Baluchi as *arzukeh*. This term is still common among Baluch women to designate both wool-spinning and the cleaning of wheat for eating.

Daily Life

The total harvest share per annum per farmer amounts to about two *kharvars*, or 1,120 kg (2,469 lbs) of wheat. This averages out to just under 700 gm (1.5 lbs) of wheat per day per member of an average four member family. This barely suffices as food for the farmer. Since the farmers also need clothing and other household necessities and obtain those by bartering some of this wheat, the standard of living of the class is extremely low. There is no opportunity to save even small amounts from their agricultural income. The Baluch farmers can never overcome their financial dependence on the landlords.

On the basis of research carried out in 1351/1973 among 25 farmers in the vicinity of Qala-i Fath, it was found that seven of the families had a milch cow and five of them had a milch sheep. Similar investigations carried out in 1353/1975 among 18 excavation workers in Rudbar showed that one in five families had a milch cow and two in three had a milch sheep.

Figure 5.5. Several Baluch workmen taking their mid-morning meal of bread and water at Qala 169, Sar-o-Tar, Nimruz Province, 1974.

The usual food of the farmers is wheat bread (Fig. 5.5) and *dugh*. In spring, summer, and autumn the clear majority of them eat bread and *dugh* at midday and evening. Despite the fact that they may have no milch animals, *dugh* is available for the farmers, since in this region it is not sold, and the farmers can obtain it for free. The khans in this area have many milch cows. They use what they need of milk, yoghurt and butter, and give *dugh* to whomever asks for it.

Figure 5.6. 'Aid Muhammad and 'Abd al-Hamid preparing *ghalu-i torsh* (an onion and potato soup) at the workmen's camp at House 183, a Timurid period site in Sar-o-Tar, Nimruz Province, 1974.

Chapter 5: Labor and Family Relationships

The farmers make another kind of food called *ghalu-i torsh* by mixing *dugh* and wheat flour (Fig. 5.6). They dampen a little flour with *dugh* and leave it for two or three days. Then they dry it and add a little turmeric. They put it through a sieve; the resulting powder is *ghalu-i torsh*. In winter when *dugh* is scarce, they boil a cup of *ghalu-i torsh* in water with some fat and make a special soup.

In Khwaja 'Ali Sehyaka they have something else called *achar*. This is made of *sabjak* (half-ripened wheat flour), coriander, turmeric, pepper,

Figure 5.7. Workman 'Abd al-Latif pulverizing the *qorut* (dried milk curd) in preparing the evening meal at the workmen's camp at House 183, Sar-o-Tar, Nimruz Province, 1974.

salt, flour, and fresh onions beaten in a mortar. If the onion juice is not sufficient to moisten this they add water. Of this paste they make cakes like round Uzbek loaves and leave them in the shade to dry for ten to fifteen days. Then they grind it and put them into a leather bag. They make soup of this with boiling water and some fat. In addition, the khans add *achar* to lentils and chicken or mutton soup to improve the flavor.

Semian is another food common in Khwaja 'Ali and Rudbar. It is made by machine of flour paste in thin strips, which are then roasted. This food is boiled like rice, drained, and eaten with a little fat. The common people

Figure 5.8. Muhammad Qarim baking bread at the workmen's camp at House 183, Sar-o-Tar, Nimruz Province, 1974.

usually eat this on feast days and nights known as "the nights of the dead."[24]

Dried whey, or in Baluchi *shalansh,* is another kind of food made from *dugh* (Fig. 5.7). In winter they dissolve this in water and eat it with bread. It can be seen that the farmers and workers of this region have a limited range of foods, their usual diet being bread (Fig.5.8) and *dugh*, and sometimes *piyaveh* or meatless soup. The farmers seldom eat meat. Most villages do not have a butcher's shop. Occasionally, a single sheep, or more usually a kid, is slaughtered. They do not sell it by weight alone but divide it into several equal portions and price these according to the value of the animal. This practice is called *vandi*. This meat is used mostly by *kashtmand* farmers, i.e., those in easy circumstances, in the period before the wheat harvest is ready. Farmers eat meat only when one of their or their neighbor's animals succumbs to sickness and is given to charity. In addition, on feast days that occur twice a year the farmers will kill and eat a chicken.

Although there are fish in the Helmand River, the farmers make no use of them due to lack of time and unfamiliarity with fishing.[25] The Baluch people also eat locusts, either boiled or roasted. They pull the heads off to extract the entrails and chew the remainder with relish. Lentils and other pulses also grow in the region from which the farmers are able to make soup. Maize is basically grown for cattle fodder, but a few poor farmers eat it boiled.

Chapter 5: Labor and Family Relationships

Figure 5.9. Drawing water from a well dug to supply the need of the expedition, between Qala-i Fath and Hauz, some 25 km from camp. Nimruz Province, 1974.

The only garden crops they grow are onions and pumpkins. Of the indigenous plants, *bajand, nalgasak, kholfa, gandomak, shurak,* and *roghanak* (mostly leafy vegetables, like spinach) grow in the spring and are available for use for a short time.[26]

Among the fruits only melon and watermelon are found in this region. The season for each of these is short, lasting for no more than a month. Dates and figs are imported from Iran but are beyond the means of the farmers. Some farmers use Iranian and Pakistani sugar with their morning tea.

In spring, autumn, and winter the people of this region get their drinking water from the rivers and canals. In the summer when the canals are dry and water scarce, areas far from the river use wells for water (Fig. 5.9). The drinking water is unsanitary and the well water usually tastes bitter.

Most farmers have only enough qilims in their houses to cover a sitting area, usually comprised of woolen Baluch qilims and woven mats of reeds. During the day the women normally fold and stack up the qilims and spread them out again at night so that they do not wear out too quickly through overuse. For two or three small children, they use a mattress and quilt. Clothes are made of imported material, and as a result very few farmers have more than two sets of clothing.

A few farmers who have succeeded in finding work in other regions such as Iran or who have family members who have done so, have not only freed themselves from debt but have even managed to obtain battery-operated radios or tape recorders.

The reader is perhaps wondering why the farmers remain in conditions where they cannot provide themselves with even the basic necessities of life. In this context it must be pointed out that in the region of the lower Helmand Valley and Afghan Sistan there is no available work except farming. Therefore, people who have not the means to leave the area have no alternative but to become farmers. Young men who can work part of the year in neighboring areas or other regions of Afghanistan and earn a better living are not content to return to farming. Often they abandon it and in some cases leave the area permanently. Nowadays, it is the traditionalists, the elderly, the infirm, and those who are indebted to the khans who continue as farmers, which has a deleterious effect on the agricultural productivity of the region.[27]

Almost every farmer and his child knows this Baluchi poem by heart, and in studying it a greater understanding can be reached of the conditions of the farmers' lives in the region:

> *Poem*
> We have no credit as much as a grain of barley
> There is no point in sowing and growing
> We have borrowed as much as possible
> Endeavors and debts are all finished
> Oh wretched year! End quickly
> So that the children can have some half-ripe barley
> Of everything we had we have sold both old and new
> In order to procure a little bread
> The eyes of my son and daughter are bulging with hunger
> In distress I went to my landlord's house
> To see if I could milk the black sheep
> As soon as I arrived at the landlord's house
> My landlord said, "Clean the byre."
> When I had finished this task
> The landlord's wife said, "Oh brother
> Bring a bit of kindling for the oven.
> There is none near here. Bring it from afar."
> I obeyed the woman
> And brought thorns and twigs for the oven
> The oven burned and the bread was baked
> They hid in the house to eat the bread
> I thought my hunger had gone beyond the limits
> They took no notice of my loud prolonged coughing

Chapter 5: Labor and Family Relationships

> When he had eaten his fill my boss belched and said,
> "Have you eaten?" I said,
> "You are my lord and my boss;
> My children are dying of hunger."
> He said, "Have you brought your one-sixth?
> You owe 100 *man*
> And are in debt 1,000 coins."
> Oh God, to whom can I turn?
> Who will give me a loan until next year?
> I said to the bailiff, "make him aware of my condition"
> But as long as I sat he did not come and my heart grieved
> My boss is an inconsiderate and unfair man
> Stubborn, with a heart harder than a rock
> My heart would not want me to go to him (?)
> Since if it should break he would not give a piece of bread
> My boss signaled to the bailiff with his eye
> And communicated a lie to him
> The farmer said to the bailiff, "let us go to the khan
> You have promised that you would feed me
> Until God fulfills the wishes of the children." (?)
> And the half-ripened barley came out for the children.[28]

The usual food of the khans consists mostly of meat and wheat bread. Rice is used less here than in other areas of Afghanistan. Every khan has a guest house. The number of guests varies with the location but probably on average two to five travelers per week visit the guest house. Ordinary food is given to travelers and special food to friends.

There is very little social life in Sistan, and a number of the upper class spend their time in private visits and in smoking opium. Some women also use opium for themselves and to pacify their children.

In addition to hunting, the khans like to collect weapons (Fig.5.10). On regular or hunting trips the khans take with them one or two armed guards. As well as attending to agricultural concerns on these expeditions, they settle disputes between people.

Most of the khans also have diesel-run mills. These mills are another source of revenue for them. The fees for these mills are very high when compared with the rest of the country. They usually take one *man* as the fee for grinding ten *man* of wheat. In Kabul a quarter of a *man* is charged for the same amount of grinding, and in Lashkar Gah, half a *man*. The annual

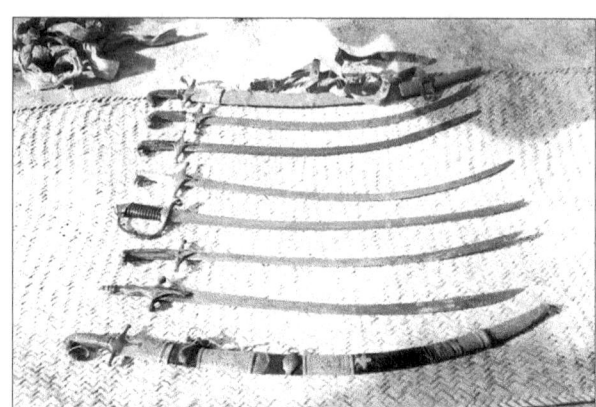

Figure 5.10. Swords from the small armory of Hajji Nafaz at Khwaja 'Ali Sehyaka, Helmand Province, 1975.

income of one such of these mills belonging to Hajji Nur 'Ali, one of the khans of Khwaja 'Ali Sehyaka, is more than 50 or 60 *kharvars* (equaling 16-19 tons) of wheat.[29] At the current rate (November 1353/1975), a *kharvar* of wheat was worth 2,500 afghanis, and 50 *kharvars* would be worth 125,000 afghanis. The total cost of a diesel mill purchased and delivered to Khwaja 'Ali Sehyaka was 120,000 afghanis. The profit from the mills is another stream of income for the landlord class, while maintenance, the provision of a mechanic, and the procuring of fuel are a nominal expense for the khans.

Trading is another favorite activity for a number of the khans of this region. Recently, the khans have added the transport of people to their sources of income. Travel in the khans' vehicles from Kandahar and Lashkar Gah costs 1,200 afghanis per person, which is several times higher for similar distances than in other parts of the country based on observations made in 1353/1975. The khan's vehicles transport people to the remotest areas of the region. They can carry up to sixty people in one Russian-built GAZ vehicle. According to these figures, they can bring in approximately 72,000 afghanis from a single journey taking less than two days. Under these conditions this source of income has a firm position on the list of income sources for the khans.[30]

Chapter 5: Labor and Family Relationships

Notes

1 This may generally reflect the truth. However, there are certainly exceptions, and some khans take considerable interest in the welfare of their farmers. WBT
2 The author recounted a substantially different version of this tale to me at the time. WBT
3 These servant/bodyguards are usually not men with family ties in the area, but are men who have been hired from more distant localities, or even purchased as boys from as far away as Pakistan. They do not marry without the khan's permission and may be required to leave his service in that event. They are charged with seeing that the khan's desires and orders are carried out, and seem to enjoy his confidence in executing these orders as they choose. Yet for the most part they seem to live harmoniously within the villages so that it may be doubted that they are the cause of habitual injustice or cruelty. At Khwaja 'Ali Sehyaka I observed that the male servants of the khan's household went about unarmed and each wore one circular earring in a pierced lobe. The bodyguards did not have the earring and, generally larger, taller men, were virtually always armed. Their rifles were usually carried in embroidered cloth cases to protect them from the fine dust of the constant winds in the region. WBT
4 Often provided with no transport by the government, these sub-governors commandeer a jeep or a pickup from a local khan for use on their inspection tours. These periodic tours are both for the purpose of hearing grievances from the khans (not the farmers or shepherds) and to maintain the presence of state authority in the region, in part to assure the regular flow of tax payments from the individual khans. WBT
5 Though their belief in and participation in the parliamentary system is exceedingly minimal. Their assessment of its efficacy appears justified. WBT
6 Every village contains a mosque of the Sunni sect. Larger villages, such as Deshu, a Sunni Pashtun village, may also contain a *madrasa* (religious school). What is most remarkable about the simple mosques in the small villages of the Helmand Valley is their apparently total lack of use. During the mission's weeks at Khwaja 'Ali Sehyaka, I never saw anyone enter the mosque for prayers. Those who pray are in the minority, and they do so singly or in groups in the open air. The Baluch of Shi'a Iran are Sunni. But there is a strong suspicion that the Baluch of Sunni Afghanistan are nominal Shi'a. A century ago the Shi'a sect was strong in all of western Afghanistan, including Herat and Kandahar. The Afghan Baluch may still have strong leanings in this direction. Traditional Shi'a names such as Ali and Murtaza are common in the region. The Sunni mullah in Khwaja 'Ali Sehyaka appeared to be the most isolated person in the village. Official patronage of the simple mosques, in terms of gifts of money and the provision of labor for maintenance and repairs, is scrupulously maintained, and a *modus vivendi* seems to have been established. An official with whom I long ago travelled in Sistan once remarked to me that the Baluch seem always to prefer mild opposition to orthodoxy. What matters to the Baluch is their Islamic faith; matters of

Shi'ism or Sunnism may be of distinctly secondary importance. WBT
7 This section was originally prepared separately and was not intended for inclusion in the ethnography. We presume this was due to political considerations at the time of writing. The reasons for this seem no longer relevant, and the editor has added it to this chapter. MA
8 Jali Robat is little more than two small clusters of shabbier than usual Baluch style houses. Whether any of the others are "fortresses" as the image of this word implies, I do not know. I have not seen them. WBT
9 The small, remote village of Jali Robat on the Pakistan border was, in 1975, also known by the name Hajji 'Isah, the elder and leader of the village. Hajji 'Isah died while on pilgrimage to Mecca that year, and control of the village passed to his son. The village lies on elevated land just inside the mountains. There is a spring of poor alkali water, and some grain is grown on small terraces. But the economic *raison d'etre* of Jali Robat is its existence along a major smuggling route from Iran. Facilities exist here for simple repairs to the four-wheel-drive American jeeps, the preferred vehicle in the *kochok* (smuggling) trade, and a fuel dump is maintained. WBT Archaeologically, the area around Jali Robat is rich with ancient copper smelting, to be described in the archaeological report of the project. MA
10 The times cannot be correct. A camel can surely traverse the 40 km in a single day. WBT
11 Chiefly motorcycles and food stuffs. WBT
12 But the camel herds are rarely used now. Motorcycles are the preferred conveyance. WBT
13 Who have received them from the government for this purpose. WBT
14 Tate, *Seistan (A Memoir on the History, Topography, Ruins and People of the Country)*, 1910–1912, pp. 289, 291. GRA. This is a summary rather than a direct quotation from Tate. WBT
15 This system of border control is the most practical for the central government in an area where its presence is barely felt. Unable to control either the border tribes or the smuggling, this system of self-policing is the only practical option open to the government. In 1971 an effort was made by the governor of Nimruz Province to exercise control of the Jali Robat corridor. It is said he dispatched seven unprepared soldiers to the region where they were promptly killed. No further attempt by the government to interfere with the border was made. The initiative had almost certainly been that of the Nimruz governor without clearance from Kabul. WBT
16 The Constitution adopted in 1964 contained a similar ostensible guarantee against forced labor in Article 37. But as may be seen, the two sentences dealing with this issue effectively cancel each other and leave the pre-Constitution condition unchanged:

> Forced labour even for the benefit of the State is not permissible. The prohibition of forced labour shall not be so construed as to affect the implementation of laws governing the organization of collective work for the public interest. https://web.archive.org/web/20110917002320/http://www.afghan-web.com/history/const/const1964.html

Chapter 5: Labor and Family Relationships

See Dupree 1973: 565ff. for a thorough discussion of the drafting and implementation of this constitution. WBT

17 Perhaps the greatest single factor contributing to the lessening of corvée labor was the prosperity in Iran during the 1970s that severely reduced the population of Sistan. The result was that fewer laborers were available to the khans, and more reasonable compensation for work was necessary. Many residents of Sistan emigrated during the severe drought of 1970–1971. With the discovery of higher wages in Iran for menial labor and feelings of liberation from the constraints of their feudal society, many others left for Iran. While there are no statistics on the percentage of Sistan residents who emigrated during the 1970s, it is generally conceded to have been in excess of fifty percent. A khan at Khwaja 'Ali Sehyaka informed us that his village, which once contained 150 households, in 1975 had fewer than 50. With the fall of the Republic, and especially since the invasion by the Russians in 1979, the depletion of population in Sistan became more acute. The majority of the remaining Helmand Valley residents fled to Pakistan, while those from Zaranj, and many even from as far away as Lashkar Gah, have moved to Iran or Pakistan. It may well be that the present population of Sistan is lower than at any point in the last several thousand years. WBT

18 By the 1970s definite signs of strain within the traditional family had begun to manifest themselves. Again, the attraction of higher wages in Iran was probably a major cause. Some who spent half of each year in Iran, apart from the family, while not unfilial in failing to send money back to the family, were likely to develop attitudes of self-interest and independence incompatible with traditional family hierarchies, especially in those cases where the father, a head of the household, failed either to exert his position of authority or became content to be supported by his sons' foreign earnings. WBT

19 As elsewhere in Afghanistan today, few men in this region had more than one wife. WBT

20 Within any such generalized social structure, there are notable, sometimes remarkable, exceptions. During the weeks we resided at Khwaja 'Ali Sehyaka in the autumn of 1975, the mission made the acquaintance of a remarkable woman. Shaparai exhibited none of the traditional attitudes of Baluch women. She traveled about the village by herself without the slightest evidence of shyness and conversed freely with the mission members. Her husband was a mild-mannered man who, though present in the village, was rarely in evidence. Shaparai was considered a phenomenon as well by the citizens of Khwaja 'Ali Sehyaka, who rarely dared to insult or criticize her. Shaparai even presented herself among the group of men assembled for employment, and for a period worked as a laborer on the excavations. Any teasing or insulting remark cast in her direction by one of the male laborers was met with scorn and sarcasm from her. Shaparai was widely traveled, had been to Kandahar and to Pakistan. She was a veritable mine of information. It was she who first told us of the places far to the south where "stones had been cooked" (copper smelting sites in the Shela Rud, Gardan Reg, and at Jali Robat), sites we subsequently visited. She had much natural curiosity and was a collector of

unusual objects. She presented us with a small ingot of copper that had been poured into a groove in the ground at one of the smelting sites. She opened her home to us to explain how the family lived and worked. She was both talented and proud of her many abilities and enjoyed discussing bread making, felt rug making, and embroidery with us. She led us about the village to meet other women engaged in various forms of craftwork. At times these women were too shy to demonstrate their work for us, and so Shaparai would seat herself at the loom and demonstrate its operation for us. She sought out the houses which had the best qilims, or the finest varieties of household goods, and bullied the occupants into letting us examine these. She had three grown sons by a previous marriage who were at that time working in Iran. By her present husband she had three more children, a bright and lively young boy, a young daughter who was rather less outgoing than her mother, and a son of perhaps three years of age who appeared to suffer from Down's Syndrome. Shaparai explained that by the birth of this last child she had had little milk left in her breasts and that the child had suffered in infancy from malnutrition. Her diagnosis was almost certainly correct. She and her daughter constructed the *tandur* for our camp, and we were frequent visitors to her own oven at bread baking time for hers was certainly the best in the village. Close to her mother's *tandur*, the daughter had a miniature one in which she played by making small pieces of bread. Shaparai cooked some of the bread for the khan's household and also made special soft bread for an old village man who had no teeth. Her life was not without sorrow, but she refused to be crushed by it. During our short residence at Khwaja 'Ali Sehyaka, a sick infant grandson cried incessantly one cold and windy night until it became silent in the early morning hours. By daylight, he had already been buried. On another day, a 14-year-old nephew accidentally drowned in the Helmand River. In this village of no more than fifty households, there were one or two burials a week in the large cemetery on a hill above the town. There were no public displays of mourning.

When we last visited Khwaja 'Ali Sehyaka in October 1976, we had a special request of the khan, to visit Shaparai. We found her in the courtyard of a house close to the Helmand River, nearly a mile from her own. She was beating into a new felt rug patterns in colorfully dyed wool. Above her head on the side wall of the house was a speaker wired to a tape recorder inside the house. Blaring out of the speaker were popular Iranian songs, the tapes of which, along with the tape recorder, one of her sons had brought to her from Iran.

Shaparai was the only Baluch woman we ever conversed with during our years in Sistan. She may well be unique, and certainly none of us will ever forget her. WBT

21 That is, providing the prospective groom has not exhibited premarital wanton extravagance in the purchase of clothing and adornments with the portion of the bride price allotted to him. If he has shown commendable virtues of frugality and moderation, the deceased bride's family will reimburse him that portion of the bride price he had spent in anticipation of the forthcoming marriage and alliance with the bride's family. WBT

Chapter 5: Labor and Family Relationships

22 The bond between the khan and his subjects formerly was preeminent, and the clergy was not considered entitled to interfere with the khan's decisions with respect to his subjects. The involvement now of the mullah in the marriage ceremony reflects less an increase in the influence of religion than the gradual detachment of the khan from such personal and familial concerns which do not require adjudication by the khan in his secular capacity. WBT

23 A cloth spread on the ground for serving meals. BA

24 This feast is not described by Amiri. MA

25 At Malakhan, fish trapped among the rocks of the *band* were collected twice a day for food. Presumably, this practice is observed at other *bands* in the river. The Baluch do not otherwise fish with line or nets. However, the Sistanis of Iran living on the shores of the Hamun-i Helmand do fish with net and line. Small balls of poison also are used, but this practice is more common in the Pashtun region of Lashkar Gah. WBT

26 The Western botanical names are not known to us. MA

27 It is abundantly clear to most khans of the region that the old order is rapidly coming to an end. Many of their farmers have left for Iran, and their wealth can no longer be based on agriculture and livestock. A number of khans have in consequence become quite impoverished. Others have turned to the lucrative smuggling trade, which has produced for them far more cash than they previously commanded. They realize that they have little to bequeath their sons but empty and useless lands, and so they have brought their sons into the smuggling business, as owners of vehicles engaged in the trade, or as agents working in Iran or Pakistan. But even the smuggling business cannot provide an adequate living for all the khans of the region, and there has been considerable rivalry and some violence connected with this activity. The trade during the 1970s was to a great extent monopolized by two families, the others having been unable to compete successfully. These families own fleets of four-wheel-drive pickups, but their success is constantly challenged by wealthier Iranians who cross the border with many more trucks accompanied by armed guards. In 1970 and 1971 Pashtuns from the Kandahar area attempted to control the smuggling business through Afghan Baluchistan, but they have largely been excluded from the trade by the Baluch khans' superior knowledge of the remote and difficult terrain and by their control of the borders. WBT

28 The text of this poem is given in both Baluchi and Dari in the original. Intended meaning is unclear in several places. According to the translators, words glossed in the Baluchi version of the poem: *Pur*: half-ripened barley which is not yet good to eat. The farmer's children ate it; *Satu*: half-ripened barley, dried and powdered. It is moistened with *dugh* and eaten.

29 This is inconsistent with Amiri's previous equivalence of a *kharvar* equalling 80 *man* or 800 lb/363 kg in Chapter 3. In this case, the author is referring to metric tons. BA

30 The transport of workers to the Iranian border is yet another aspect of the smuggling business. For the most part, the khans transport their own villagers, thus devastating the local economy based on farming. Four-wheel-drive

pickups are usually employed, but one large Russian Gaz truck was also in service in 1975. The trips are made at night and are not without hazard. Breakdowns in the desert far from water are not unknown. The khans have arrangements to pay Iranian police to permit workers delivered by them to cross the border. The Iranians prefer Baluch laborers as peaceful, hardworking men. But by the mid-1970s, the supply of available Baluch had much diminished, and increasing numbers of rough and destitute Pashtuns from the Kandahar area were being brought down the Helmand for transport to Iran. The Iranians believe the Pashtuns are less willing workers and frequently resorted to crime within Iran. Once inside Iran, life is not necessarily congenial for the Baluch guest workers. They must bribe the Iranian police for the privilege of staying. They must pay an exorbitant amount for the return journey. They have difficulty in sending their earned money back to Afghanistan and normally cannot risk carrying it with them for fear of robbery at the border. Normally it is sent back through a relative or friend who has been fortunate enough to purchase a passport and is thus able to travel by commercial services. If an Afghan stays for a long period in Iran, he may be arrested by the Iranian police intent on confiscating his accumulated earnings. Afghans who attempt to cross the border alone, without paying for the protection provided by the khans' transport, are arrested and imprisoned if caught before being turned over to Afghan police at Zaranj who, convinced their prisoner has accumulated a fortune in Iran, in their turn imprison him under frequently appalling conditions and attempt, by beatings and/or starvation, to extort money from him, of course without avail. WBT

Chapter 6
Education, Health, Religion, and Cultural Norms

Education

A superficial look at the conditions surrounding the advanced peoples of today and a comparison of them with the backward nations shows that those nations that are among the advanced and who have attained great power in the world did not suddenly and accidentally achieve that position, but their development was born of a series of events which prepared the economic and social ground for it.

The influence of education on the improvement of the economic, political, and social life of mankind is a vital one. With the acquisition of knowledge and the grasping of scientific principles a people can overcome those factors that are an obstacle in the road to progress, light up the dark corners of society, and illuminate them with the guidance of science.

Our country, which is among the developing nations of the world, does not sufficiently enjoy the benefits of education. Until a few years ago most of the remote areas had no secondary schools, and the people there had no share in the advantages of reading and writing. With only slight improvements this situation continues today, and in the villages, schools, teachers, and educational necessities are not available to fill the students' needs.

The region which we are at present discussing is also one of these remote and educationally impoverished areas. Compared with the population the number of schools and teachers is minimal. According to statistics compiled in 1351/1973, in the province of Nimruz there were in total 207 teachers and 6,909 students, male and female, and 65 schools.[1] In the same year in the province of Helmand, which includes a portion of Sistan, there were 554 teachers, 23,348 students and 40 schools,[2] which compared with the census figures for the same year for the two provinces —134,336 and 348,839 respectively—is a very low number. According to this data, 5.14 percent of the population of Nimruz and 6.69 percent of the population of Helmand is being educated.[3]

According to the author's own findings, in 1352/1974 in the region of Qala-i Fath and Dashtul there were two village schools—in Mehrabad and Jui Nao— serving 18 villages, and one elementary school in the village of Hauz. The two village schools in Mehrabad and Jui Nao were founded in 1350/1972, and the elementary school in Hauz, in 1347/1969. The number of students at this elementary school was 201[4] according to my survey that year. In the 18 villages connected with the Qala-i Fath Canal (Mehrabad, Baluchan/Maluchan, Baghak Pa'in, Baghak Boland, Mateh Jat and Shuri, Na 'Ilaj, Shahr, Taushakh, Maddi, Malakhan, Delanguk, Hauz, Zandak, Godri, Shuri Pa'in, Shuri Bala, Shahr-i Nao, and Sabzgozi) and Dashtul (400 families) there were in total 1,462 families. According to these figures one child from every 7.2 families was receiving an elementary education.[5]

According to counts made in 1351/1973 among the families of 25 excavation workers in the region of Qala-i Fath, and in 1353/1975 among the families of 19 excavation workers in Rudbar, there were 4.8 and 4.9 members of each family respectively who made their living by agriculture. According to these calculations, there were 7,017 people in the region, and one in 34.5 attended elementary school. Therefore, if those at school all completed their education, with no dropouts, there would be less than 3 percent of the population who had attained sixth grade literacy. The top three graduates from grade six have their way paid by the province to attend middle school or to a lycée in Lashkar Gah, Zaranj, or elsewhere. The rest must pay their own way, and 90% of the people of Sistan cannot afford it. One of the village schools is for girls and does not go beyond grade three. Only boys who graduate from a village school go to the elementary school at Hauz. Thus the girls' school was not included in the above figures.[6]

The elementary school is quite distant from most of the villages it serves, and because of the lack of motor transport, travel to it is on foot or by donkey and is very difficult. The distances between several villages and the school are as follows: from Mehrabad to the school at Hauz is 17.5 km, from Sabzgozi 16 km, Baluchan/Maluchan 15 km, from Baghak Pa'in 11 km, and from Baghak Boland 8 km. The above distances are as the crow flies between the school and the students' homes. But because of the sand and the irrigation channels the roads are not direct and the distances which the children must cover twice a day are perhaps one and a half times those given here.

Chapter 6: Education, Health, Religion, and Cultural Norms

Table 6.1

Middle, Elementary, and Village Schools along the Helmand from Darwishan to Zaranj

Name of School	# students	# teachers
1. Seh Mu'alameh Village School of Sorkh Dez	130	3
2. Hazar Joft Agricultural Lycée	287	23
3. Hazar Joft Middle School	437	9
4. Yek Mu'alameh Vil. Sch. of Deh Zakarya	46	1
5. Darwishan Elementary School	270	8
6. Village School of Kuchnai Darwishan	40	1
7. Village School of Miyan Pushtu	64	1
8. Laki Elementary School	206	6
9. Bartaka Elementary School	91	2
10. Safar Elementary School	190	8
11. Banadar Village School	70	1
12. Khan Neshin Elementary School	266	6
13. Bagat Village School	42	1
14. Taghaz Village School	93	1
15. Deshu Village School	30	1
16. Upper Khwaja 'Ali Village School	40	1*
17. Upper Rudbar Village School	35	1
18. Lower Rudbar Elementary School	200	5
19. Guludand Elementary School	37	1
20. Khajau School	40	1
21. Charburjak Elementary School	210	7
22. Bandar-i Kamal Khan Elementary School	230	8
23. Hauz Elementary School	49	1
24. Mehrabad Elementary School	49	1
25. Hauz Elementary School for Girls	25	1
26. Jui Nao Elementary School	50	1

*The author visited this school in 1355/1977 and found that the one teacher had departed during the previous year, leaving a substitute, and had not yet returned.

The above figures represent the official figures for the schools and do not reflect the large number of chronic absentees.

Enrollment at a Sample School

The following are the official class by class enrollment figures for the Khan Neshin Elementary School.

      1. The number of students in grade 6 was 34.
      2. The number of students in grade 5 was 32.
      3. The number of students in grade 4 was 39.
      4. The number of students in grade 3 was 48.
      5. The number of students in grade 2 was 31.
      6. The number of students in grade 1 was 82.

The official enrollment figure for the school was 266, but considering that 55 of those were chronic absentees 211 would be a more accurate figure.

Figure 6.1. The new *maktab* (school) at Hauz, with its two classrooms and office. Two additional classrooms are under construction. Nimruz Province, 1974.

The school building at Hauz has four 5 by 3 m rooms made of unbaked brick. Two of the rooms are offices, and the other two are classrooms (Fig. 6.1). Because of the lack of space, there is a morning session and an afternoon session for lessons.

Another oval room, 5 by 3 m, made of matting, branches, and daub like the Baluch houses, is located 20 m from the main school and serves as the girls' school (Fig. 6.2). This school had one teacher with a tenth-grade education and, including the permanent absentees, had 80 students.

Most people in Afghan Sistan have not been keen on education for women. They believe that female education should not go beyond reading religious texts, because girls would use writing for wicked purposes. This is the way they argue: The daughter of King Qutb ad-Din, who was very beautiful and enamored of the famous conqueror Timur-i Leng (Tamerlane), after Timur had besieged Zahedan for some time without taking it, wrote a letter describing the underground water system that the people of the city had used during the siege. She wrapped the letter around an arrow and fired it to Timur. The condition of this treachery was that Timur would agree to take her as his wife. He cut the city's water supply, captured it, and married the woman.[7] Up to now there have been no female teachers in the girls' school, and the people are reluctant to send their daughters to a male teacher. Perhaps another cause of the early marriage of Baluch girls is this same antipathy towards female education. Because the law exempts girls

Chapter 6: Education, Health, Religion, and Cultural Norms

Figure 6.2. A typical Baluch dwelling serves as the girls' school at Qala-i Fath, Nimruz Province, 1974.

from school attendance after their marriage, families marry their daughters young as a means of keeping them from school.

In most areas of the country the mullahs and other religious leaders also have a role in the education of children. In the villages children are sent to the mosques before the age of seven to learn reading, writing, and religion. This type of education continues for male students until the age of ten or twelve. After this the children who are not enrolled in school give up mosque education and go to work with their fathers. Those who are enrolled in school continue their studies. Although the main purpose of mosque education is religious, at the same time the children acquire basic literacy. Unfortunately, in the lower reaches of the Helmand Valley and Afghan Sistan, the mullahs and other religious leaders are not involved in educating the children. They merely lead prayers and occasionally preach. The teaching of religious thought and reading and writing is not common in the Sistani mosques.[8]

As a result, on the one hand the people lead hellish lives, and on the other hand the knowledge and education that could aid them in removing the obstacles in their path to progress are extremely deficient.

There are several factors blocking progress in education in this area:[9]

1. In Afghan Sistan most of the people are Baluch and their mother tongue is Baluchi, but in the schools all the teaching and the textbooks are in Dari.[10] Most of the children do not understand

The Helmand Baluch

Dari and so gain little from their schooling. As a result, they fail. This failure by the children dampens their parents' interest in education.

2. Another reason for the stagnation of education and the general disenchantment with learning is the unsettled lifestyle of most of the people, meaning the farmers and the other villagers. It has been mentioned before that, except for the khans, no one has his own house to enable him to put down roots in one area. If a farmer leaves farming, goes to another area to find work, or is obliged by the khan to leave, it takes several days of his time to transfer the children from one school to another. What is more, since the number of schools in the region is very limited due to the widely scattered population, the farmer's dwelling will probably be far from the new school. Traveling to and from school is very difficult and sometimes impossible for the children. For this reason, another group of school children is deprived of education, and the parents whose children have derived no benefit from spending several years at school lose interest in education.

3. Some of the Sistani khans and teachers contribute to the pessimistic attitude towards education. These khans allocate a few *jeribs* of agricultural land near the school to the teacher and the head teacher so that their meagre stipends may be augmented by producing at least some of their own food. Although the khans grant this land out of a sense of fellowship with the teachers and believe they are furthering the cause of education, the teachers have no aptitude for farming, and they make use of the students' labor and their parents' agricultural equipment. In this way, the teachers and students are concerned with agriculture instead of occupying themselves with academic pursuits. On the other hand, this requisitioning of the services of the children's parents is imposed as a duty and disinclines them to enroll their children in school. At the same time the teachers and administrators are unwilling to dispense with the unsuccessful and older students who work well on the school farm.

4. In spite of the fact that the Baluch people have, when compared with the other peoples of the country, less religious fervor, yet they are influenced by the predominant mentality in the country, although the spread of modern education has to some extent weakened religious belief. For this reason the Baluch people believe that

Chapter 6: Education, Health, Religion, and Cultural Norms

enrolling their children in school contributes towards diminishing the children's religious faith and counts as a sin.

5. Graduating from the sixth grade of elementary education is fruitless for the majority of people in this region since they are poor. They cannot afford the expense of living in town away from their families in order to attend a middle school or lycée beyond sixth grade. Therefore, most of them join their fathers at work after leaving sixth grade and forget everything they have learned without ever having used it.[11]

Public Health

In the province of Nimruz there is one clinic at Zaranj, the capital, which in 1351/1973 had 15 beds, an X-ray machine, and two doctors.[12] The population of the province in the same year was 134,336.[13] According to these figures, there was one doctor for every 67,168 people and one hospital bed for every 8,655, which is extremely inadequate. In the province of Helmand in the same year there were two clinics (in Lashkar Gah and Girishk), three doctors, 70 beds, 3 laboratories, and one X-ray machine.[14] The population of this province was 348,839,[15] which works out to one doctor for every 116,279 people and one hospital bed for every 4,983 people.

These clinics are in the provincial capitals. Most of the farmers and villagers in the lower Helmand Valley and Afghan Sistan are unable to take advantage of them because of the distance involved, lack of transport, and insufficient time and money. As has been mentioned already, because of the sand, transport routes are extremely limited and generally unsuitable for motor transport. It is thus very difficult for the Baluch people to get their sick to the clinics in proper time.

One day in 1349/1971, while we were occupied with our research in the ancient fortress of Qala-i Sirak, located on the right bank of the Helmand near Deshu, an old man entered the fortress. Seeing that all the members of the expedition were busy, he leaned against the wall and slowly sat down. I and several expedition members approached the old man. From the bulge under the right side of his cloak it was apparent that he was carrying something. On questioning him we learned that the man had a child under his cloak who had fallen into a hot oven when his mother was not looking and had been severely burned.

The peasant asked whether we had any medicines to give to his child. When the whole expedition was gathered around him questioning him, the old man brought the injured child out from under his cloak for inspection by the expedition team on my request. The child's body had been wrapped several times in a cotton shirt and he seemed to be exhausted and in great pain. The old man lifted the wrappings to show us the sick child's burns. From under the shirt his skinny body and burnt right side were revealed. The treatment of the child was beyond the ability of the expedition, none of the members of which had medical training, much less adequate medical supplies for the critical treatment required. We implored the old man to take the child as quickly as possible to the clinic at Lashkar Gah, which was the nearest, but the old man shook his head sadly and said "It is not possible." He had no way of getting to Lashkar Gah, and since it was the wheat planting season and the beginning of the agricultural year, his absence from work would mean that he would be unable to farm that year and would be out of work for the entire year.[16]

In addition to the lack of doctors, the scarcity of hospital beds and the unjust increase in the price of drugs, there is another difficulty which besets these people and prevents the administration of modern scientific medicine. In the whole of the province of Nimruz there is only one pharmacy; in Helmand there are four. These pharmacies are not properly supervised, and the prices of drugs are very high for the people.[17] Because of the lack of facilities for administering modern and effective drugs, villagers are obliged to make use of their traditional methods of healing. Disorders that cannot easily be identified (particularly nervous disorders), that require more careful study and diagnosis, are thought mysterious and sinful, and villagers believe that they are caused by jinn (spirits) and by occult and invisible presences. They believe that these disorders are not treatable.

Sometimes the ill think that someone is hostile to them and has worked witchcraft on them, believing that an adversary has hurt them by means of amulets or talismans. Such disorders are more prevalent among women who are more repressed.[18]

If someone overworks and becomes sick, he believes that he has been afflicted with the evil eye.[19] Sometimes through carelessness, wounds or sores become infected and worsen the condition. In this case they think that the sick man has heard some evil sound, and to avert the evil eye they set about burning seeds of rue, an indigenous bush that grows throughout the country, and reading scrolls of holy writings. In the last case they burn *barbau* or *badrau*, a bush that grows wild in the central mountains of Afghanistan and produces smoke very pleasant to inhale. *Barbau* is considered pure and sacred. Or they hang special amulets, usually made of

Chapter 6: Education, Health, Religion, and Cultural Norms

precious stones, about the necks of the sick. Such remedies are, of course, unscientific with no tangible benefits.[20] Many sick people turn to the mullahs for scrolls and amulets as remedies. The mullahs give patients almost every kind of amulet and scroll. Occasionally, a sick person recovers, and as a result, they believe more strongly than ever in the efficacy of amulets and scrolls. Fortunately, it is not customary to pay for amulets and scrolls. But if the sick person should give a token of gratitude, it would of course not be refused, and approximately 90 percent of the people give as big a gift as they can. Some of the Sayyids in the district are also in the business of dispensing amulets and scrolls.[21] The Sayyids who currently enjoy the best reputation for performing incantations and handing out amulets are Mullah Safar in Bandar-i Kamal Khan, Khwaji 'Abd al-Hakim in Khwaja 'Ali, Agha Muhammad 'Umar Khan in the village of Maddi, Agha Gholam Khan in the village of Shahr associated with Qala-i Fath, Maulawi Khan Muhammad in the village of Lop-i Rudbar, and Akhond 'Abd as-Samad in Khwaja 'Ali Sehyaka. During the fifth season of excavations, in 1353/1975, one of the workers named Muhammad Rasul had a triangular amulet in a leather case around his neck. This he had obtained from Agha Muhammad 'Umar Khan. He firmly believed that it protected him, and that after a year of illness (probably a nervous disorder), he was cured as a result of obtaining the amulet (Fig. 6.3).

In addition to obtaining amulets and scrolls, these people also go to shrines to effect cures. Women, who are less free than men to approach

Figure 6.3. Muhammad Rasul, an excavation workman, at Qala 169, Sar-o-Tar, Nimruz Province, 1974. He wears a triangular *tumar* amulet around his neck.

Figure 6.4. The Shrine of Adam Khan in Maktab, near Safar, Helmand Province, 1976.

Figure 6.5. A typical regional grave near the Shrine of Adam Khan, near Safar, Helmand Province, 1976. Prayers are knotted in a cloth suspended by the cord between the poles at the grave ends.

Chapter 6: Education, Health, Religion, and Cultural Norms

the mullahs and Sayyids, seek help more from shrines. They light candles at the shrine and sometimes beat in wooden nails and make their requests to them.[22] Sometimes they wrap a string around head stone of the shrines, and then they collect these and wear them around their necks. Many of the sick believe that they can be cured by eating the earth around a shrine.

The famous shrines in this region include Shaykh Hosein in the village of Delanguk, Khwaja Bidar in Jui Nao, Bad Shao near Godri, Adam Khan in Bagat (Figs. 6.4, 6.5), Mir Gadu and Mullah Ijab in Khan Neshin, and Lajvard Jan in Khwaja 'Ali Sehyaka.

The people of this region do not confine themselves to visiting local shrines, but go also to those which are far distant, maybe even one or two days' journey, from their homes. Among such shrines having an important position in the hearts of the people are: Balanush in Chaghi, Baluchistan; Hajji Fayz Muhammad on the left bank of the Helmand opposite Jui Nao; and Amiran Sahib in the Dasht-i Amiran near Zaranj (Fig. 6.6). This last-mentioned shrine is located in the middle of a flat, waterless, and infertile playa to the northeast of Zaranj, the capital of the province of Nimruz, and is about 25 km by motor road from Zaranj.

This shrine is situated next to a historic mosque of the Timurid period, of which a large portion of a minaret is still standing.[23] Next to the Timurid mosque there is a second mosque in the north portion of which

Figure 6.6. Ziyarat-i Amiran, the Shrine of Amiran Sahib in the Dasht-i Amiran in central Sistan, Nimruz Province, 1974.

Figure 6.7. Ziyarat-i Amiran, with the pile of horns marking the place of sacrifice, Dasht-i Amiran, Nimruz Province, 1974.

Figure 6.8. Ziyarat-i Amiran. The horns of sacrificed goats at the shrine. Dasht-i Amiran, Nimruz Province, 1974.

is the shrine of Amiran Sahib, his brother, and his sister, where they are buried. According to the keeper of the shrine, Amiran Sahib originally came from Arabia by way of Herat. He fought against the non-Muslims and was martyred.

Approximately twenty meters to the south of this shrine there is a mound of bones of goats, sheep, and cattle next to an animal slaughtering-place (Figs. 6.7 and 6.8). People bring their sick from far and near to this shrine and seek to cure them through the sacrifice of animals. Some of the pilgrims bring their sheep and goats with them and slaughter them near the shrine and give them to charity.[24] Since there is no running water or

Chapter 6: Education, Health, Religion, and Cultural Norms

well near the shrine, pilgrims also bring the necessary water with them. This is a kind of spiritual healing, and it is sometimes effective.

Herbal medicine, which in our country is called Greek Medicine, is also common in this area. Experience has taught these people that certain herbs and plants have medicinal properties, which are efficacious against certain diseases. In the past almost everyone used this kind of remedy as several ancient books attest. Usually, the famous learned men make up their prescriptions according to those books and administer them to the sick. In Sistan people do not use only those remedies which are found near at hand, but also bring them from great distances. Among the population there are individuals who specialize in this. A number of old women also engage in this practice, but their activities are limited to the families or villages where they live. They do not go beyond these precincts. However, there are learned men in the region whose activities are not confined to one village but who have influence over a wide area. One of these men is called Rajah Jahil; he lives in the village of Delanguk on the Qala-i Fath Canal (Fig. 6.9). He not only gives out medicine, but also sets bones, meaning that in a basic and rudimentary fashion he performs the functions of an orthopedist and evidently possesses a certain facility in setting broken bones. In addition to setting bones, Jahil Hakim treats sick people with local medicaments which he concocts from herbs.

Figure 6.9. Jahil Hakim in Delanguk, a village near Hauz, Nimruz Province, 1974.

Such potions sometimes have medical value for the villagers, but sometimes they have detrimental effects. Since these remedies are not scientifically prepared, but are mixed extempore, it is possible that one of the ingredients will cure the sickness from which the patient is suffering, but on the other hand may bring on an incurable side effect. In any event, while these remedies have chance benefits they also frequently occasion much harm. In order better to clarify conditions I wish to make a short list of the method of preparation of the drugs used in treating the sick in this region.

Following traditional wisdom, for stomach ailments the people use:

1. Aniseed, or dry anise, mixed with rose petals. They beat it to a powder and every day give a little of this, mixed with water, to the patient who is suffering from stomach pains.
2. *Khaleseh* and *kalpureh* (two indigenous plants) are mixed and beaten together and given to the patient with water.
3. *Chapru* (the root of a wild plant) is another kind of local medicine in this region. This is dried and powdered and given to the patient suffering from a stomach ailment, to eat with yoghurt.
4. They boil dragon-wort and use the water in which it was boiled, considering this efficacious for gastric ailments.
5. Mint root is also used as a stomach remedy by these people. They boil it well and administer the water to the patient.
6. They feel that eating cumin mixed with water is of some benefit against gastric disorders.
7. *Puzhu* and *marmut*, two wild plants that grow in the Kuh-i Malik Siyah, are mixed together and served with milk against stomach upsets.
8. They grind *damichakeh* (a wild shrub) and consider it efficacious against stomach trouble.
9. *Anj* is the sap of a tree which grows in the Kuh-i Malik Siyah. They eat it with butter, raisins, and water to alleviate stomach aches.
10. In Khwaja 'Ali Sehyaka they also use *gavatek*, which grows in the mountains on the Pakistani border, to cure stomach ailments.
11. Another mixture used against stomach disorders is *tusu* and milk, mixed together.

Chapter 6: Education, Health, Religion, and Cultural Norms

They use these remedies to cure fevers:

1. They mix flea-wort seeds with sherbet and drink it.
2. They soak dried Bokhara plums in water overnight and drink the water before breakfast.
3. The water in which a wild shrub named *karkavok* has been soaked overnight is used against fever; the patient drinks part of it and washes in the rest.
4. They heat a knife in the fire and singe the back of the ears of the patient until they burn.
5. They wrap the sufferer in the freshly skinned hide of a kid or lamb, and he is obliged to remain that way all night until he is cured.
6. They soak branches of seven fruit trees in water overnight, and give the patient the water to drink before breakfast.
7. Plants such as mallow, endive, chamomile and camel thorn are soaked for a specific time in hot water and the water is given before breakfast to relieve the fever. This remedy is called *charbikh*.
8. Sometimes they believe that their sickness results from an impurity in their blood. In this case they tightly bind the arm at the elbow and open one of the veins in the wrist or any part of the lower arm. They let the patient bleed freely so that his blood will be purified, and he will be cured.

They also have remedies for other sicknesses which would take too long to list. The method of treatment for the great majority of people of this region is as described above. It is clear that these remedies are not very effective and that few diseases will be cured in this way. For this reason, minor ailments such as the common cold, influenza, measles, and whooping cough, which would be curable in the cities, are often fatal in this region.

According to my study of 25 excavation workers in 1352/1974, the average life expectancy in the area of Qala-i Fath was less than 43 years. Our investigation of 19 excavation workers in 1353/1975 showed that in Rudbar the average was 44.2 years. The age of the oldest living family members who took part in the study was reckoned as 60 years. In Afghanistan since people generally do not know the year of their birth, they do not know for sure how old they are. For this reason it is impossible to be entirely accurate in computing the average life expectancy of the population, but with effort a close approximation can be reached.

Religious Practices

The Baluch of Afghan Sistan are, like most of the population of Afghanistan, Sunni Muslims.[25] Instruction in religious matters begins at the age of three in Baluch families, and the parents gradually teach their children the important tenets of their belief. Children's curiosity about their surroundings, which usually begins at this age, is directed towards religious questions. By the age of seven, the children are to some extent familiar with religious knowledge and mosque practices. At the age of seven most children, equipped with this degree of understanding from their home environment, go to school, and they are taught religious studies along with other subjects. After the age of ten, children are expected by the parents to participate in religious activities. In this way, Baluch learn religious matters over a number of years.[26] In their youth Baluch are less subject to religious influences than are people who live in the cities, since their knowledge of religion is very limited and does not exceed that of their parents. There is no extensive religious instruction available in the centers of religious learning. Religious practices are less noticeable among the Baluch of Afghan Sistan. Throughout this region only one mosque exists in Khan Neshin, and another in Charburjak.[27] Perhaps one of the reasons for this is the impermanence of the villages in the area which is not conducive to the building of a large permanent mosque.[28] There are no madrasas or large mosques in the whole of the area from Darwishan to Charburjak and Zaranj. Friday prayers, common in other parts of the country, do not take place in most areas of the Helmand Valley. Prayers on feast days take place in the large squares in the villages where the khans live. The majority of people in the area pray individually, since it is difficult for them to assemble in mosques. For a month, I lived near the mosque of Khwaja ʿAli Sehyaha and did not once see a group of more than four attending the communal prayers. The mullahs and learned men in Sistan belong to the middle class, are less active than in other areas of the country, and are not very active in society. Leading prayers, attending funerals, washing the dead in the villages, performing marriages with the khan's permission, giving sermons and speeches on holy days such as feast days, Fridays, and the birthdays of religious figures, are among the duties of the mullahs. Teaching children after the age of seven and giving them religious instruction is part of the mullah's duty in most other parts of the country, but in Afghan Sistan this is not the case. In some areas of this region the mullahs are occupied with the cultivation of a plot of land equivalent to that of a farmer given to them by the khans.

Chapter 6: Education, Health, Religion, and Cultural Norms

For these reasons, the Baluch people, when compared with the people in the rest of the country, have very little religious feeling. In addition, as has been said before, the region is remote and under the influence of powerful men who use religion for political ends. G. P. Tate has written concerning the religion of these people:

> In general, the Seistanis are by no means fanatical in religious matters. Portions of the same tribe are in many cases settled on both sides of the boundary, and those who are subjects of Persia conform to the State Church and are Shiahs, while their bretheren, as Afghan subjects, profess the Sunni doctrines. All alike are extremely superstitious, and resort largely to "Ziarats" or shrines.[29]

To the same degree that the Baluch people are free and unfanatical in religious matters, in other ways they are very superstitious. A number of Sufis who call themselves Sayyids exert a great influence among the Baluch people. Under the name of *pir* they have acquired many followers in Baluch society, who believe that the *pir* can help them on all occasions and especially that at the time of death they can protect them from Satan's evil.[30] In the hope that with the help of the *pir* they will depart this life in safety, they set great store by the orders of the *pir*. A *murshid* (spiritual advisor) sets out a daily schedule of religious observances for a disciple. For some they prescribe repeating one of the names of God one hundred times a day, and for others recommend reciting the Qur'an and praising God. These practices are in addition to the regular observances required of all Muslims. Discipleship does not depend on a person's knowledge, but more on his piety. For most of the *pirs*, the title is hereditary. Their fathers and grandfathers were also famous as *murshids*, and their disciples believe in their venerability even after their deaths. Their burial places are revered as places of pilgrimage.

A number of these *pirs* live today in Baluchistan and have come from great distances to Afghan Sistan. In 1353/1975 I had a conversation with two *pirs* named Mostanshah and Shahbanshah who had come from Chaghi in Baluchistan to Khwaja 'Ali Sehyaka (Fig.6.10). From Mostanshah I learned that he had left a month and a half earlier from Chaghi in Baluchistan to check on his disciples and had spent several days in Bagat. Afterwards, he went by camel to Chakhansur by way of the Dasht-i Margo.[31] From there he went to visit his disciples who lived in villages along the Helmand Valley, and after a month and a half had arrived in Khwaja 'Ali Sehyaka, where I met him. This news gathering about disciples usually

Figure 6.10. Itinerant holy man Sayyid Mostanshah between two of his devotees, Khwaja 'Ali Sehyaka, Helmand Province, 1975.

takes place toward the end of autumn, which is the best season in Afghanistan for having guests.[32] At this time the harvest is in, and the villagers can share part of it with the guests. In Sistani villages most of the people rear a sheep or a kid for a year, and at the end of autumn they kill it and dry the meat, a tradition known as *qaqi* or *landi* in most parts of the country. Families who cannot afford to eat meat even once a month throughout the year have some *landi* meat. Since the harvest season is not long past, they still have several *man* of flour in store. Families who have a milch cow or sheep also have saved some dried milk products at this time for the winter. The favorite foods in this region are these three things: wheat bread, mutton, and clarified butter, all of which are more plentiful at this time of the year than at any other. In these favorable circumstances the *murshids* seek out their disciples and bless their followers with their presence in their lowly dwellings.

The *pirs* take some of their brethren with them on these journeys. The *pir* and his entourage usually spend a day and a night in the house of a disciple, and on leaving, go straight to the home of another one. The disciples are not content merely to invite the *pir*, but also give gifts such as meat, fat, and flour, so that the *murshid* can send them back to his family. If a disciple neglects to give provisions, one of the *pirs'* brethren will inform him of that. Sometimes, the *murshid* himself, while relating dreams, is

Chapter 6: Education, Health, Religion, and Cultural Norms

reminded by the sight of an animal such as a kid, sheep, or donkey with specific desirable qualities, which was given to him in his dream. In such a case the disciple feels himself obliged to find the animal and give it to the *Pir*. Finding such an animal is not difficult as the *pir* probably saw the animal first when he was awake and afterwards in his dream![33] Some beautiful and valuable furnishings in the disciple's house also sometimes figure in the *murshid*'s dreams. After two or three weeks, all the provisions and animals are collected and sent to the *murshid*'s house with one of his brethern (Fig. 6.11), and the *pir* usually spends the autumn and winter in these wanderings.

According to the people of Khwaja 'Ali Sehyaka, several other people from Baluchistan (Sakhi Muhammad Mazar, Hajji Delshad, La'l Shah, and others), are considered to be famous *murshids* in the lower portions of the Helmand River. Every year they visit their followers. Usually a person will follow a single *pir,* and he is free in his choice since there are several *murshids* in a village, each with his separate following. These *murshids* have brought some *khordeh* (shrine soil) with them from the Chaghi District in Baluchistan and give it to their followers as a gift.[34] The disciples believe it to be blessed and that they and their families derive benefit from it. They believe that it will protect them from sickness and calamity. Soil from the shrine of Balanush is particularly highly esteemed among the Baluch of the lower Helmand Valley.[35]

Of the supplies that the *pir* collects on his travels and sends home, a portion goes to guests and to the people who transport them back to his house. Some of these *pirs* also have a *khangah*. A *khangah* is a place where people gather for instruction in various Sufi practices. The *pir* provides the food in a *khangah*. The existence of a *khangah* has a great effect on the fame and popularity of a *pir*. People who visit the *pir* in his home usually donate as much as they can to the *khangah*.

In the village of Shirak connected with upper Rudbar in 1975, I spoke with an old man named Sayyid Muhammad who had recently returned from a four-day journey on foot. On questioning him I learned that he had gone to see the survivors of Saleh Baba who had been his pir. Since he believed that he was not wealthy, he had given them only 400 afghanis in aid. Some *pirs* receive many such gifts and own flocks of animals and possess great wealth.[36]

Figure 6.11. Sayyid Mostanshah, accompanied by his son Shahbanshah, seen leading several camels in the direction of Chaghi, Baluchistan (Pakistan), loaded with wheat and household effects obtained in Khwaja 'Ali Sehyaka, Helmand Province, 1975.

Folk Customs

A large number of customs have been mentioned already under different headings. Several others current among the Baluch and the inhabitants of Afghan Sistan that the author considers worthy of note will be mentioned here. Some of these customs are common and exist also in other parts of the country, but several are unique to this region.

Just as birth control is unimportant to most of the people of the area, they are delighted by the birth of a son. The more sons a family in Afghan Sistan has, the more fortunate they consider themselves to be. In order to find out whether a pregnant woman is carrying a boy or a girl they take auguries from dead snakes. They take the dead snake by the tail and twirl it around three times, and throw it eight or ten meters. If the snake lands belly down and looks lifelike, they believe the pregnant woman will have a boy. If it lands belly up the woman will have a girl. The birth of a boy, at whatever time of day or night, is announced to the people of the village by gunshots. For her confinement a pregnant woman seeks the assistance of an older experienced woman with a reputation as a midwife. On the

Chapter 6: Education, Health, Religion, and Cultural Norms

sixth evening after the birth the close relatives are invited to the home of the newborn, and they hold a gathering in which some of the guests play and sing local music for the baby and celebrate. The baby is also usually named at this party. In some areas, the mullah of the mosque and several of his students and children, following a special custom, visit the baby's family and are given tea and sweets. One person, usually the mullah, recites verses especially composed for the occasion, and the others join him in repeating the last lines of the verses. The local people call this custom "Bringing *nashrah*." At the age between five and ten years, usually in the spring or autumn when the weather is mild, the ceremony of circumcision of the male child takes place. This event is also the occasion for a special celebration in which the relatives and friends of the child's family participate with local music and dancing. The operation is performed in a primitive manner by the barber.

The celebration of feast days in this area does not differ greatly from other areas of the country. On these days, in addition to all the people of the village congratulating each other on the happy day, families gather in each other's houses and visit. People who have been at odds during the interim between two feasts put aside their quarrels and reestablish good relations. Young engaged people go to the houses of their betrothed's parents on the second day of the feast and are given sweetmeats, kerchiefs, and colored boiled eggs, some of which they usually give to their own relatives.[37]

Marriage Customs

In marriage customs, people with no immediate family enlist the aid of the village elders to mediate marital engagements. For the marriage ceremony, the people of the village and the near relatives of the boy and girl do not stint in providing all that is necessary. Although the expense of the wedding falls on the boy's family, or on the groom himself, the affair does not stop there. In the cooking of food and in the distribution of it in the morning, noon, and evening, many of the people of the village lend a hand. Usually, the barber takes responsibility for the preparation of food, and others help him in providing water for cooking and for washing dishes, distributing the food, and furnishing cooking utensils.

Cooking equipment, carpets and dishes, a sitting place, or several rooms necessary for the guests, are provided free and voluntarily by the people of the village or by the relatives of the bride and groom. If there is music, almost all the young people join in the fun with foot stomping and dancing. Some people also come from a considerable distance to take part in the wedding. Because of the distance, they cannot return home in the middle of the night after the ceremony. In this case, some of the villagers take a few guests each and put them up in their houses so that the guests will not be left without a place to sleep, and so the difficulties of the wedding organizers are alleviated.

On the third day after the wedding, another festival takes place called "The Third Day." Most of the women who had attended the wedding ceremony return and gather where the newlyweds are then residing. They take turns to give money and a gift called *siyali* to the bride. With the sum of this money and the gifts that the men give to the groom under the name of *bijar*, a portion of the wedding expenses are defrayed. This custom, with little variation, is also current among the Baluch of Iran. The *bijar* of wedding assistance is one of the most useful and pleasing customs among the Baluch people and one not to be found among the more advanced peoples and nations.[38] *Bijar* means assisting young men who wish to marry and start a family. Both rich and poor benefit from *bijar*, but it is obvious that the wise Baluch instituted the custom to aid poor young men. They began the custom so that the bridegroom should not be embarrassed by his poverty. On the other hand, a young man who gets married and has his wedding expenses paid by the local people is obliged to contribute to the *bijar* of other young men in the future and thus repay his social debt. *Bijar* gifts are made in accordance with a person's wealth and no one is exempt.[39] This custom is seen in several guises in various parts of the country. In the areas of Bini Hisar, Shiwaki, Hud Khel, some parts of Lugar, some parts of Chahar Dehi, and elsewhere, the people carry out this custom on the eve of the wedding. In some areas, especially in the towns, this aid has recently taken the form of goods rather than money, so that in fact it provides the household necessities for the bride and groom.

Burial Customs

There are also customs among these people that are seen in times of affliction. On the death of an old person, someone, usually the barber or a close relative of the deceased, informs the village. With infants, a few people gather for the shrouding and burial. For this situation there is a Baluch saying which goes, "He came from one grave and went to another." One or two other people inform the relatives of the deceased in outlying villages. On this day the village people do not go about their usual work. Close

Chapter 6: Education, Health, Religion, and Cultural Norms

friends and wealthy acquaintances of the deceased go to his family and express their readiness to lend money to defray expenses out of charity and at no interest, or in the case of ongoing need, to lend money to the family of the deceased. Villagers congregate somewhere, usually the mosque, to recite prayers for the dead, and others gather to prepare the body for burial according to custom. Some people occupy themselves with digging the grave and making the necessary preparations. Three or four more help the bereaved to purchase necessary items. Before the burial the distribution of *isqat* takes place. *Isqat* is money that the bereaved distribute among the religious and the poor. In some cases one of the near relatives of the deceased assumes the responsibility for paying these sums. The amount of money distributed depends on the wealth of the bereaved family. At the time of my research in 1353/1975, farmers give from 200 to 500 afghanis, *kashtmands* from 600 to 1,000 afghanis, and khans from 2,000 to 10,000 afghanis, or more.[40]

After the distribution of *isqat* the deceased is buried. In most parts of Afghanistan the grave is dug in *shaq ya shami* fashion, where the body is placed at the bottom of the pit and covered with a stone slab, but in Sistan it is generally built as a tomb with an angled side chamber at the bottom of the burial pit and covered with a slab. Because stone slabs are very scarce in this area, they close the mouth of the tomb with bricks made of a mud and straw compound. They pile a heap of earth on top of that until the grave forms a mound above ground level. In order that the soil should not blow away they cover it with small stones.[41] There is also another kind of grave in Sistan, which is built above ground in the form of a small vaulted room. In these graves skeletons of from two to five people have been found. Nowadays, this kind of tomb is not used in Sistan, and we ourselves came across them for the first time in the environs of Shahr-i Gholghola (Sar-o-Tar). Subsequently, more of these tombs were found during the course of the survey near Bandar-i Kamal Khan. The people of this area associate this kind of tomb with previous inhabitants of the region.

In the villages the funeral rites generally last for three days from morning to sunset, and in the towns for two days from morning to noon. Village people do not leave the prayer assembly on the first day until the end of the day. On the second and third days, everyone attends the ceremony for one or two hours and then returns to their daily occupation. Close friends and the family of the deceased attend the gathering on all three days.[42] In the area under discussion, the family of the deceased is not obliged to cook or prepare food for three days. Every household in the village feels itself obliged to send a portion of food three times a day to the home of the bereaved family. The amount of food sent is in proportion to the size of the family of the deceased and its guests. The guests and family of the deceased use this food for three days. At the end of three days, the funeral rites come to an end, but the obligations of the family continue. Every Friday for 40 days they are expected to provide food for the people. The villagers and family friends help out with this. All travelers, villagers, and anyone else can take advantage of this charity. Failing to take advantage of it is not a fault for those who have no need of it. After the 40 days, the relatives of the deceased in their turn invite the family. The intention of all this hospitality is that the bereaved family should have no opportunity to be overwhelmed by the loss of the person who has died. For this reason this custom is known as *ya'is keshi* (removing sorrow).

Collective Practices

Among the farmers there is a custom worthy of note called *hashar*. A farmer for some reason is behind in his farming, or needs to irrigate some rough and difficult land to prepare it for cultivation, a very difficult task to accomplish alone, or encounters a task that is beyond the powers of one or two people and yet has to be completed within a specific time—in these cases the farmer, according to an exchange system which the Baluch have, invites the necessary people to help him in the above work. The people invited to work gather at a specific time to do the work and carry it out together. *Hashar* itself is an Arabic word and means "to gather together." In the past it was used to designate an irregular army of organized villagers for fighting. In *hashar* the farmer who is being helped is responsible only for providing the midday meal for the day or days when the work is being done. It is not usual to make any payment to the helpers during *hashar* days. In other parts of the country, this system is also used in repairing and building houses.

Until recently, there were also tribal councils in Sistan. One or two khans, or tribal chiefs, usually took part in these councils. The council members also chose one of their number for his wide experience, wisdom, and perspicacity as a spokesman. Some clerics were also invited to serve on the council. These councils were formed to solve major issues. The khans dealt with small matters concerning the people and the farmers. The tribal councils were mostly called to settle differences between the khans in the event of a dispute continuing for a long time. Most of the disputes

Chapter 6: Education, Health, Religion, and Cultural Norms

for which the tribal councils were convened concerned matters of family honor or murder. As far as the people of Khwaja 'Ali Sehyaka were aware, the last time a tribal council was called was in about 1330/1952, because of a dispute over a woman between Shir Muhammad Khan, who lived in Khwaja 'Ali Sehyaka, and Taj Muhammad Khan of Upper Khwaja 'Ali.

Notes

1 As with all official government statistics in Afghanistan, those which reflect favorably tend to be grossly exaggerated, those reflecting poorly upon development as equally grossly underestimated. A rule of thumb is to apply, at a minimum, a fifty percent reduction or increase, accordingly. WBT
2 *Statistical Data on Afghanistan (Years 1350-1352)*, pp.161–2, 164, 165. GRA
3 The largest town in Nimruz Province almost certainly had a population of under 10,000 in 1975. The members of our mission believed it quite impossible that the total population of Nimruz Province could have exceeded 60,000. Helmand Province, on the other hand, with two towns of approximately 10,000 population, and one of perhaps 5,000, and with a much greater number of smaller villages, might have had a population of close to 100,000. These figures were approximately half the numbers claimed by the Afghan government. The Demographic Project's calculations did not, we believed, reflect the massive emigration of Afghans, especially from Nimruz Province, beginning in 1970. The ratios, if not the actual figures, are both more accurate and more significant. WBT
4 Officially enrolled. However, the school contains only two small classrooms, and it did not appear that more than 35 to 50 children attended at any one time. Because the school served a large district, it is unlikely that children living up to ten miles from the school ever attended. WBT
5 I myself counted the inhabitants of the villages of Delanguk, Hauz, Godri, Zandak, Maddi and Malakhan, and information about the other villages was obtained from 25 excavation workers living in these places. GRA.
6 The large number of students officially enrolled in grade one in comparison to those of grades two through six adequately reveals that no more than half the eligible students even remain on the rolls beyond the first year. The highest absenteeism is undoubtedly among the grade one students, suggesting that a substantial proportion of eligible and enrolled children receive no education at all. WBT
7 Tate, *The Frontiers of Baluchistan*, 1909, p. 229. GRA. Amiri omits the subsequent killing of the lady on the grounds that she was capable of treachery, quite apart from her education, and this is surely an equally important point of the anecdote. WBT

8   This may as well be a reflection of local ambivalence toward the Sunni sect represented by the village mosques. WBT
9   The progressive attitudes of the author are particularly manifest in this statement. The problems are certainly more complex, for education does not per se inevitably lead to progress and better lives. The twentieth century has provided many examples to support this. The very few men responsible for the present (1980s) tragedy in Afghanistan all belonged to the educated elite of the country, and the country has undergone incalculable suffering as a result of their efforts to force their personal concepts of progress upon it. Lack of formal education does not automatically condemn one to a "hellish" life, and it is extremely doubtful that the lives of the urban Pashtuns, Tajiks, Hazaras, and others are superior to those of the rural tribal groups. Many, including the majority of the tribesmen themselves, would consider the opposite to be true. WBT
10 While this seems incredible, it is true. WBT
11 There is still another factor contributing to the failure of rural education, not only in Sistan, but in other parts of the country as well. The teachers come from the major cities of the country and belong to the urban culture where they received their education. They are totally unprepared to work among rural populations, especially those with whom they do not even share a common language. Under such circumstances, it is difficult for the teacher to survive, let alone adjust, to the rural environment. In many cases, a teacher's rural assignment may represent his first experience of life outside the city. Few are truly dedicated to their profession, and fewer still are intellectually or emotionally capable of enduring the privation of the life they enter suddenly, without preparation or transition. Some even feel menaced by the rustic populations they have never encountered before. Under the circumstances, it is not unusual for the teacher to leave his post for a short visit to the city, without the slightest intention of returning. Many of the rural schools have no teachers at all for long periods. WBT
12 *Statistical Data on Afghanistan (Years 1350–1352)*, pp. 171-3. GRA
13 *Statistical Data on Afghanistan (Years 1350–1352)*, pp. 171-3. GRA. See note 1 above re population statistics. WBT
14 *Statistical Data on Afghanistan (Years 1350–1352)*, p. 91. GRA
15 *Statistical Data on Afghanistan (Years 1350–1352)*, p. 91. GRA
16 See the description of another incident with an injured child in the Note on Translation and Transliteration in the front matter. That case turned out better for the child. WBT
17 Doctors and pharmacists, like teachers, generally are not interested in employment in rural areas. Foreign educated doctors wish to remain in Kabul where they may maintain contact with aspects of foreign life they enjoyed while studying abroad. There are also few opportunities to earn salaries in rural Afghanistan commensurate with those they observed among members of the medical professions in the countries where they attended school. Kabul offers the only possibilities for generous financial rewards, and there

Chapter 6: Education, Health, Religion, and Cultural Norms

is no reason to expect members of the Afghan medical profession to have less interest in those aspects of the good life medical practice offers than do their counterparts in Western countries. Locally trained doctors are seldom more interested in rural practice. Consequently, the doctors who work in the provinces are more likely to be less capable than those of the major cities. The same may be said of pharmacists. Medicines that require prescriptions in Western countries are generally openly available in Afghan pharmacies, and in most cases, even in the cities, Afghans tend to avoid the cost of a doctor's diagnosis and accept medicines from pharmacists who may have little or no diagnostic training. The best an Afghan entering a pharmacy can hope for is a lucky guess; the worst that can happen is that he will be given medicine which exacerbates his complaint and may possibly result in harmful, or even fatal, side effects. While the shortage of competent doctors is acutely felt in Helmand and Sistan, the absence of pharmacies outside Lashkar Gah and Zaranj is not altogether a misfortune. Little attention is paid to the dispensing of outdated medicines, and informed advice on proper dosages is almost totally lacking. Storage of drugs under proper temperature and light conditions is practically impossible, and the hygienic conditions of all but a few pharmacies in Kabul are far from satisfactory. WBT

18 Perhaps because of their inferior status, women have greater need to believe in magic causes and cures for diseases. Husbands are much less likely to seek professional medical advice or aid for their wives and daughters than for themselves and their sons. In consequence, folk medicine and appeals at the grave shrines of holy men are more commonly practiced among women. In most cases, other options simply do not exist. I do not mean to create the impression that men are universally unconcerned with the health of their womenfolk. It is by no means uncommon for a husband to journey a considerable distance to a particularly efficacious shrine in the hope that she may be cured through offerings and prayer. But a girl is less likely than a boy to be taken to the city for whatever degree of professional advice may exist there, and the mortality rate is certainly higher among women than men. WBT

19 This is not always the case. Malaria is endemic in Sistan and nearly all of our workmen complained of periodic attacks of fever. While they had no exact knowledge of the cause of the disease, they did not believe it to be the result of intemperate living or the evil eye, perhaps because nearly all are so afflicted. WBT

20 They have, however, powerful psychological effects, and as is well recognized, in many illnesses the patient's belief in the efficacy of the treatment can be an important factor in recovery. WBT

21 Those who are reputed to be direct descendants of the Prophet, and therefore to possess special powers. WBT

22 Strips of colored cloth symbolizing imprecations are also frequently tied to wooden poles inserted in the ground about the tombs. WBT

23 The Ziyarat-i Amiran is perhaps the most important shrine in Sistan. It is evidently of great age. The ruined fifteenth century Timurid mosque is not

the oldest structure on the site. Foundations of eleventh century Ghaznavid structures are also present, and the site undoubtedly held religious significance still earlier. The shrine is constructed to contain the graves of three martyrs: Amiran Sahib, his brother, and a sister. According to legend, it was Amiran Sahib who first brought Islam into the Sistan region. The archaeological and architectural elements of the shrine will be described and discussed in greater detail in the archaeological reports of the Helmand Sistan Project. WBT

24 Charity in this instance is for the lone keeper of the shrine, who is dependent upon these gifts of food, and also of water, which does not exist in this truly spectral landscape. WBT

25 This is not strictly true. Sunni is the official nominal sect, as evidenced by the Sunni mosque in every village. But the Baluch of the Helmand Valley may better be described as Muslim. They lean strongly toward Shi'ism, which until comparatively recent times was the predominant sect of western Afghanistan. WBT

26 And from diverse sources, which may account for eclecticism in their religious belief and practice. WBT

27 There is a problem in nomenclature here. See ahead in the author's text. I, myself, have visited the "mosque" in Deshu and the one in Khwaja 'Ali Sehyaka. Perhaps the author would use a different term to describe these humble structures. Yet there may be substance to what the author has said. We were very struck by the absence of mosques among the ruin fields of Sistan. Apart from the mosque at the Ziyarat-i Amiran, which has existed since Ghaznavid times at least, we found only remains of only two other mosques within the great Sar-o-Tar tract, an elaborate Ghanznavid one inside the inner city of Shahr-i Gholghola and a simple Timurid mosque in the community labeled Houses 338. To the north, between the Hamun-i Sabari and the Hamun-i Puzak, there is a ruinous mosque at Peshawaran. Religious observance may always have been in Sistan what it largely is today, a faith tied more to charms, prayers, and saints' graves than to architectural forms. WBT

28 This cannot be the reason. While villages move about frequently, they move within a very constricted radius, never moving beyond their toponymic zone. That is, a village in the Lop district of the Rudbar region will not move outside its district except in unusual circumstances (floods, sanding). The villages of the Helmand Valley are extremely small and yet an examination of maps of the valley made as long as 150 years ago gives the same village names in the approximate places where they exist today. Cf., for example, the otherwise quaintly inaccurate map in Perrin (1842) or Ferrier (1856). WBT

29 Tate, *The Frontiers of Baluchistan*, 1909, p. 228. GRA. "...and the custodians of such places derive no small profit from their visitors" completes the quotation, deleted by Amiri perhaps because there is absolutely no evidence to support this contention today. The shrines are poor, ruinous places, and the custodians eke out a meager living from the equally poor who, usually in some condition of desperation, visit them. WBT

Chapter 6: Education, Health, Religion, and Cultural Norms

30 At Khwaja 'Ali Sehyaka, a <u>pir</u> lived apart in a simple hut near to the cemetery. Burials were conducted in accordance with his instructions rather than those of the mullah who was not in attendance. WBT
31 A direct distance of approximately 220 km, but longer if following established tracks through the desert. WBT
32 Following the rains of spring, the intense heat and wind of summer, and before the cold and storms of winter. As the author notes, food is also more plentiful at this season. WBT
33 This cynicism is probably justifiable. WBT
34 Small cakes of earth from holy shrines are standard furnishings in mosques. In Iran, for instance, earth from Karbala and Mashhad is both sold in the bazaar and available in mosques. At prayers, the small cake of sanctified earth is placed on the floor or ground in front of the prayer. When during the course of the prayer the forehead is touched to the ground it rests upon this small cake of earth, and the prayers thus are spiritually enhanced through this contact with the ground of a holy shrine. In the same fashion, the blessed water in Christian churches is held to possess certain spiritual qualities. WBT. This is true only of Shi'a Muslims. BA
35 The geographical location of this shrine is not given by the author, but presumably it is in the district of Chaghi in Pakistani Baluchistan. WBT
36 That is, relative to local criteria. WBT
37 Colored eggs are especially popular at the celebration of Eid, which marks the end of the traditional month of fasting. These are given as presents tied in especially embroidered kerchiefs. The custom is much the same as the colored Easter eggs in the Christian West. Both solid colors and paintings of intricate geometric design are employed. The eggs, having been accumulated slowly over a considerable period of time, are not meant for eating. Children play a game with these eggs which consists of each striking with his egg the one held by the other. The winner is one whose egg is not broken. WBT
38 That is, elsewhere in Afghanistan. But this is not strictly true. What the author means is that *bijar* is institutionalized among the Baluch. WBT
39 Nasih, *Baluchistan in the Year 1344/1966*, p. 94 GRA
40 All of this is conducted with dispatch, since by custom the deceased is buried by sundown on the day of his death. WBT
41 Considerable attention is paid to the selection of the stones. Normally rounded pebbles are collected from the banks of the river, and these are selected for the purity of their color (usually black). The most highly esteemed stones are translucent white travertine pebbles from the region of Golichah, far to the south near the Pakistan border. If the family can afford it, travertine from Golichah will be acquired as soon as possible after the burial. Normally, pieces are brought over a period of time by travelers passing through the Golichah area. Most graves have only a few pieces of this stone on them, but in some parts of the Helmand Valley, the majority of the graves are covered with these beautiful gleaming stones. Carved travertine antiquities of the third millennium BC are often found among the pebbles covering a grave. These

have been, in most cases, found accidentally by travelers passing through the Gaud-i Zirreh and Shela Rud regions where cemeteries of this date exist. These antiquities are usually in the form of fragmentary mortar-shaped vessels and grooved concave pestle-shaped objects of unknown function. These objects will be discussed at greater length in the archaeological reports of the Helmand Sistan Project. The grave type may consist of a simple vertical excavation, about a meter in depth. But "catacomb" burials are also common. From the bottom of the excavated pit, a passage sloping downward is excavated, and beyond this a chamber is excavated for the body. The sloping passage is filled with stones and earth before the surface excavation is filled. A cross-section of this type of grave appears in Savage Landor (1902, II, p. 402). WBT

42 These prolonged obsequies are not observed on the occasion of the death of an infant or young child. WBT

Conclusions

The geographical area under discussion in this work used to be called the "granary of Asia," but now it is part of a region desecrated by wind and sand. If care is not taken, it will become still more completely a desert. The desert region, which at present covers one third of the area of the earth, is constantly increasing. According to the 1,500 delegates from 110 countries attending a United Nations conference in Nairobi, during the last half century 650,000 square km (250,000 square miles) of agricultural and pastoral land on the southern fringes of the great Afro-Asian desert belt have been transformed into desert. In Indian Rajasthan the area inundated by sand has increased by 8 percent over a period of 18 years. UN specialist Hugh Lamprey reports that prior to 1333/1955, the city of Khartoum was surrounded by acacia trees and was a green area, whereas now around this city, which has only a few inches of rainfall a year, no such trees are to be seen for a distance of 90 km (56 miles). Faruq al-Baz, an Egyptian specialist, has measured the advance of sand in the Nile delta at 13 km (8 miles) per annum.[1]

Most people in the United States and other developed countries do not consider the threat of the encroaching sand to be very important, but for the 78 million people who see the desert sand eating up their farmland it is not an insignificant event. The problem of desertification of farmland, especially since 1348/1970, has assumed increasing importance and has become a familiar story, threatening every aspect of the lives of the 630 million people who live in these regions.[2]

The Baluch people of Afghanistan are also numbered among these unfortunates, and Afghan Sistan is one of these areas.

Some scholars ascribe the destruction of wide tracts of agricultural land and consequent loss of livelihood in Afghan Sistan to climatic changes. New research shows results that conflict with this, namely that the destruction of the irrigation system by human forces such as the Mongols,

The Helmand Baluch

Timur-i Leng, and others is a major cause of this change.[3] Today, more than ever agriculture is regressing, and most of the farmers of the area, who suffer greatly from the lack of social and economic equality and from others with vested interests that conflict with supporting prosperous agriculture in the region, are unsuccessful in their farming and seek seasonal work in other regions. The cleaning of the few remaining irrigation canals necessitated by the effects of wind and sand and other natural forces, which fell exclusively on the shoulders of the farmers, has been neglected due to the rise in wages and the increasing availability of work in other regions,[4] and because of the paucity of farmers in some regions, the canals have become blocked and have even disappeared. The only way to solve this problem is to initiate a program of repairing the earthworks and finding employment for the inhabitants.[5] Curtailing of the emigration of our fellow countrymen to Iran will not come about as long as the area of the southwest border is under the control of the local khans. The landowners cannot utilize their land to the extent necessary to support even its reduced population, and the agricultural produce of this region is insufficient to meet the needs of the khans and the people. The lack of farmers has resulted in most landowners leaving their lands unplowed. The region of Guludand, downstream from Rudbar, which was previously owned by Ghulam Dastgir Khan, a landowner from Charburjak, went uncultivated for several years as the result of the blocking of a canal. In 1353/1975, the province of Nimruz, with the approval of this khan, divided the land of Guludand among landless Baluch. The new landowners, with the help of the province, unblocked the irrigation canal. This land is now being cultivated and is yielding a profit. There are many large and small tracts of land suitable for agriculture in this region that, through the blocking of the irrigation canals, have ceased to be cultivated but that, with a little attention to their irrigation, could be transformed into fertile and profitable agricultural land. So if these areas were considered first for agricultural development, great results might be achieved quickly and at small expense. In order that the canals of this region should no longer be blocked by the effects of wind and sand, it would be better for the entire system of irrigation to be changed. The digging of open canals, as is customary in this region, has not been successful. Each year they have disappeared under the onslaught of the sand and have had to be cleaned out. It would probably be better in this region to excavate subsurface canals,[6] or to transport the water in cement pipes in conjunction with the existing system. But this also would be a temporary solution and does not address the root of the problem, which is the

Conclusions

continuing encroachment of the sand. Even if the irrigation system were salvaged, the sand would still engulf the agricultural land.

The essential solution to this problem lies in stopping the wind and removing the source of the sand.[7] Care must be taken not to empty the basin lakes of water to the extent that the sand and silt deposited there by the river, which constitutes a major source of sand, is exposed by low water levels and is carried by the wind to other areas. On the other hand, wind breaks could be planted to mitigate the effects of the wind over the agricultural land. In this way the area under discussion might, under an accountable government, once more become a rich agricultural area. In order to develop this region, and to achieve high agricultural profit goals, some basic requisites may be noted:

1. The increase of agricultural land.
2. The increase in yield per acre by means of better seed, and the use of fertilizer and the elimination of reeds that choke canals.
3. Raising the status of agricultural work by means of changing the feudal ownership and the various kinds of tenancy, and by addressing the other unnecessary problems arising from the uneven distribution of land.
4. Exchanging less valuable crops for more valuable ones.
5. Diversification of production: for example, along with farming encouraging chicken rearing, animal husbandry, market gardening, and silk worm production.

If the above recommendations are not heeded, no "Green Revolution" will take place in this region. It is an astonishing thought, but if the Baluch landowners and farmers and other people in the area were knowledgeable about modern farming and irrigation methods they could not only provide food for themselves, but for three or four other provinces as well, and perhaps the country would not have to import wheat. In comparison with other areas of the country, in the lower Helmand Valley and environs there is more pasture land. Even the Khash Rud, a small river in the area, is mentioned in the Avesta, Yasna 68:15, and called *Khwastra*, meaning "abounding in good pasture land." But this does not mean that the Helmand Basin should be exempt from further development. Since this area is most suited to pasturage, it is necessary to develop veterinary capacity, improve the milch animals and cattle breeding, and establish a small cheese factory.

The economic power of smugglers and their associates and the presence of a black market in this area have obstructed the development of indigenous handicrafts.[8] Weaving of famed Baluch carpets, which was formerly a noteworthy industry in this region, is now in decline and will possibly disappear altogether unless steps are taken. To develop carpet weaving it is necessary to teach the art in girls' schools and to prevent the export of wool to Iran.

Another craft which would be beneficial to this area is stone craft and carving, since there are abundant sources of fine travertine in the border area near Golichah and the proximity of the Helmand River would provide favorable conditions for the development of this industry.[9]

For the development of pottery there is also ample fuel for kilns and a particular clay (75 percent clay and 25 percent sand) conducive to ceramic production is present in most areas of the region. Unfortunately, the people of this area obtain their necessary earthenware vessels from Kandahar or Farah.[10] This is no doubt good news for the tradesmen of those areas. The existence of raw materials for a glassmaking industry, i.e. the pure, clean sand of this region, which can scarcely be equaled anywhere in the world, and the greater availability of water in this region than in other areas of the country for establishing industry, should also be mentioned.[11]

The new road between Yakhchal and Deshu will to some extent lessen the remoteness of this region,[12] but in some areas roads are distant from the Helmand Valley, and this circumstance cannot contribute to an increased population returning to the Valley. In order to facilitate communication between these people and others in the country, it would be better to make use of the navigable lower reaches of the Helmand River. Dr. Klaus Fischer, a German archaeologist, has remarked about sailing on this river: one of the major channels of the Helmand River is called Tim Yaqiam, which runs from the right bank of the river near Rudbar and Charburjak and flows down to Nishk. The gradient along this stretch ranges from 1 foot per 1,000 feet to 3 feet per 1,000 feet. From the name of this channel the possibility of sailing on it is apparent. In fact, in the accounts of Islamic historians of the Middle Ages, sailing on this waterway is mentioned.[13] Because of the lack of bridges below the upper stretches of the Helmand, communications between the inhabitants on the two sides of the river are infrequent and difficult except at low water.[14] Therefore, in addition to the bridge that is projected near Deshu in connection with the construction of the new

Conclusions

road, another bridge near Charburjak would be of great help in alleviating the difficulties.

In the field of education, although some attention should be paid to giving instruction in the children's native tongue, the making available of the means of further education for poor children graduating from sixth grade would be of great benefit under present conditions.[15]

There are many other difficulties, great and small, that have been mentioned in the various chapters. Only those that have played a major role in the history of this region and its people and that can be solved under present conditions have been suggested here.

Notes

1. Sand, however, is not everywhere being created at such a prodigious rate. In some cases it is a question of shifting sands, encroaching at one point on fertile agricultural land while leaving behind elsewhere sand-free but damaged land that cannot readily be restored to usefulness. In the closed Tarim Basin, for instance, it seems unlikely that the vast quantities of sand that have engulfed the southern perimeter of the basin during the last 1500 years represent that substantial an increase in the total sand existing in the basin. A more likely explanation is that only a portion of this represents newly formed sand, and that the major mass has simply moved, chiefly through wind, from further to the north, leaving behind barren and moderately sterile plains and badlands. WBT
2. "The Creeping Deserts," *Time Magazine*, September 12, 1977. GRA
3. *International Commission for Irrigation and Drainage Bulletin*, July 1974. GRA. This persistent popular belief is, of course, untrue. A highly developed, efficiently operated irrigation system is virtually indestructible by the means available to such conquerors as Tamerlane. It is recorded that he destroyed the dams in the Helmand River, the reservoirs of which fed the vast network of canals in Sistan. But this destruction of the Helmand dams was an almost yearly occurrence anyway during spring floods in normal years, and these simple, but ingeniously constructed *bands* were easily repaired. It is recorded also that his armies destroyed the canals, but a moment's reflection would reveal that such would have been quite impossible. The Sistan Basin was watered by hundreds of miles of major gravity fed canals and literally thousands of miles of subsidiary canals, a system which had to have consumed centuries in its construction. Certainly the major canals could have been breached by military work gangs and large tracts of land temporarily flooded. But such efforts conducted during the course of brief campaigns could not have damaged canals beyond repair or farmlands beyond rehabilitation,

and quite possibly, with a larger labor force, they were restored more quickly than they had been damaged. Destruction of dams and breaching of canals can be an important factor only so long as an invading and/or occupying army prevents their repair. The fact that the Sistan Basin enjoyed one of its greatest periods of prosperity during the century following the conquest of Tamerlane is sufficient testament to the fact that whatever havoc he may have wreaked upon the area served only the purpose of conquest, and that within a short while the entire region had regained its former prosperity. One must not consider acts associated merely with conquest as factors in the destruction of prosperous irrigated lands. The reasons for the decline and eventual abandonment of the well over 1,000 square km of irrigated farmland in the Sistan Basin lie elsewhere. It did not come about through the agency of a single event, be it conquest or climate change (for which there is no evidence during historic times in Sistan), but through a complex series of interrelated physical, political, and economic causes. This subject is examined in greater detail in Whitney's (2006) geological monograph and will also be addressed in future Helmand Sistan Project publications. It is disturbing to read in a recent report by a German hydrologist, who himself conducted researches in Sistan among the widespread remains of prosperous Timurid settlements, that Tamerlane had been the cause of the final destruction of the agricultural prosperity of Sistan (Radermacher 1974). There can be no logically acceptable foundation for such a carelessly traditional conclusion. WBT

4 For irrigated lands to be farmed efficiently, a minimal labor force is an absolute necessity. When this labor force is attracted away from the land by the lure of higher wages elsewhere, like Iran, the land cannot be maintained. This depletion of the labor force is perhaps the greatest single factor in the destruction of labor-intensive farmlands, and it was certainly a major factor in the rapid abandonment of Sistan by the beginning of the sixteenth century. Extensive irrigated tracts of land cannot survive the gradual movement away of the labor force. Where great canals must be maintained, it is not a question of the lands slowly passing into smaller and smaller farms. There comes a definite moment when the labor force falls below the minimum to maintain the system, and at this point the land must fail and the entire residual population be forced to leave the land quite suddenly, to take up residence in areas closer to sources of water, where reduced numbers of people can maintain smaller tracts of farmland requiring fewer people to maintain the simplified irrigation arrangements. Even these much reduced acreages cannot be maintained beyond the point where the remaining farmers are too few in number to maintain these smaller irrigation systems. At this point irrigation farming can no longer be sustained. WBT

5 That is, of attracting them back to the abandoned lands. WBT

6 Considering the possible return on the investment, I personally don't think this would be a viable undertaking. WBT

7 While the former is manifestly impossible, much progress could be made in controlling the problems associated with sanding. WBT

Conclusions

8 That is, by the import of inexpensive machine made textiles from Iran. The smuggling trade, of course, through its enormous profits not based on production, has deleterious effects on all aspects of the local economy. WBT

9 Water mixed with abrasive is required for the cutting of the stone. Large deposits of travertine exist on the Pakistan side of the border as well, particularly in the remote region of Zeh (the quarries of which are owned by the Agha Khan), and the travertine industry is far more developed in Pakistan than in Afghanistan, even though the production is of poor quality and not generally appealing to Western tastes. Pakistan, however, exports large quantities of travertine to Italy, while the small production in Afghanistan, apart from trinkets for the tourist trade, is consumed locally and demonstrates little taste. WBT. Carved travertine objects from Pakistani Baluchistan are now, in the twenty-first century, a standard commodity in South Asian retail stores in the West. MA

10 The increasing availability of cheap aluminum imports from Pakistan suggests that an indigenous ceramic industry is highly unlikely to be developed in the future. WBT

11 However, roads to transport products to markets and other infrastructure are completely lacking. The same factor renders the construction of even small industries in the region an unattractive business proposition. WBT

12 If it is constructed, which presently seems unlikely. WBT

13 The lower Helmand is navigable for small shallow draft vessels only, and the stretch from Rudbar to the vicinity of Zaranj would amount to communication from one insignificant point to another. At present, there would be nothing to transport and arrival at Zaranj does not bring one close to a significant market. The navigation would be utterly impractical, for in flood the river is too swift, and at low water it is obstructed not only by *bands*, but by shallow fords of considerable dimensions. While Amiri's enthusiasm in laudable, this is not a useful proposition. The suggestion doubtless derives from the fact that during periods of prosperity in Sistan, grain was probably transported on small barges along the major canals of the region to riverside depots where it was loaded on camel caravans for transport far beyond Sistan. WBT

14 There is no bridge over the Helmand downriver from Darwishan. WBT

15 Since instruction is not in Baluchi, but in Dari, which few, if any, children understand, for all intents and purposes education in this region is presently useless. WBT

Afterword
The Helmand Baluch as Native Ethnography

Mitchell Allen

Why read G. R. Amiri's ethnography of the Helmand Baluch close to half a century after it was written? Other than a snapshot of the lifeways of a small community of Central Asian villagers, does his work have a broader meaning for the study of anthropology? In this chapter, I demonstrate that Amiri's study is an important piece of native ethnography, written well before the idea of scholars native to a country studying their own peoples became fashionable or even widely possible. In this sense, Amiri's work stands at the beginning of a revolutionary change in the ethnographic study of the less-developed peoples of the world and an important model for much that has followed it.

What Is "Native Ethnography"?

The terms 'indigenous ethnography' and 'native ethnography' have been much discussed in recent anthropological literature. The most commonly agreed definition, coming out of a Wenner Gren workshop in 1978, would be "the practice of anthropology in one's native country, society, and/or ethnic group" (Fahim 1982). Fahim's (1977) previous work distinguished between "indigenous" anthropology, which implies both ethnicity and nationality, and "native" ethnography, which implies only ethnicity. In more recent decades, the term "indigenous" has become associated with the inhabitants of the more rural, least developed parts of nation states and the indigenous ethnographer members of those less developed communities. Thus, we find ourselves more comfortable with the term "native ethnography" to describe Amiri's work, the work of a scholar native to the country in which the research took place. During the time that Amiri did his field work, ethnographic work on less developed societies like Afghanistan was done almost exclusively by European or American researchers (Shalinsky 1991, p. 2). In contrast,

Afterword: *The Helmand Baluch* as Native Ethnography

Amiri's book is a distinctively Afghan approach to describing a cultural setting in his country.

Native ethnography extends back to the beginnings of the field of anthropology. The collaboration between George Hunt, a high-status Tlingit-English Canadian, and Columbia University anthropologist Franz Boas is legendary in the anthropological literature, though Hunt's central role formulating the ethnographies of the Kwakwaka'wakw published by Boas has only recently been recognized (Berman 1997). Boas is widely considered the founder of American anthropology, so Hunt certainly earns the title of its first native ethnographer, based upon the thousands of pages of field notes he provided to Boas. Bruchac, though, points out that Hunt's contribution was not solely his, but made possible by information collected by other family members, especially his mother, sisters, and wives (Bruchac 2014).

Native Ethnography in Global Context

Afghanistan was not the location of the founding of native ethnography, though close to one of its earliest known sources. In India, the practice goes back to the founding of the anthropology department at the University of Calcutta in the 1920s, though most early studies were censuses or village studies and were closely tied to British colonial rule (Mahapatra 2006). M. N. Srinivas, the best known Indian scholar to produce early native ethnographic work, lived and studied in Rampara, near Mysore, between 1948 and 1964 and wrote the classic ethnography *The Remembered Village* (Srinivas 1976, 1997). That ethnographic tradition has continued to the present, for example in the work of Indian-American anthropologist Kirin Narayan, who studied in Kasik and in Kangra in the early-mid 1980s (Narayan 1993).

India produced many of the early native ethnographers due to a lengthy scholarly tradition of its own and with support of British scholars who trained many of these ethnographers in western anthropological techniques either on the subcontinent or in England. But there were others. Kofe Abrefa Busia of Ghana and Jomo Kenyatta were both trained in anthropology in the UK and conducted ethnographic fieldwork in the 1930s and 1940s before becoming presidents of their respective countries, Ghana and Kenya. Egyptian Hussein M. Fahim studied Nubian populations in Egypt and Sudan beginning in 1963. Jesus Salinas Pedraza was a Nahnu school teacher who worked with American anthropologist H.

Afterword: The Helmand Baluch as Native Ethnography

Russell Bernard to create the first book written in Otomi, an ethnography of his people in the 1980s (Salinas Pedraza 1989). Similar cases can be found of scholars in East Asia, Latin America, the Pacific, and North America (Fahim 1982).

In the 1970s, problems with funding, ethics, and host countries increased the number of Western ethnographers who stayed at home and studied their own complex Western societies rather than the Others of the Global South. Harry Wolcott, an educational anthropologist at the University of Oregon and one of the earliest American "native" ethnographers, outlined the differences for the scholar who worked in his own country, including different strategies for note taking, length of the fieldwork, confronting sensitive issues directly, and attempting to alter unfair circumstances (Wolcott 1981). Delmos Jones (1970) introduced similar themes in discussing the differences between his work as an African American anthropologist in Thailand and in the African American community in Denver.

The issues posed by native ethnography have been discussed more by anthropologists and other ethnographers since Western researchers began to study their own cultures (Messerschmidt 1981). The booming qualitative research industry in Europe and North America is largely pointed toward institutions, communities, and subcultures of Western society: urban street corners for William Foote Whyte, schools for Harry Wolcott, hospitals for Howard Becker, and thousands of other settings, all examined in the past three decades. These scholars have now had to wrestle with making the familiar strange and with the many methodological, theoretical, and ethical concerns that raises. Women, scholars of color, immigrants, and the occasional non-Westerner studying a western society (Bhattacharya 2019) have raised additional questions of identity, othering, and power.[1]

Key Issues in Native Ethnography

Still, the issues raised by native ethnography of the West differ considerably from those of native scholars who operated in less developed nations.

Hannoum (2011) and Narayan (1993), among others, point out that even the most culturally integrated native ethnographer actually has a double sense of belonging, both to their native culture and to the culture of anthropology, which has its own priests, rituals, adherents, and a holy site of pilgrimage, the annual meeting. Even those who return to their

AFTERWORD: *THE HELMAND BALUCH* AS NATIVE ETHNOGRAPHY

native village or region for fieldwork still represent difference, they are those who moved away and are returning to do research on those who stayed. Often class differences come into play as well, as noted in Srinivas's fieldwork experience, where his Indian Brahmin background created expectations of certain behavior both from and toward him (Srinivas 1976, pp. 33-40). Narayan (1993) notes that factors such as gender and education also separate the native ethnographer from the population studied. Additionally, ethnographic studies by native ethnographers are almost always written in European languages to appear in Western journals, from Western scholarly presses, and find homes in Western libraries. Fahim (1977, p. 81) goes further, suggesting that any non-Westerner who has lived and studied in the West is incapable of providing a value-free, non-Western perspective of problems in his native country. Amiri's work, originally written in Dari and published in Kabul, and whose scholarly development came from work with an Afghan mentor, shows its distinctiveness by violating these rules.

Many native ethnographies are conducted in the home nation of the scholar, but on a different cultural group in a different region than the researcher's home territory. This is true of Amiri's work with the Baluch. In India, with its numerous native scholars trained in the British tradition and usually at British universities, this is also the case. Guneratne (2011) was Sri Lankan studying Nepal. Narayan (1993, p. 674) was a bicultural Indian/American who grew up in Mumbai but did her fieldwork in Kangra in the Himalayan foothills.

Native ethnographers are typically considered people with power when they enter a field site. Chidi Ugwu, a Nigerian from Nsukka, found himself an outsider when returning to his native region to conduct his PhD research. The mere fact that he carried a voice recorder, paper, and camera, and asked community members detailed questions about malaria, created distance between him and his community. The applied nature of his work studying the Roll Back Malaria program in southeast Nigeria in 1998 gave him "an identity of the authority and power of the state and the global North" (Ugwu 2017, p. 2635). This included both community members' self-censorship in offering him information as well as suggestions those members made to him that would benefit them and that he was expected to pass along to the government, on the assumption that his role gave him the authority to do so. Fahim (1977), doing research on Nubian communities in Egypt and Sudan, describes receiving the same reactions from his informants

Afterword: The Helmand Baluch *as Native Ethnography*

as Ugwu when he became principal investigator for a Nubian resettlement project connected with the construction of the Aswan Dam in 1971. He found his Nubian informants more formal and reserved, though he had worked with them before. They could not disassociate him from the government sponsorship of the resettlement project. He contrasted his work with that of Gunnar Sorbo, a University of Bergen graduate student working simultaneously in the same area. Nubians had no expectations of a foreigner who was both powerless and neutral (Fahim and Helmer 1980, p. 646). In contrast, they viewed Fahim as someone who was able to advocate for their views to higher authorities, whether he had that power or not. (Fahim 1977, p. 85). Srinivas echoes the same opinion, that his villagers "had assumed that as an educated, urban and well-off (by their standards) Brahmin, I would behave like the officials who, during their brief visits to the village, met and talked with only a few leaders" (Srinivas 1976, p. 332). Amiri, a government official from the Afghan Institute of Archaeology, must have been viewed similarly to the others described here by the Baluch villagers with whom he interacted.

There are, though, some distinct advantages to being a native ethnographer. Understanding the symbols and value systems of your country and even slight familiarity with histories, traditions, language, and of other ethnic groups not your own allow for more nuanced questioning and understanding of the responses (Fahim and Helmer 1980, p. 646). Srinivas adds one more crucial element, empathy:

> Successful fieldwork involves not only the sociologist's painstaking collection of a vast amount of the minutiae of ethnography, but also his exercising his powers of empathy to understand what it is to be a member of the community that is being studied. In this respect, the sociologist is like a novelist who must of necessity get under the skin of the different characters he is writing about...this involves not only his intellect but his emotions as well. (Srinivas 1969, p. 152)

Here is another place in which Amiri's work excels. He struggles with the economic inequalities that allow village khans and others to claim over 90 percent of the harvest, leaving the farmers themselves in a perpetual state of serfdom. Amiri states "the share of the peasants in the produce is negligible, so that they cannot assure themselves of even the lowest standard of living, as the peasant is always considered superfluous by the landlord" (p. 64).

Afterword: *The Helmand Baluch* as Native Ethnography

Native Ethnography in Afghanistan

The best known native ethnographies in Afghanistan contemporary with Amiri's are the works of two Afghan scholars trained in the United States.

M. Nazif Shahrani conducted twenty months of fieldwork in 1972–1974 in the Wahkan Corridor and Pamir Mountains of eastern Afghanistan with Kirghiz and Wakhi pastoralists. Shahrani grew up in an Uzbek village in northeastern Afghanistan, was educated at boarding schools in Kabul, then at Kabul University. He finished his undergraduate degree at the University of Hawaii, then enrolled for graduate work at the University of Washington, where he was awarded a PhD in 1976. After five years in the United States, he returned to Afghanistan in the mid 1970s, coterminous with Amiri's work, to conduct his fieldwork as part of his PhD program. Befriending a Kirghiz khan, he traveled under the khan's patronage into the Little Pamir area, where he surveyed a majority of the 250 households in that area. A second trip was in the company of a Wakhan deputy to the Afghan parliament representing this area. This restricted frontier area bordering on the Soviet Union and China was not accessible to Western researchers. His dissertation, *The Kirghiz and Wakhi of Afghanistan*, was published by the University of Washington Press in 1979 and reissued in 2002 (Shahrani 1979, 2002). He has contributed numerous other books, articles, chapters, and presentations on Afghanistan over his scholarly career. Like many other Afghan academics, his later work examined the impact of changing political regimes on Afghan life. He taught and researched at several American universities before ending at Indiana University, where he has been on the faculty since 1990. Like Amiri, Shahrani came from a more privileged background than the groups he studied and received his initial academic training at Kabul University, which had no anthropology department. Unlike Amiri, Shahrani received anthropological training in the United States before conducting his field work. In the preface to his first edition, he thanks equally his Afghan and American mentors and funders for their assistance in facilitating his fieldwork and improving the final product (Shahrani 1979, pp. xxxiv–xxxvi).

Ashraf Ghani is better known as the current president of Afghanistan than as an anthropologist. Born in Loghar Province and a Pashtun, he went to the United States as an exchange student in high school. His college education was at American University of Beirut, and he pursued graduate degrees at Columbia University, from which he received a PhD in 1975. His dissertation, *State Building and Centralization in a*

Afterword: The Helmand Baluch *as Native Ethnography*

Tribal Society: Afghanistan, 1880–1901, while claiming to be ethnographic, "mediates between theoretical discourse and detailed historical investigation" (Ghani 1982, p. xi). The majority of his data comes from archival sources, though he confirmed some of his theoretical notions of production economics with on-the-ground fieldwork observations. After stints at UCLA, Johns Hopkins University, and the World Bank, for whom he conducted extensive fieldwork, he returned to Afghanistan in numerous governmental capacities, including Minister of Finance and Chancellor of Kabul University and was elected president of the country in 2014.

Baluch Ethnography before Amiri

The Helmand Baluch have been known to the West for some time now based on the visits by European travelers, diplomats, surveyors, soldiers, and spies in the nineteenth and early twentieth century. Many of these foreign visitors to Sistan were British because it bordered the Northwest Province of India, now Pakistan, under British rule and was important to England's strategy in the nineteenth century "Great Game" with the Russians. Lieutenant Henry Pottinger's 1816 book *Travels in Beloochistan and Sinde* (based on the visit of his colleague Captain Christie through the region in 1810) was the first account published. It was a "flat sandy country, in some places overgrown with Jungul" (Pottinger 1816, p. 315). His writing sets the tone for later nineteenth century European works, a land suffering from excessive heat and wind, a plague of flies, and a home of robbers and outcasts, yet a promising location for growing crops because of the fertility of the soil and the consistent water flow from the Helmand (Pottinger 1816, p. 316).

Three decades later, French adventurer and mercenary J. P. Ferrier visited Sistan in 1845, just after the first Anglo-Afghan War. He had to continually assure his hosts that he was not a British deserter or spy (Ferrier 1856, p. 294). He, too, complains about the heat and insects and reinforces Pottinger's comments about the agricultural potential: "this is not because wheat is scarce in Seistan, or that the consumption is small; there is, on the contrary, a very fair breadth of it sown, but the inhabitants sell their corn at Herat, Kandahar, and Kerman" (Ferrier 1856, p. 413). His negative assessment of the Baluch villagers and herders might have come from the fact that his party was chased by a Baluch mob and saved only by hiding in a well at the ancient site of Malakhan (Qala-i Sirak), visited and mapped by the Helmand Sistan Project and Amiri in 1971 (Ferrier 1856, p. 407).

AFTERWORD: *The Helmand Baluch as Native Ethnography*

Most ethnographic information from this continual stream of European observers came from two extended visits of the British Boundary Commissions trying to establish the border between British India, Persia, and Afghanistan. The first commission was led by Sir Frederic John Goldsmid between 1870 and 1872; the second by Sir Henry McMahon in 1903–1905. While primarily conducted for political reasons and heavily weighted toward the then-current controversies between various parties involved, each report contained much valuable ethnographic information, naturally tinted by the colonial ideology of the day.

Goldsmid's 1876 report includes a lengthy description of the region by Major Euan Smith, who spent six weeks with the boundary commission along the Helmand. A separate set of ethnographic descriptions were published by Surgeon Henry Walter Bellew, who traveled independently through the region in 1872. Bellew was the more detailed observer of village life, describing at length the method of constructing houses (Bellew 1874, p. 183), desalinating soil (p.167), windmill operations (p. 235), villager superstitions (p. 192), and economics of herding (p. 169), among other topics. His description of the relations between village khans and their attendant farmers anticipates Amiri's descriptions a century later:

> Each of these chiefs had a number of dependants or subjects, consisting of various Baloch tribes. Their number amounted to several hundred families, and they were collectively styled *tawci* or bondsmen. They cultivated sufficient land for the supply of their immediate wants, and for the rest, were mainly occupied in tending their herds of camels and flocks of sheep, in plundering their neighbours, and in protecting themselves from reprisals. (Bellew 1874, p. 208)

Yet Bellew was still a nineteenth century British colonialist, and his assessment of the Baluch villages he visited clearly reflected that:

> It is a pitiful fact that the ruins in this country, from their extent, and superior construction, and frequency, constantly impress upon the traveler the former existence here of a more numerous population, a greater prosperity, and better-established security than is anywhere seen in the country, whilst the wretched hovels that have succeeded them as strongly represent the poverty, lawlessness, and insecurity that characterize the normal condition of the country under the existing regime. (p. 191)

Smith's writings on Sistan are less ethnographic, but still provide us with useful information, for example, a detailed description of the construction and maintenance of Sistan's canal system, also are similar to Amiri's descriptions (Smith 1876, pp. 281–282).

The later boundary commission had the advantage of including George Passman Tate, a surveyor attached to the Survey of India, whose four volume description of Sistan in the years of the commission's work (1903–1905) is the basic document from which all later history, archaeology, historical architecture, and ethnography about the region stems (Tate 1910–1912). Amiri cites Tate's work extensively in this volume. After sections on the history, ruins, and topography of the region, Tate addresses *The People of Seistan* in volume 4. Much of the volume outlines the different tribal groups, their locations, leaders, population, broader ethnic affiliations, and languages, important for Tate's survey work. The volume also contains numerous important photographs of village life at the time.

Chapter 6 of volume 4 (Tate 1910–1912, pp. 325–335) describes the typical Baluch village structure and labor relations. A detailed description of the *pago* system (*pagao* in Amiri's volume) is included here and fleshed out by Amiri in greater detail sixty years later (pp. 326–327). In Tate's book, the *pago* is left with 20 percent of the grain it raises (p. 330) after paying off the landowner, the mullah, and various community specialists. In the 1970s, that percentage is almost unchanged (see Table 3.3 in this volume). Each *pago* was obligated to provide labor for canal maintenance in both eras (p. 332). Tate estimates about 27 people per square km (69 people per square mile) in Afghan Sistan at the turn of the twentieth century (p. 334); Amiri estimates half that amount in the 1970s in the present work (p. 85). Tate notes the very extensive use of opium (p. 328), a claim that Amiri challenges in this work (p. 85). While Tate's work suffers from the same Eurocentrism as his contemporaries, it contains far more detailed data about the population and lifeways of the Helmand Baluch than any of the writings of his contemporaries.

Modern Ethnography of the Baluch

While Amiri's ethnography was not the first to look at Baluch villages, it was the first and only modern one to study this ethnic group specifically within Afghanistan. Most studies of the Baluch have been done across the border with the much larger Baluch populations in former British India, now Pakistan, and in Iran. Pastner (1979) wisely identifies the differences with those studying the Pakistani Baluch. Having been part of British India, any foreign researcher is automatically be assumed to

Afterword: *The Helmand Baluch* as Native Ethnography

be related to the British colonial project. Pastner's amusing interaction with Pir Mahmud is a good example. The aged dry goods shop owner welcomed the American Pastner's arrival "because he assumed we were the vanguard of a British army that would soon reoccupy Baluchistan and boot out the Panjabis and Pathans who held most of the key positions of authority" (Pastner 1979, p. 44).

Modern anthropology of the Baluch began in the late 1950s (Spooner 2013b, p. 143), and its studies were largely done by EuroAmerican scholars (Spooner 1998a). Best known are the early works by Pehrson (1966), the Swidlers (1968, 1973), and Spooner (1969). Though his field work was done in northeast and southeast Iran, Spooner's work foreshadows Amiri's in the way he describes the political, social, and economic conditions of the Baluch across three nation states. Spooner notes:

> all the locations with some ten hectares or more of cultivable soil and surface water that could be used for irrigation had been taken over by one or another leading tribal family (khans) who managed the land with people who had been reduced to the status of peasants, helots or serfs (their status varied from place to place), while the remaining parts where there was insufficient surface water to irrigate crops were roamed by nomadic groups of varying sizes. (Spooner 2013a, p. 7)

Beyond their boundaries, "They were now administratively integrated into a nation-state that they did not choose, and formally subordinated to a central urban authority in each country, with minimal representation at the center" (p. 11). He differentiates the Baluch populations of Afghanistan as being propped up in their ethnic identity because of their role in the conflicting imperial interests of the British and Russians (p. 24).

In contrast, Nina Swidler's description of the Brahui Baluch, based on her research in the Kalat district of Pakistan, highlights the collective ownership of land by "large kin groups who hold collective grazing rights to extensive territories which are often vaguely banded" (Swidler 1973, p. 302). Proprietary land rights, the *botari*, has remained collective and prevented powerful landlord families from controlling large swaths of land (p. 303) in contrast with Afghan Sistan. Similarly, building of *karez* systems, rather than irrigation canals, is financed by groups of men rather than by a single household, and water rights are separately held (p. 310).

This difference does not surprise Spooner, who sees the various Baluch communities as "remarkably heterogeneous in terms of economy, local political organization, and even religion and showed no evidence of

Afterword: The Helmand Baluch as Native Ethnography

nationalism before the middle of the twentieth century" (Spooner 2013b, p. 142). The few criteria for Baluch identity within this diversity are "Islam, the use of the Balochi language for public purposes, and a political relationship with one of the leading families in the agricultural settlements" (Spooner 2013a, p. 8).

The Helmand Baluch as Native Ethnography

It is in the context of the larger issues concerning native ethnography and previous studies of the Baluch and of Sistan that we can consider Ghulam Rahman Amiri's work. It allows us to admire his descriptive ethnography of the Baluch villages along the lower Helmand Valley as a unique ethnographic project of its time and place.

Amiri was not an anthropologist, rather, he was trained in history at Kabul University. Thus, his skill at eliciting cultural information was self-taught. The other ethnographic studies done by Ghani and Shahrani were conducted as part of dissertation research from American universities and by native ethnographers trained in anthropological fieldwork at those universities. In Amiri's case, he had spent a brief period at Ohio University and an even briefer stint at Harvard, the latter only after having completed his fieldwork.

Helmand Sistan Project Director William B. Trousdale, who provided extensive notes to Amiri's work here, does not recollect many discussions with Amiri in the field about how to conduct his ethnographic study. Nor could Trousdale mentor Amiri. He was not an ethnographer himself, despite the detailed ethnographic descriptions in the notes of this volume. Rather, he was trained in East Asian art history and archaeology and had conducted no ethnographic studies of his own prior to launching the Helmand Sistan Project. Most evenings, Trousdale sat with Amiri in evening discussions in the field camp over events of the day and included notes of these discussions in his field notebooks.

In the acknowledgements to this work, the author thanks Hasan Kawun Kakar (better known as M. Hasan Kakar), at the time a lecturer in history at Kabul University, who served as his mentor. Kakar (1928–2017) was a very well-known Afghan historian and author of a dozen books on Afghanistan in Dari, Pashto, and English, including *Afghanistan: The Soviet Invasion and the Afghan Response, 1979–1982* (University of California Press, 1995) and *Government and Society in Afghanistan* (University of Texas Press, 2011). A Pashtun from Laghman trained in history at University of London, Kakar

AFTERWORD: *THE HELMAND BALUCH* AS NATIVE ETHNOGRAPHY

was a central figure in, and chair of, the Kabul University History Department before being arrested by the Soviet-supported regime. He later fled the country for the United States, where he served as an academic historian and political advocate. From the nature of Amiri's thanks, it appears that Kakar's assistance with the project occurred after the completion of Amiri's field work. We believe the two might have done this work at Harvard in 1976, where they overlapped. Thus, the field work strategy, interview questions, and organization of cultural topics were devised by the author, choices made without the influence of 50 years of Western anthropological field techniques. The richness and depth of Amiri's work is even more impressive given this knowledge. Unfortunately, his original field notes were lost when he was imprisoned by the Soviet-backed regime and then forced to flee to New Delhi, so we will never know what other information he gathered that did not end up in the final text.

Amiri's work was external to his role as the representative of the Institute of Archaeology to the Helmand Sistan Project. While we are unaware of the reasons behind his selection to accompany us to Sistan, it certainly would not have been considered a plum project for someone as well situated in the institute's hierarchy as he was, the Director of Excavations for the institute. At the time there were numerous other foreign archaeological projects (British, French, German, Italian) in process, each of which required an accompanying Afghan government representative, and any one of which would have been more comfortable for the urban and urbane Amiri than to camp in the desert for three months each fall for four years with a handful of American researchers and Baluch workmen.

Amiri was our designated representative and was with us for each field season from 1971 to 1975 except 1972. His full involvement in the project and its fieldwork was evident. While we have no way of comparing his work with that of other institute representatives working with other foreign missions, we suspect that most of them were not as actively involved in the archaeological fieldwork as Amiri was with us. Certainly, none of them produced a document like this one. We were assigned two other institute representatives in 1972, the one year that Amiri could not accompany us. Neither was particularly interested in our project and one worked diligently to get himself reassigned out of Sistan, a difficult task because of our remote location and the related difficulty of his transmitting his desires (and self) out of the field and back to Kabul.

Amiri notes in this text that many of his sources were workmen who were hired by the Helmand Sistan Project to help us with survey and

Afterword: The Helmand Baluch as Native Ethnography

excavation work along the lower Helmand River and the deserted Sar-o-Tar basin to its east. In 1972-1974, we were based in Sar-o-Tar, outside the ruins of the large Islamic fortress city of Shahr-i Gholghola. In these years, we went to the nearby town of Hauz and hired about twenty men to work with us, almost all of them from Hauz or from one of the other eighteen villages along the Qala-i Fath Canal that Amiri mentions in the book. These workers lived near us in tents in the desert, twenty-five miles from Hauz. Thus, Amiri was given a set of informants who had ample time after work to be interviewed, and he could draw on the comparative experiences of inhabitants of several neighboring villages. Amiri was the only person on the professional team who could speak to them in Dari—none of the Americans knew the language—so he was considered their primary employer, despite the fact that he himself spoke no Baluchi, their primary language. Problems of work, health, wages, or any other employment or personal issue were directed through Amiri to Trousdale, the project director. Instructions on how and where to excavate similarly passed through Amiri. The nature of these artificial interactions in a remote desert camp—where Amiri served both as their boss and as an ethnographer—likely had an influence on Amiri's data collection. We were not embedded in a village and able to observe social conditions ourselves. Nor did we have direct contact with anyone other than work-aged able male laborers in those seasons, which likely skewed the information Amiri gathered.

The situation in 1975 was entirely different, as field work in that season was conducted near two villages along the Helmand Valley, Khwaja 'Ali Sehyaka near Deshu and Lat by Rudbar. In the first case, we lived in the courtyard of the compound of the village khan Hajji Nafaz, hired workmen with his guidance and blessing, and were "gifted" with an older woman, Shaparai, who was responsible for baking bread and washing clothes for us, among many other tasks (See chapter 5, note 20). Visits to various craftspeople—carpenter, blacksmith, rug weaver—were possible, as well as observations in some homes, the school, mosque, and cemetery because of our location within the community. Amiri and our photographer, Chip Vincent, took advantage of these opportunities. The situation at Lat was intermediate between the other two settings. We lived in a field camp at the foot of Kona Qala II, our excavation site, but it was reasonably close to the village of Lat, whose ruler, Bibarg Khan, permitted us to hire workmen from his community. Still, not being embedded in the village allowed for a less rich ethnographic experience than we had in Khwaja 'Ali Sehyaka.

Afterword: *The Helmand Baluch* as Native Ethnography

Archaeological survey work took up much of each season and allowed for observations and interviews by Amiri in other villages along the Helmand during these periods of mobility, though in much more superficial ways than our lengthy encampments described above. Thus, while much of Amiri's data comes from the villagers of Hauz, Khwaja 'Ali Sehyaka, and Lat, his universe of contacts spanned much of the Helmand Valley, from Lashkar Gah to the Hamun Lakes, and to the west as far as Jali Robat, as both he and Trousdale point out in the text and related notes.

Key Themes in *The Helmand Baluch*

Despite his being educated in Kabul, Amiri's book makes it clear that he was a strong proponent of the international development ideology prevalent among foreign missions of the time. He believed that with enough modernization, education, training, and resources, Afghanistan could make great leaps forward in its social and economic conditions. This belief appears numerous times in the book. It is part of his statement of purpose for the book:

> Since no books or even articles have been found concerning Afghan Sistan and the way of life of its inhabitants in Dari or Pashto languages, since knowledge of this area and the way of life of its inhabitants is necessary for the progress and prosperity of the region... (p. xxiii).

Later on, he elaborates:

> A superficial look at the conditions surrounding the advanced peoples of today and a comparison of them with the backward nations shows that those nations which are numbered among the advanced and have attained great power in the world did not suddenly and accidentally achieve that position, but their development was born of a series of events that prepared the economic and social ground for it (p. 159).

Education, more than any other element, was the key:

> The influence of education on the improvement of the economic, political and social life of mankind is a vital one. With the acquisition of knowledge and the grasping of scientific principles a people can overcome those factors that are an obstacle in the road to progress, light up the dark corners of society and illuminate them with the guidance of science (p. 159).

and

Afterword: The Helmand Baluch *as Native Ethnography*

on the one hand the people lead hellish lives, and on the other hand the knowledge and education that could aid them in removing the obstacles in their path to progress are extremely deficient (p. 163).

Amiri describes the underdevelopment of this region in numerous ways. At a time when population in most of the less developed world, including Afghanistan, was spiraling upward, he documents population decline in the region and suggests several reasons for it, including poor health care, the costs of marriage causing delays in child bearing, emigration to neighboring areas with higher wages, and drought conditions that increased sanding and disabled the irrigation canal system. Similarly, he surveys the schools in the region and finds only one in every seven families is sending a child to school. He posits several reasons for this, including the mismatch between Baluchi speaking communities and textbooks in Dari, the mobility of the population and distance from the few extant schools, the poor payment, training, and treatment of teachers, and the conflict between secular education and religious beliefs, among others.

Amiri is not shy in decrying the lack of development in the region:

> It has been intended that this research should shed light on one individual and geographically small area with regard to people and human resources, which are considered some of the major factors in progress and the understanding of society. People can make great use of resources and treasures to make for themselves favorable and effective grounds for the propagation of economic activities. The results are increased production and a rise in the standard of living. From an economic standpoint, this area is now backward, with a standard of living lower than the Asian average (p. 83).

He notes that the agricultural methods are "ancient and primitive" (p. 51) and that crafts like carpentry are done at "a mediaeval level" (p. 105). Merchants do not exist in an area that produces no agricultural surplus and has only the most sparse transportation infrastructure (p. 116).

Gender inequality based on tradition is called on the carpet. "Baluch men in this region consider women unintelligent, weak-willed and incapable of performing fine or difficult work" (p. 141). Sistani men also do not believe in educating women beyond reading religious texts because "girls would use writing for wicked purposes" (p. 162).

Religion is not spared critique. He points to the popularity of itinerant Sufi faith healers, *pir,* who often ask poor farmers to provide them with materials far beyond their means. A vision that requires the gift of a calf to avert catastrophe is easier to prophesy when the *pir* had seen such a calf outside the house at the beginning of the visit (p. 177). The link between clergy and the powerful landowning class is also noted: "The clergy try to put a religious face on the privileges of the powerful men, and they encourage the people to acquiesce in the wretchedness of their lives" (p. 133).

The Afghan government was complicit in this backwardness by its support of economic inequality and repressive taxation. The government was also responsible for the failure to provide proper resources for education and health care. The entire province of Nimruz had one hospital with two doctors at the time of the research; Helmand had two clinics and three doctors (p. 165). Drugs and vaccinations that could alleviate some of the more common illnesses were unavailable, priced beyond the reach of most farmers, or at such a distance away that accessing them in time for use was impossible. The use of folk medical remedies described by Amiri are understandable in this context.

But the author saves his greatest rancor for the small landowning class, 3 to 4 percent of the population, who through political and economic means created a feudal system in Sistan so extreme that "the Baluch famers can never overcome their financial dependence on the landlords" (p. 145).

In the introductory historical chapter, he traces the development of this system back to pre-Islamic times and follows its recurrences in more recent eras. And he lays the blame for Sistan's economic and social situation in the laps of this group over and over:

> The khan despises the farmer and thinks that his only function is to provide profit for the landowner. If the khan treats him other than harshly, then the farmer will slyly and deceitfully trample on the landowner's privileges. The landlords as a whole believe that if they take one unnecessary step towards the wellbeing of the farmers, the farmers will consider this a sign of weakness in the landlords and will not support the landlords' interest. With the exception of a few enlightened landlords they do not believe that education, health care, and better housing are necessary for the farmers (p. 131).

and

> The burden of corvée labor, which is one of the principal factors in feudal oppression, is still laid by the landlords on the shoulders of the peasants (p. 139).

Some of the blame he places on the farmers themselves:

Afterword: The Helmand Baluch as Native Ethnography

> The farmer himself is also a great traditionalist and remains very backward. Whenever he is confronted by an attempt to change his ancient ways and customs, he remains intransigent, even when this change might improve his way of life or his agricultural techniques (p. 131).

This egalitarian stance fits well with our knowledge of Amiri as a progressive social reformer. His ideology led him to stay in Afghanistan with the ascent of a Marxist regime, followed by the Soviet invasion. While many of his educated colleagues fled the country, Amiri was made national Minister of Tourism. Trousdale relates, though, that his long experience with Americans and fluent English made him suspect to the new regime, as did his willingness to host Western visitors to Afghanistan in his official role of fostering tourism. These activities led Amiri to be removed from his post, thrown in jail, and later forced to flee the country. (Private correspondence, Amiri to Trousdale, January 29, 1989)

Still, this egalitarian philosophy allows him to side with Baluch farmers and exhibit the empathy that Srinivas mentions, noted earlier:

> The reader is perhaps wondering why the farmers remain in conditions where they cannot provide themselves with even the basic necessities of life. In this context it must be pointed out that in the region of the lower Helmand Valley and Afghan Sistan there is no available work except farming. Therefore, people who have not the means to leave the area have no alternative but to become farmers (p. 149).

and

> The difficulties of the farmers in the ditch-cleaning season are increased because the work is far from their homes and they have no transport. They have to carry their daily necessities with them and spend day and night at the work site. For most of them, bed is an old quilt and food a small amount of wheat, some *ghalu-i torsh,* and tea (p. 50).

He also points to strategies the Baluch farmers use to help each other through a system built to exploit them:

> Among the farmers there is a custom worthy of note called *hashar*. A farmer for some reason is behind in his farming, or needs to irrigate some rough and difficult land to prepare it for cultivation, a very difficult task to accomplish alone, or encounters a task that is beyond the powers of one or two people and yet has to be completed within a specific time—in these cases the farmer, according to an exchange

system which the Baluch have, invites the necessary people to help him in the above work (p. 182).

He was also diligent in correcting errors of previous researchers as to behavior of the villagers, notably Tate's claim of massive opium use, largely on the grounds that most farmers could not afford it:

> In my observations, not more than 10 percent of the inhabitants of Afghan Sistan may be addicts. For example, of the 25 excavation workers, representing various parts of this region, employed by us in 1351/1973, only one was an opium addict (p. 85).

If the local farmers were unable to improve their status, there were many more identifiable culprits than opium addiction:

> The problems connected with opium have far less effect on birth rate than do other problems in the region: lack of modern medical services, poverty, propagandization of the people with regard to material needs, physical afflictions, exhaustion from day-to-day physical labor, lack of energy, and poor nutrition (p. 86).

The Importance of this Book

Amiri was much a product of his time. A believer in the power of Western technology, education, and democracy to create a better world, a critic of the backwardness of a region of his country and the various political actors who preserved it, and a supporter of socially just solutions to economic inequalities, Amiri sounded much like Western anthropologists of the era.

Yet, Amiri has provided anthropologists, scholars of non-Western cultures, policy makers, native scholars, and historians with an invaluable contribution. The 1970s world of the Baluch village has been overwhelmed by the tidal wave of political and military conflict since 1978. Helmand Province became, and still is, a center of Taliban activity and of opium production. The American and its allies' invasion of Afghanistan after the World Trade Center disaster focused numerous troops in the area around Lashkar Gah, and Helmand Province became one of the fiercest battlegrounds. The social configuration described by Amiri no longer exists. Thus, his work—historical description, village surveys, and thick description of the economic and social life of the villagers—is well worth his report's publication over four decades after the fieldwork took place. Equally important, his empathy for the inhabitants of the Helmand Valley, and his unshaken hope for the future of the region despite

Afterword: The Helmand Baluch *as Native Ethnography*

the innumerable social and economic problems his research documents, should bolster our hope for the future of Afghanistan despite what has beset that county since the time of Amiri's field work.

Note

1 The recently established Pyburn-Wilk Parallax Research Grant specifically supporting non-Western scholars studying the United States as a cultural setting should increase the pace of this work. https://www.facebook.com/openant.org/posts/the-pyburn-wilk-parallax-research-awardparallax-the-effect-whereby-the-position-/689802718184029/

Appendix A

Tribes of the Lower Helmand Valley

Name of Tribe	Ethnic Group	Approx No. of Families	Place Inhabited	Comments
1. Sanjrani	Baluch	120	dispersed between Khwaja 'Ali and Qala-i Fath	
2. 'Aidozai	Baluch	300	dispersed between Deshu and Qala-i Fath	
3. Khwabgani	Baluch	20		previously based in Kanak but have been dispersing since 1952 when their lands became inundated
4. Sargulza'i	Baluch	600	mostly in Qala-i Fath and Charburjak	
5. Guleh Bacheh	Baluch	500	mostly in Charburjak and Chakhansur	
6. Rashkhani	Baluch	200	mostly in Kanak	
7. Shirza'i	Baluch	200	mostly in Kanak	
8. Zahruza'i	Baluch	300	mostly in Chakhansur	most fled Afghan Sistan after a two-year drought period
9. Isizi	Baluch	300	mostly in Chakhansur	
10. Kashani	Baluch	400	mostly in Chakhansur and Khash Rud	
11. Bajizi	Baluch	500	mostly in Guludand	
12. Sizi	Baluch	500	mostly in Sikhsar	
13. Nautani	Baluch	500	mostly in Chakhansur	
14. Sarbandi	Baluch	4	mostly in Karuki	since 1952 when their lands were inundated, they have gone elsewhere
15. Rudani	Baluch	200	mostly in Zaranj	
16. Ajbari	Baluch	800	mostly in Kash Rud	
17. Kutkhail	Baluch	10	mostly in Zaranj	
18. Rigi, or Riki	Baluch	600	mostly in Zaranj	
19. Yamari	Baluch	—	—	a number once lived in Zaranj, but they have gradually left
20. Naru'i	Baluch	900	mostly in Kanak	
21. Balichi, or	Baluch	100	mostly in Kanak and	G.P. Tate (1910–1912, p. 314) calls this group the 'Jats.'
22. Shahuzi	Baluch	200	mostly in Charburjak	
23. Karimdadza'i	Baluch	150	mostly in Chakhansur	
24. Malkukza'i	Baluch	200	mostly in Chakhansur	
25. Laja'i	Baluch	100	mostly in Chakhansur	
26. Salarza'i	Baluch	300	mostly in Chakhansur and Sabzgozi	
27. Kaukdani	Baluch	450	mostly in Sabzgozi and Dikeh Dileh	
28. Arbab	Baluch	1000	mostly in Chakhansur	
29. Zarut	Baluch	300	mostly in Kanak and Dikeh Dileh	
30. Makaki	Baluch	1000	mostly in Kanak and Chakhansur	
31. Shaykh Visi	Baluch	100	mostly in Nad-i 'Ali and Kanak	

Appendix A

Name of Tribe	Ethnic Group	Approx No. of Families	Place Inhabited	Comments
32. Siyasuli	Baluch	200	mostly in Upper Rudbar	
33. Bilar	Baluch	500	mostly in Nad-i 'Ali	
34. Khareh Ku'i	Baluch	3500	mostly in Deshu	
35. Avazi, or Gurgaj	Baluch	3000	dispersed throughout Afghan Sistan	
36. Deh Murdeh	Baluch	500	mostly in Chakhansur and Charburjak	
37. Dalkheh Ki	Baluch	400	mostly in Chakhansur	
38. Abil	Baluch	900	mostly in the area of the Hamun-i Puzak	most are cattle herders
39. Uzbak-Za'i	Baluch	800	mostly in Khash Rud and Chakhansur	although calling themselves Baluch, are probably of Uzbek origin; many are carpet weavers
40. Naru'i	Baluch	2000	mostly in Kanak	
41. Barakza'i	Pashtun	30	mostly in Kanak	
42. Achguza'i	Pashtun	200	mostly dispersed about Afghan Sistan	
43. Sakaza'i	Pashtun	700	dispersed	are nomads and tent dwellers
44. Nur-Za'i	Pashtun	900	dispersed	
45. Dah Bashi	Pashtun	10	formerly in Kanak	departed after agricultural lands were inundated in 1952
46. Ghalza'i	Pashtun	800	mostly in Kanak	
47. Sipar-Za'i	Pashtun	120	mostly in Chakhansur	
48. Sumal-Za'i	Pashtun	150	dispersed	
49. Musa-Za'i	Pashtun	50	mostly in Chakhansur	
50. Abdali	Pashtun	200	mostly in Chakhansur	
51. Barahauvi	native Sistani	800	mostly in Bugat and Khwaja 'Ali	
52. Sayyid	call selves Arab	200	mostly in Jauvin	
53. Kundeh	call selves Farsivan	300	mostly in Chakhansur	
54. Shahryari	call selves Farsivan	1200	dispersed	
55. Taular	call selves Farsivan	5	Qala-i Fath	
56. Mir	call selves Farsivan	30	dispersed	
57. Karim Kashteh	call selves Farsivan	1000	mostly in Nad-i 'Ali	weaving, once common, is in decline; many have left area; G.P. Tate (1910–1912, p. 297) calls them 'Kharajis' and puts their numbers at 2,300 families.
58. Khazari	call selves Timurid	600	dispersed between Chakhansur and Qala-i Fath	
59. Tajik	—	700	mostly in Chakhansur	G.P. Tate calls these people 'disciplined' and 'agricultural'

Total number of families: 30,549

Appendix B

Climate Data from Zaranj and Deshu Meteorological Stations

Zaranj Station

	Jan	Feb	Mar	Apr	May	Jun	Jul	Aug	Sep	Oct	Nov	Dec
Monthly Mean Temperature in °C												
1973	4.3	12.4	15.8	25.6	32.3	37.4	35.0	33.5	26.4	21.6	12.2	7.7
1974	6.9	5.3	14.1	25.8	29.8	36.8	35.0	31.2	28.3	20.3	14.8	5.0
1975	6.5	10.1	14.2	21.2	29.5	32.8	35.7	33.1	27.9	19.1	11.2	7.6
Monthly Mean Pressure in MB												
1973	968.2	961.1	959.2	954.0	947.2	936.6	937.1	937.8	947.9	957.9	962.8	965.5
1974	967.6	969.8	964.5	955.7	950.2	942.2	937.3	940.5	946.2	953.8	953.7	953.1
1975	959.5	961.3	954.3	950.3	949.9	945.0	942.3	944.3	951.4	957.5	961.3	964.5
Maximum Relative Humidity in Percent												
1973	96.5	91.7	92.5	82.3	50.18	43.2	46.19	47.30	52.25	62.28	78.30	80.25
1974	95.19	95.21	86.8	82.2	50.16	45.8	37.31	47.30	53.11	49.8	50.26	80.26
1975	98.26	90.6	74.9	70.21	92.15	55.24	50.3	44.13	42.17	78.18	79.00	96.00
Minimum Relative Humidity in Percent												
1973	29.10	21.16	20.18	19.30	20.23	14.15	20.3	19.21	25.4	29.29	26.5	29.20
1974	31.28	33.22	24.28	22.25	22.31	17.27	14.4	21.9	20.4	26.28	27.26	29.00
1975	28.18	19.28	12.14	12.21	9.30	9.28	8.7	9.6	10.3	13.13	17.00	20.00
Maximum Speed of Wind with Direction and Date in m/sec												
1973	14.26	N	12.10	NNW	N	N	N	N	N	N	N	N
	N	18.7	N	10.14	25.9	15.26	24.15	22.18	28.11	10.1	18.7	10.14
1974	N	N	N	N	N	N	N	N	N	N	N	N
	14.12	9.4	16.13	18.11	10.30	12.23	20.1	17.14	14.9	14.2	14.18	14.2
1975	N	N	N	N	N	N	N	N	N	N	N	N
	12.21	11.4	20.10	18.6	13.19	19.10	19.1	19.18	18.24	20.00	24.00	16.00
Monthly Average of Precipitation in mm												
1969	0	—		2.4	0	0	0	0	0	1.4	6.4	0
1970	26.6	0	28.5	0	0	0	0	0	0	0	0	0
1971	9.4	15.0	0	0	0	0	0	0	0	0	0	2.3
1972	1.2	0.1	14.1	15.0	0	0	0	0	0	0	0	1.4
1973	0	0	3.6	0	0	0	0	0	0	0	0	1.4
1974	44.9	59.4	0	5.6	0	0	0	0	0	0	0	0.1
1975	15.4	0	0	0	0	3.4	0	0	0	0	0	0.1

Appendix B

Deshu Station

	Jan	Feb	Mar	Apr	May	Jun	Jul	Aug	Sep	Oct	Nov	Dec
Monthly Mean Temperature in °C												
1973	4.1	13.5	17.6	24.6	29.6	34.6	34.4	31.5	25.1	19.5	12.3	7.5
1974	6.9	7.8	18.4	25.1	28.9	32.6	34.4	30.5	27.3	16.5	12.1	8.0
1975	7.4	11.3	17.1	22.2	29.6	32.4	34.1	31.5	26.7	17.4	13.2	7.2
Monthly Amount of Precipitation in mm.												
1973	10.4	2.0	4.4	1.8	0	0	0	0	0	0	0	0
1974	23.6	16.5 2.7	0.1	3.0	0	0	0	0	0	0	24.9	0
1975	30.5	4.5	2.3	3.8	0	0	0	0	0	0	2.5	3.3
Monthly Mean Pressure in M.B.												
1973	—	—	—	942.0	938.3	932.3	930.5	933.6	941.1	947.0	950.8	953.5
1974	950.2	950.9	947.1	941.3	939.2	934.2	932.5	934.5	940.3	948.4	950.7	951.1
1975	951.5	948.0	945.4	944.0	939.3	933.1	930.6	932.7	938.8	946.6	950.3	952.1
Maximum Relative Humidity in Percent												
1973	—	—	—	45.3	46.2	29.11	31.13	30.31	34.27	47.30	51.28	76.00
1974	85.25	64.1	62.84	63.4	53.12	30.10	29.17	34.2	39.24	54.26	62.24	82.00
1975	68.31	66.1	69.9	66.2	45.15	34.13	39.26	44.17	34.23	61.18	76.30	81.00
Minimum Relative Humidity in Percent												
1973	—	—	—	6.1	5.18	5.5	5.11	6.6	7.6	8.5	8.4	6.11
1974	7.29	4.8	3.17	4.10	5.22	6.4	8.1	8.13	10.21	10.22	12.21	8.31
1975	7.5	7.20	4.25	5.14	6.19	7.13	7.9	9.26	8.11	7.23	11.26	16.00
Maximum Speed of Wind with Direction and Date in m/sec												
1973	W	NW	NW	NNW	N	S	W	NNW	NW	N	NW	SW
	12.25	17.7	9.9	12.20	5.5	7.11	18.25	19.7	11.7	8.18	5.7	7.23
1974	N	SSW	W	WSW	NW	NW	W	NNW	NNW	NNW	NW	S
	17.25	8.2	18.30	24.1	12.31	15.23	20.11	20.13	16.9	12.14	10.1	24.27
1975	NNW	NW	W	W	N	WNW	NW	W	W	NNW	NW	W
	18.14	12.27	30.3	28.24	18.19	18.21	16.15	16.18	18.25	14.21	16.29	10.00

Source: Afghan Meteorological Institute 1975.

Ed. note: A copy of these climate charts can be found in US National Oceanographic and Atmospheric Administration library at https://library.noaa.gov/Collections/Digital-Docs/Foreign-Climate-Data/Afganistan-Climate-Data#03897652. Some data missing in Amiri's original have been filled in from the NOAA charts to nearest whole number. In case of discrepancies between the two sources, we have kept Amiri's.

Appendix C

Monthly Water Flows at Charburjak Station

water year	Oct	Nov	Dec	Jan	Feb	Mar	Apr	May	Jun	Jul	Aug	Sep
1. 10/1973–9/1974	115.0	85.6	62.0	113.3	174.7	167.5	109.3	120.6	73.4	64.8	54.8	59.6
2. 10/1972–9/1973	119.7	—	—	318.3	323.9	371.4	410.9	364.9	—	153.9	—	—
3. 10/1971–9/1972	14.9	18.6	16.5	107.0	124.0	329.0	—	—	—	—	118.0	118.0
4. 10/1970–9/1971	—	—	—	—	41.8	—	33.9	46.3	17.2	15.2	13.0	15.0
5. 10/1969–9/1970	—	—	109.0	215.0	225.0	173.0	138.0	—	—	—	—	11.4
6. 10/1968–9/1969	55.1	56.9	174.0	107.0	144.0	195.0	674.0	572.0	312.0	189.0	—	—
7. 10/1967–9/1968	—	—	104.0	172.0	201.0	398.0	261.0	528.0	—	140.1	119.0	86.0
8. 10/1966–9/1967	—	61.2	59.2	61.0	170.0	109.0	—	—	—	—	—	—
9. 10/1965–9/1966	80.2	150.0	189.0	190.0	175.0	149.0	146.0	136.0	53.6	43.2	47.9	—
10. 10/1962–9/1963	13.9	27.6	55.4	92.8	134.0	122.0	69.6	159.0	—	—	—	63.5
11. 10/1961–9/1962	67.0	92.4	164.0	175.0	147.0	139.0	89.0	85.0	85.3	47.3	21.0	21.0
12. 10/1960–9/1961	70.0	146.0	168.0	171.0	157.0	119.0	428.0	626.0	226.0	75.0	63.0	61.0

Figures provided in cubic meters/second. Data for parts of 1963–1965 missing.

Author's note: during the summer months the daily water flows sometimes fell below 50 cubic meters per second.

Source: Venkata, Rao Mullaqudi, *Review Report on the Design of Check Structure at CH-5200 across Lashkary Canal*.

Glossary

Most of the terms explained below are used in this treatise, while the rest are frequently used in the region by the Baluchi population of Afghan Sistan.

achar	Paste made of *sabjak*, coriander, turmeric, pepper, salt, flour, and fresh onions beaten in a mortar and formed into round cakes
anj	Tree sap used as herbal medicine
arti	Amount of grain, usually 5 *man* of wheat, given to a camel-driver for the maintenance of each camel
arzuka (arzukeh)	Assembly of women gathering for the purpose of spinning wool or the grinding and sifting of grain
ashkin	Wetlands
asp	Frame made from three pieces of wood and forming the basis of a dam on a riverbed
azhghon	Aniseed
badi	Type of riding camel, see *mari*
badil	Compensation, especially for corvée labor
bagjat	Camel driver
bagri	Equivalent to 2-3-*man*-seed-worth of land in addition to the *pagao* is allocated to each farmer.
bajand	Indigenous vegetable
banak	Part of a plow; a piece of wood upon which fortunes may be read
band	Weir; dam
barbau	Kind of wood that is considered sacred and is burned as incense
barek	Type of pine tree
bigham	"Dead men." Two men of the *pagao*. Original duties were services to landlord.
bijar	Gift to the groom; shared cost of wedding celebration
bughmeh	Disease of the liver and lungs in camels
chanak	Shrub used in tanning
chapar	Woven mat made from tamarisk twigs
chapru	Indigenous plant used as herbal medicine
charbikh	Medicinal remedy using indigenous plants soaked in hot water
chawa	Marker separating two parts of a sown field, placed after tilling by two farmers to distinguish their own portions

Glossary

chawak	*Mirab*, or one whose duty it is to see that everyone with a right to water gets his share
chawat	Footwear made of felt
chawband	Roofless shelter for animals
chem	Scummy mud
chogh	Yoke
chol	Waterless, barren plain or desert
chur	Camel pasture
chut	Shoes given to a camel man by the owner of the camel
chuti	Type of money of varied value to purchase shoes
dag	Land that is rocky and too elevated for irrigation
dagal gardi	"Searching the ground" for ancient artifacts
damichakeh	Indigenous plant used as herbal medicine
daup (dup)	Comb used in beating back warp in qilim weaving
dik	Mound or earthen ruin
do-kirch	Wooden-handled shears used for shearing carpet knap
dudni	Wild rue
dugh	Drink made of yoghurt or whey
duzdan (dozdan)	Woolen bag in which women keep personal items
fal	Part of a plowshare
galaw	Kind of melon
galgir	Piece of agricultural land from government to be farmed tax-free
gandomak	Indigenous vegetable
gardan gao (gardani)	Hiring rate of an ox
gavatek	Indigenous plant used as herbal medicine
ghalu-i torsh (ghalau)	Mixture of *dugh*, wheat flour, turmeric, potato, onion
ghaminha	Three men of the *pagao* who do all the farm work
gorwan	Cowherd
guyi	See *vatar*
hak	Prepared oil kept in a *mashk*
hashm	Animal dung
ishkana	Soup consisting of sour curd or hen's egg, *piyawa* in Dari
ishtan	Wooden fork used to fan threshed grain
isqat	Money distributed to the religious and poor before a burial
janin	Married woman

Glossary

jar	Driving the weft in the weaving of qilims and rugs
jaunat	Cradle
jerib	Measurement of land
jilak (jalak)	Wooden instrument used in spinning wool
jilat	Grain storage bin made of tamarisk branches
jinak	Young girl, virgin
jogan (jugan)	Wooden mortar or mallet used for grinding
jugh	Double yoke made of wood
jui	Canal
jung	Very young camel
kalpureh	Indigenous plant used as herbal medicine
kamunuk	Child's playpen
kang	Land of too high an elevation to be easily watered
karkavok	Indigenous plant used as herbal medicine
karu (kalu)	Wooden measure for wheat
kashtmand (kashmandi)	Farmer who owns farm tools and equipment and obtains his own seed. A landlord provides the land.
kesheh	Winnowing fork
khahsi	Bullock
khakao	First water given to a field following sowing and germination
khaleseh	Indigenous plant used as herbal medicine
khameh khuri	A local bush from whose seeds rennet is made
khanaqah	Place where people gather for instruction in various Sufi practices
kharvar	Measurement of wheat
khatmi	Indigenous plant used as herbal medicine
khazgar	Fiancée
khig	Leather bag in which oil is kept
kholfa	Indigenous vegetable
khordeh	Soil from a religious shrine
kirakesh	Hired camel transporter
kisheh	20 to 25 *satri*
kod	Baluchi village or hamlet
kodik	Baluchi dwelling made from branches, wattle, and daub
kori	Bunches of tamarisk branches used in house construction

Glossary

kram	Storage pit to bury wheat
kumach	Bread baked on sand
kurgh	Below ground storage in which grain is kept beneath straw and reeds
kutwal	Foreman of the canal cleaning operation
laka tao (*lakehtab*)	Suspending by the feet as a punishment
landi	See *qaghi*
langar	Plowshare
lari	Bundle of tamarisk branches forming the basic frame of a Baluchi dwelling
lidau	A "regular" camel
lulak	Caterpillar-like worm that infests wheat fields
madag	Locust
mahghau	Disease in cattle caused by eating melon rinds
maktab	School
maleh	Harrow; wooden platform attached to yoke
mamateh	Method of farming arrangement between landlord and farmer
man	Measurement of seed, equivalent to 10 *pav* (pounds)
maneh	Large wooden and reed platform attached to the house for sleeping
mangal	Sickle
mangasha	Wooden forked stick used in threshing grain; pitchfork
marak	Type of liver worm
marghak	Disease in camels
mari	Type of riding camel, see *badi*
marmut	Indigenous plant used as herbal medicine
mashk	*Sinach* which has be transformed into dressed leather; leather bottle used to make *dugh*
mayeh	Load-bearing camel
mirab	Superintendent of water
murshid	Spiritual advisor
mushrif	Inspects, certifies, and controls wheat harvest for landlord
nalgasak	Indigenous vegetable
nashrah	Custom of reciting verses by the family and friends following the birth of a child
naswar	Mixture of powered green tobacco leaf and lime paste, a stimulant
pachao	Wooden pole used to drive a *tutin*
pagao (*pagau*, *pagav*)	Six farmers working the same land

Glossary

pakhal	Roots or stalks of wheat or barley remaining in the field after harvest
pakhali	Harvested wheat field
palas	Goat hair tent or tarpaulin
patun	Worm infestation; see *lulak*
pav	Weight measurement, 1/10 of a *man*
peshkash	Money paid by the groom to his fiancée's proxy
pir	Sufi holy men
piyawa	Local food made from oil, fried onions, water, and salt meat
pizwan	Semi-circular piece of decorated metal worn suspended from a ring in the middle of the nose
pukka	Chaff
pulu	Half-ripe wheat roasted in the husk
puluk (polik)	Small star-shaped metal pin worn by a woman on one side of her nose
pur	Half ripened barley that is not yet good to eat
puzhu	Indigenous plant used as herbal medicine
qaghi	Autumn tradition of drying meat for harvest celebration; also called *landi*
qorut	Dried milk curd
qurs	Type of disc lozenge hat
rakhmi	Dried condensed whey
rakht	Piece of wood that joins the plowshare to the yoke
rakul	Trowel or spade
rash	Pile of sifted and winnowed grain
rashtan	Wooden forked stick used in threshing grain
rawgiz	Sieve used for cleaning wheat
reshkeh	Plant eaten by camels
rishta	Team of cattle used for the purpose of stamping and threshing harvested grain
roghanak	Indigenous vegetable
rudang	Indigenous plant used to dye wool, produces the color brown
sabjak	Half-cooked wheat flour
salar	Head of a *pagao* group of farmers
sangao	Women's bracelet
saruk	Woolen or cotton cloth to carry wheat to the threshing floor
satri	Handful of ripened wheat
sattu	Half ripened barley, dried and powdered
shal	Qilim or carpet used directly on the ground.
shalansh	Dried whey

Glossary

shamshirak	Wood which joins together and holds household linen
shawanak	Shepherd
shekanjeh	Two pieces of wood used to geld sheep and cattle
shireh	Worm that eats the tendrils and vines of watermelons
shod	Soap-like shrub used to launder clothing
shurak	Indigenous vegetable
sinach	Method of skinning sheep or goat
sir	Unit of measuring weight equaling 7 kg
siyali	Money/ gift to the bride
spikar	Baluch qilim with a white border
tabila	Shelter for cattle, horses, or donkeys
taghaz	Tree used for firewood
taratkeh	Shrub for fattening sheep
tashnab	A washing area outside a home
tavileh	Trough
tawil (tuyul)	Piece of land owned by landlord and worked by *pagao* group
taytak (tatik)	A triangular metal ornament worn on the heads of women
tayyak	Anvil
tazi	Variety of Afghan hound
teppor	Quantity of wool used to make a felt rug
tesh (tish)	Metal plowshare
tikar	Shards of glass or ceramic
to'ma	Court land grants
tumar	Type of amulet
tupak	Cattle disease
tusu	Indigenous plant used as herbal medicine
tutin	Boat used for freight, guided by a fixed rope
ushlan	Indigenous plant used to dye wool
vandi	Practice of selling meat by value of portions instead of by weight
vatar	Land which has sufficient water for germinating seeds
wadan	Woolen bag in which salt is kept
ya'is keshi	"Removing sorrow" grieving custom
zang	Small child
zardi	Wheat disease
zelir	Indigenous yellow spring flower used to dye wool
zobak	Year-old camel that has never borne a load

References

English / European Language References

Al Sharifi, Al Idrisi. *India and the Neighbouring Territories*. Leiden: E.J. Brill, 1960.

Atlas of the Classical World. London and Edinburgh: Thomas Nelson and Sons, 1959.

Ball, Warwick. *Archaeological Gazetteer of Afghanistan, Revised Edition*. Oxford: Oxford University Press. 2019.

Baluch, Sardar Muhammad Khan. *History of the Baluch Race and Baluchistan*. Karachi: Process Pakistan, 1958.

-----. *The Great Baluch*. Karachi: Lion Art Press, 1958.

Bellew, Henry Walter. *From the Indus to the Tigris: A Narrative of a Journey through the Countries of Balochistan, Afghanistan, Khorassan, and Iran, in 1872*. London: Trubner, 1874.

Berman, Judith. "George Hunt and *The Social Organization and the Secret Societies of the Kwakiutl Indians*." 1997. Unpublished paper accessed 03.13.2020 at https://lingpapers.sites.olt.ubc.ca/files/2018/03/1997_Berman.pdf

Bhattacharya, Kakali. "Unsettling Imagined Lands: A Par/des(i) Approach to Decolonizing Methodologies." In *Oxford Handbook of Methods for Public Scholarship*, edited by Patricia Leavy, 175–215. Oxford: Oxford University Press, 2019. DOI: 10.1093/oxfordhb/9780190274481.013.36

Bosworth, C.E. *Sistan Under the Arabs: from the Islamic Conquest to the Rise of the Saffarids*. Rome: IsMEO, 1968.

Bruchac, Margaret. "My Sisters Will Not Speak: Boas, Hunt, and the Ethnographic Silencing of First Nations Women." *Curator: The Museum Journal* 57, no. 2 (2014): 153–71.

Codrington, Oliver. "Note on Musalman Coins Collected by Mr. G. P. Tate in Seistan." *Journal of the Royal Asiatic Society of Great Britain and Ireland* (October 1904): 681–6.

-----. "Note on Musalman Coins Collected by Mr. G. P. Tate in Seistan." *Journal of the Royal Asiatic Society of Great Britain and Ireland* (July 1905): 547–553.

-----. "Coins Collected by Sir A. Henry McMahon, K.C.I.E., in Seistan." *Journal of the Royal Asiatic Society of Great Britain and Ireland* (July 1911): 779–784.

Conolly, Edward. "Journal Kept While Travelling in Seistan by the Late Captain Edward Conolly." *Journal of the Asiatic Society of Bengal*, (1841): 319–340.

Daffinà, Paolo. *L'Immigrazione dei Sakas nella Drangiana*. IsMEO Reports and Memoirs 9. Rome: IsMEO, 1967.

Dames, Longworth. *The Baluch Race*. London: Royal Asiatic Society, 1904.

Debets, G.F. *Physical Anthropology of Afghanistan I–II*. Russian Translation Series of the Peabody Museum V:1. Translated by Eugene V. Prostov. Cambridge MA: Peabody Museum, 1970.

References

Dewindt, H. *A Ride to India Across Persia and Baluchistan*. London: Chapman and Hall, 1891.
Dupree, Louis. "Population Review 1970: Afghanistan." South Asia Series vol. 15, no. 1, New York: American Universities Field Staff, 1971.
-----. *Afghanistan*. Princeton, NJ: Princeton University Press, 1973.
Elfenbein, Josef. "A Linguistic Mission to Helmand and Nimruz." *Afghan Studies II* (1979): 39–44.
The Encyclopaedia Britannica. 11th ed. New York: Cambridge University Press, 1911.
The Encyclopaedia of Islam, Vol. 4. Leiden: Brill, 1936.
"Environment: Earth's Creeping Deserts." *Time Magazine*, September 12, 1977.
Fahim, Hussein M. "Foreign and Indigenous Anthropology: The Perspectives of an Egyptian Anthropologist." *Human Organization* 36, no. 1 (Spring 1977): 80–6.
-----, ed. *Indigenous Anthropology in Non-Western Countries*. Durham NC: Carolina Academic Press, 1982.
Fahim, Hussein M. and Katherine Helmer. "Indigenous Anthropology in Non-Western Countries: A Further Elaboration." *Current Anthropology* 21, no. 5 (October 1980): 644–63.
Fairservis, Walter. "Archaeological Studies in the Seistan Basin of Southwest Afghanistan and Eastern Iran." *Anthropological Papers of AMNH* 49 (1961): 30–7.
Ferrier, J.P. *Caravan Journeys and Wanderings in Persia, Afghanistan, Turkistan, and Beloochistan*. London: John Murray, 1856.
Fischer, Klaus. *Nimruz: Geländebegehungen in Sistan 1955–1973 und die Aufnahme von Dewal-i Khodaydad*. Bonn: Rudolf Habelt Verlag GmbH, 1974, 1976.
Ghani, Ashraf. "Production and Domination: Afghanistan, 1747–1901." PhD diss., University of Pennsylvania, 1982. Accessed 03.13.2020 at http://citeseerx.ist.psu.edu/viewdoc/download?doi=10.1.1.694.6197&rep=rep1&type=pdf
Gold, Milton, trans. *The Tarikh-e Sistan (History of Sistan)*. Persian Heritage Series 20. Rome: IsMEO, 1976.
Goldsmid, Frederic John. *Eastern Persia: An Account of the Journeys of the Persian Boundary Commission, 1870–71–72*. London: Macmillan, 1876.
Government of Afghanistan and the United States Agency for International Development. *Helmand River Basin Soil and Water Survey Study Report*, Part I, 1976.
Grace, Jo. "Who Owns the Farm? Rural Women's Access to Land and Livestock." *Working Papers Series*. Kabul: Afghanistan Research and Evaluation Unit, 2005.
Gregorian, Vartan. *The Emergence of Modern Afghanistan: Politics of Reform and Modernization, 1880–1946*. Palo Alto; Stanford University Press, 1969.
Guneratne, Arjun. "Plain Tales from the Field: Reflections on Fieldwork in Three Cultures." In *The Anthropologist and the Native: Essays for Gananath Obeyesekere*, edited by H.L. Seneviratne, 397–422. London: Anthem Press, 2011.
Hackin, Joseph. "Recherches archéologiques dans la partie afghane du Seistan." In *Diverses recherches archéologiques en Afghanistan (1933–1940)*, edited by J. Hackin, J. Carl, and J. Meunié, 23–38. MDAFA VIII. Paris: Presses Universitaires de France, 1959.

References

Hannoum, Abdelmajid. "The (Re)Turn of the Native: Ethnography, Anthropology, and Nativism." In *The Anthropologist and the Native: Essays for Gananath Obeyesekere*, edited by H.L. Seneviratne, 423–43. London: Anthem Press, 2011.

Hughes, A.W. *The Country of Baluchistan*. London: George Bell and Sons, 1877.

Jones, Delmos J. 1970. "Towards a Native Anthropology." *Human Organization* 29, no. 4 (Winter 1970): 251–59.

Kakar, M. Hasan. "Afghanistan in the Reign of Amir Abdal Rahman Khan." PhD diss., University of London, 1975.

-----. *Afghanistan: The Soviet Invasion and the Afghan Response, 1979–1982*. Berkeley: University of California Press, 1995.

-----. *Government and Society in Afghanistan*. Austin: University of Texas Press, 2011.

Konieczny, M.G. *Textiles of Baluchistan*. London: British Museum, 1979.

Kramer, Carol. *Village Ethnoarchaeology: Rural Iran in Archaeological Perspective*. New York: Academic Press, 1982.

Mahapatra, Lakshman Kumar. "Anthropology in Policy and Practice in India." *NAPA Bulletin* 25 (2006): 52–69.

McMahon, Henry. "Recent Survey and Exploration in Seistan." *The Geographical Journal* 28, nos. 3–4 (1906): 209–28; 333–40.

-----. "Seistan Past and Present." *Journal of the Society of Arts* 54, no. 2790 (1906): 657–682.

Messerschmidt, Donald A., ed. *Anthropologists at Home in North America: Methods and Issues in the Study of One's Own Society*. Cambridge UK: Cambridge University Press, 1981.

Narayan, Kirin. "How Native Is a 'Native' Anthropologist?" *American Anthropologist* 95, no. 3 (September 1993): 671–86.

Pardind, Edoardo. "Anthropological Research in Sistan." *East and West* 25, nos. 3–4 (September–December 1975): 267–286.

Pastner, Stephen L. "The Man Who Would Be Anthropologist: Dilemmas in Fieldwork on the Baluchistan Frontier of Pakistan." *Journal of South Asian and Middle Eastern Studies* III, no. 2 (Winter 1979): 44–52.

Perrin, Narcisse. *Afghanistan, ou description géographique du pays théatre de la guerre*. Paris: Arthus Bertrand, 1842.

Pehrson, Robert N. *The Social Organization of Marri Baluch*. Chicago: Aldine. 1966.

Pottinger, Henry. *Travels in Beloochistan and Sinde*. London: Longman, 1816.

Radermacher, H. "Historical Irrigation Systems in Afghanistan." *International Commission for Irrigation and Drainage Bulletin* (July 1974).

Rapson, E. J. "Note on Ancient Coins Collected in Seistan by Mr. G. P. Tate, of the Seistan Boundary Commission." *Journal of the Royal Asiatic Society of Great Britain and Ireland* (October 1904): 673–80.

Salinas Pedraza, Jesus. *Native Ethnography: A Mexican Indian Describes His Culture*. Newbury Park CA: Sage, 1989.

Salzman, P.C. "Continuity and Change in Baluch Tribal Leadership." *International Journal of Middle East Studies* 4, no. 4 (1973): 428–39.

References

-----. "Islam and Authority in Tribal Iran; a Comparative Comment." *The Muslim World* 65, no. 3 (July 1975): 186–195.

SAUTI, I.C.E. "Helmand Valley Extension Road." Report 1, 1974–1975. (Unpublished manuscript.)

Savage Landor, A. Henry. *Across Coveted Lands: A Journey from Flushing (Holland) to Calcutta, Overland.* 2 volumes. New York: Scribners, 1902.

Seltzer, Leon E. *Columbia Lippincott Gazetteer of the World.* Morningside Heights NY: Columbia University Press, 1952.

Shahrani, M. Nazif. *The Kirghiz and Wakhi of Afghanistan.* Seattle: University of Washington Press, 1979.

-----. *The Kirghiz and Wakhi of Afghanistan, Revised Edition.* Seattle: University of Washington Press, 2002.

Shalinsky, Audrey C. "The Aftermath of Fieldwork in Afghanistan: Personal Politics." *Anthropology and Humanism Quarterly* 16, no. 1 (1991): 2–9.

Singhal, Damodar P. *India and Afghanistan.* Brisbane: University of Queensland Press, 1963.

Spooner, Brian. "Politics, Kinship and Ecology in Southeast Persia." *Ethnology* 8 (1969): 139–152.

-----. "Ethnography." *Encyclopædia Iranica* 9, no. 1 (1998a): 9–28. Retrieved from http://repository.upenn.edu/anthro_papers/128

-----. "Baluchistan: Geography, History, and Ethnography." *Encyclopædia Iranica* 3, no. 6 (1988b): 598–632. Retrieved from http://repository.upenn.edu/anthro_papers/127

-----. *Investment and Translocality: Recontextualizing the Baloch in Islamic and Global History.* Crossroads Asia Working Papers Series, No. 14. Bonn., 2013a.

-----. "The Baloch in Islamic Civilization, Western Ethnography, and World History." *Journal of the Middle East and Africa* 4 (2013b.): 135–151.

Srinivas, Mysore Narasimhachar (M.N.). *Social Change in Modern India.* Berkeley: University of California Press, 1969.

-----. *The Remembered Village.* Berkeley: University of California Press, 1976.

-----. "Practicing Social Anthropology in India." *Annual Review of Anthropology* 26, no. 1 (1997): 1–24.

Statistical Year Book. New York, UN Publishing Service, 1973.

Sweetser, Anne T. *Family Formation Attitudes among High School Girls in Kabul: A Study of Population and Social Change.* Occasional Paper 9. New York: Afghanistan Council of the Asia Society, 1976.

Swidler, Nina. "The Political Context of Brahui Sedentarization." *Ethnology* 12, no. 3 (July 1973): 299–314.

Swidler, Warren W. "Technology and Social Structure in Baluchistan, West Pakistan." PhD diss. Columbia University. 1968.

Tate, George Passman. "Coins and seals collected in Seistan, 1903–4." *Journal of the Royal Asiatic Society of Great Britain and Ireland,* (October 1904): 663–72.

-----. *The Frontiers of Baluchistan.* London: Witherby, 1909.

References

-----. *Seistan: A Memoir on the History, Topography, Ruins, and People of the Country*, 4 vols. Calcutta: Superintendent Government Printing, India, 1910–12.
Thomas, David C., and Fiona J. Kidd. "On the Margins: Enduring Pre–Modern Water Management Strategies in and Around the Registan Desert, Afghanistan." *Journal of Field Archaeology* 42, no. 1 (2017): 29–42. http://dx.doi.org/10.1080/00934690.2016.1262188
Ugwu, Chidi. "The 'Native' as Ethnographer: Doing Social Research in Globalizing Nsukka." *The Qualitative Report* 22, no. 10 (2017): 2629–37. Retrieved from http://nsuworks.nova.edu/tqr/vol22/iss10/7
Venkata, Rao Mullaqudi. "Review: Report on the Design of Check Structure at Ch–5200 Across Lashkary Canal." 1974. Unpublished manuscript.
Ward, T.R.J. *Untitled Manuscript Concerning the British Boundary Commission Work, 1903–1905*, Unpublished manuscript. Library and Records Department, Foreign and Commonwealth Office, London. 1906.
Webster's New Geographical Dictionary. Springfield MA: G. & C. Merriam 1972.
Whitney, John W. *Geology, Water, and Wind in the Lower Helmand Basin, Southern Afghanistan*. Scientific Investigations Report 2006–5182. Reston VA: US Geological Survey, 2006.
Wolcott, Harry F. "Home and Away: Personal Contrasts in Ethnographic Style." In *Anthropologists at Home in North America: Methods and Issues in the Study of One's Own Society*, edited by Donald A. Messerschmidt, 255–66. Cambridge UK: Cambridge University Press, 1981.
Yate, Charles Edward. *Khurasan and Sistan*. Edinburgh and London: William Blackwood and Sons, 1900.
-----. *Baluchistan*. London: Proceedings of the Central Asian Society, 1906.

Dari and Pashto References

Bahar, Malik al-Shu'ara, ed. *The History of Sistan*, Tehran: Zavar Press. 1314/1936. Comprehensive edition of anonymous work written roughly 445–725/1067–1347.
Central Statistical Office of Afghanistan. *Statistics of Afghanistan, 1350–52*, 1353/1975.
-----. *Statistics of Afghanistan, 1351–53*, 1354/1976.
The Demographic Report Project of the Prime Minister's Central Statistical Office. *Atlas of Villages, With an Explanation of Local Administrative Districts* 3, 1353/1975.
Farmanfarma, Firuz Mirza. *A Journal of Travel in Kirman and Baluchistan*. Farmanfarma'iyan Tehran: Foundation Press, 1342/1964.
Ghobar, Mir Gholam Muhammad. *Afghanistan in the Course of History*. Kabul: Books Publishing Institute, 1346/1968.
Ghobar, Mir Gholam Muhammad and 'Ali Ahmad Na'imi. *The History of Afghanistan*, Vol. 3. Kabul: Public Printing House, 1346/1968.

References

Heravi, Ma'il, ed. *The Geography of Hafiz Abru*. Tehran: Publications of the Cultural Foundation of Iran, 1349/1971.

Jahanyani, Sepahbod Aman Allah. *The Story of Baluchistan and its Borders*. Tehran, 1338/1960.

Kohzad, Ahmad 'Ali. *The History of Afghanistan*, Vol. 2. Kabul: Public Printing House, 1325/1947.

-----. *Afghanistan in Proto-History*. Kabul: Books Publishing Organization: Government Press, 1331/1953.

Lambton, Ann Katharine Swynford. *Landlord and Peasant in Persia*, trans. Minuchihr Amiri. Tehran: Translation and Publishing Foundation, 1339/1961. (Original English edition, Oxford: Oxford University Press, 1953.)

Literary Society. *Kabul Magazine Calendar, 1332-33*. Public Press of Kabul. 1333/1955.

Literary Society. *Kabul Magazine Calendar, 1333-34*. Public Press of Kabul.1334/1956.

Literary Society. *Kabul Magazine Calendar, 1334-35*. Public Press of Kabul.1335/1957.

Nasih, Zabih Allah. *Baluchistan*. Tehran: Ibn Sina Press, 1344/1966.

Organizational Divisions of the Kingdom of Afghanistan. Kabul: Niyugrafi Press, 1300/1922.

Poliyak, A.A. *Economic Organization of Afghanistan*. Soviet Academy of Sciences, Institute of World Economics and International Relations, 1964.

Public Relations Office, Ministry of Information and Culture. *History and Documents Pertaining to the Helmand River Water*. 1352/1974.

Sistani, Muhammad A'zam. "Natural Geography of Iran." *Aryana*, Joint Issue 274 (Dalv-Hut 1346/1968).

-----. "Sistan in Sina Border Literature." *Aryana*, Joint Issue 295 (Asad-Sambola 1350/1972).

-----. "The Decline of the Kayanids and Sistani Conditions." *Aryana* Joint Issue 295 (Asad-Sambola 1350/1972).

-----. "The Economic Conditions in Sistan During the Islamic Expansion." *Aryana* Joint Issue 270 (Hamal-Saur 1350/1972).

-----. "Zareh Lake." *Aryana*, Joint Issue 258, (Hamal-Saur 1343/1965): 176-7.

-----. "A Peep at Nimruz." *Aryana* 262 (Qaus-Jadi 1343/1965).

-----. "The History of a Great River." *Aryana* Joint Issue 266-267 (1344/1966).

-----. "Traces of a Lost City in Sistan." *Aryana* 268 (Qaus-Jadi 1344/1966).

-----. "Historical Geography of Zaranj." *Aryana* Joint Issue 272-273 (1345/1967).

-----. "Sistan in Farsina Literature." *Aryana* 275 (Hamal-Saur 1345/1967).

Zahri, 'Abd al-Hamid Nahif. *Famous People of Ancient Sistan*. Afghan Milat Official Printing House, 1346/1968.

Index

'Abbasid period, 37–42
'Abd ur-Rahman Khan, 12, 15, 40, 59
Abdul-Rahman bin Thamara, 8–9
Abdullah bin 'Umar, 8–9
Adam Khan (shrine), vii, 105, 168, 169
agriculture, see farming
Ahmad Shah Durrani, 40
Amanullah Khan, 41–42, 60
amulets, 166–167
Amurjizis, 7–8
animals, animal husbandry, 40, 64–74, 191; animal products, 27, 118–119; animal skins, 111–113, 118; domestic animals, 64–71; gelding, 65–66; impact on environment, 32; wild animals, 72–73. See also: cooking; diseases; food; livestock; tanning; trade
Arabs, xxiv, 7–8, 17, 25, 37–38, 182; conquest of Sistan, 8–10, 61, 75
Ardeshir, 8
artifact hunters, 129
Asak, vi, x, 67, 71, 78, 98

Bad Shao, 169
Bagat, xxvi, 6, 134, 169, 175
Baghak Boland, 160
Baghak Pa'in, 160
bagri farming, 55, 58, 64. See also: farming systems
Balanush (shrine), 169, 177
Baluchan, 25, 45, 160
Banadar, 44, 136, 161
Band-i Rustam, 10, 25 (dam)
Bandan, 7, 13–15
Bandar-i Kamal Khan, xxv, 4, 13, 15, 16, 23, 27, 43, 44, 100–101, 117, 127, 167, 181
barber, 61–63, 178–180. See also: religion
Bellew, Surgeon Henry Walter, 204
Bibarg Khan, x, 51, 126, 132, 209
blacksmith, 61–64, 84, 106, 209. See also: metalworking
boar, xxv, 73, 82. See also: animals
boats, 100–101, 126. See also: transportation
bodyguards, 80, 132, 133, 134, 153. See also: security
border control, 133–135, 154. See also: security
bride, 120–121; 143–144; 156; 179–180. See also: bridegroom; marriage; wedding
bridegroom, 62–63, 142–144, 180. See also: bride; marriage; wedding
British involvement, boundary commission, 12–16, 69, 83–89, 203, 204–205; British Rule and the Partition of Sistan, 12–16; settlement, 16
burial customs, 180–182; burial money, 181; funeral, 181–182; grieving custom, 181–182
Bust (Qala–I Bist), x, 5, 7, 8–9, 17, 18, 26–27, 33

camels, 64, 65, 68–71, 73–74, 79, 81, 97, 128, 135, 178, 204; disease, 69; pasture, 70; personnel, 65, 70; products, 111, 118; transportation, 99–100, 117, 125, 133, 139–140, 154, 175, 195; transporters, 70, 97, 98, 99; types, 69–70
canals, xxv–xxvi, 2, 18, 19, 25, 43–50, 52, 57–61, 75, 76, 77, 82, 89, 94, 123, 139, 149, 189–191, 193–194, 195, 204–206, 208, 211; canal foreman, 61; dredging, 45–50. See also: irrigation
carpenter, 54, 59, 61–64, 103–105, 132, 209. See also: carpentry; feudal system/feudalism
carpentry (woodworking), 103–105, 211. See also: carpenter
cattle, xxv, 32, 53, 58, 64–68, 73–74, 78, 81, 118, 140, 145–146, 148, 170, 176, 191
chador (women's covering), 141. See also: clothing; women
Chaghi (District or Hills), 16, 17, 169, 175, 177, 178, 187
Chahar Kiseh Basin, 21
Chakhansur, xxvi, 5, 13, 23–25, 34, 53, 56, 63, 66–67, 78, 87, 116, 138, 175, 216
Charburjak, 1, 4, 6, 13, 23, 45, 46, 59, 60, 63, 88, 100–102, 117, 125, 127, 128, 133, 137, 174, 190, 192–193
chief, 11, 27, 204; chieftains, 37; tribal 182–183; tribal organization 37–42
childbirth, birth customs, 178–179; birth rates, 85–86; breastfeeding, 86. See also: marriage; women
clergy, 39, 58, 120, 133, 157, 211–212. See also: religion
climate, 28–32, 64, 73–74, 82, 128, 193–194; arid, 13, 28–32; humid, 29, 123; precipitation, 29; semi-arid, 28–32, 64, 68; snow, 29, 33. See also: rain; weather; wind

233

Index

clothing, 114–115
collective action, work group, 182–183, 213
commerce, 116–119. *See also*: economy
communication, 99–102. *See also*: newspaper; radio; telephone
Conolly, Captain Edward, 5, 19
corvée labor, 139–140, 155, 212
crops, xiii, 37, 47–48, 51–53, 55, 58–62, 87, 99, 124, 149, 191, 203, 206; types of, 157, 149. *See also*: food; harvest

dams, xxv–xxvi, 13, 22–23, 25, 33–34, 42–45, 61–62, 75, 76, 87, 123, 126, 193-194; *band*, xxv, 42–43, 75–76, 157. *See also*: irrigation
Darwishan, 4, 6, 21, 42–45, 51, 57, 63, 89, 101, 128, 135, 136, 174, 195
Dasht-i Amiran, 2, 5, 89, 123, 126, 169, 170
Dasht-i Margo, 5, 17, 18, 23, 27, 33, 129, 175
"dead men," 56–58
death, 140, 175; mortality, 81, 82, 185. *See also*: burial customs; health care; occult; *pir*; population decline
Delanguk, viii, 160, 169, 171, 183
Demarda, x, 126
Deshu, x, 1, 5, 27, 82, 88, 100–101, 117, 127, 137, 153, 165, 186, 192, 209
dik (ancient mound), 6
Dilaram, 101
disciple, 175–177
diseases, animal, 66–69, 139–140; crops, 54–55; human, 66–67, 85, 120, 171–173, 185
divorce, 141–142, 144
dogs, xiv-xv, xvi–xvii, 64, 71–72, 79–80, 82, 125; Afghan hounds, 64, 71–72
donkeys, 64, 70–71, 73, 79, 128, 139, 160, 176–177
Drangiana, 7–8, 17, 117
dung, 51–52
dyes, 107–111

economy, 38, 75, 77, 83, 99–100, 102, 157, 192; challenges 43, 128, 192; conditions, 133; economic arrangements, 41–42; economic structures, 37–38, 41–42, 90
education, 159–165, 193; impediments to, 163–165; elementary schools, 160; female education, 162–163; gender make up, 159–160; girls' schools, 162; religion, 163–165. *See also*: religious education; schools; teachers; women
embroidery, 113
emigration, 8, 183, 190, 211
ethnography, Baluch, 203–207; methods ix–x, xii–xxiii; modern, 205–207. *See also*: native ethnography

family, 83–86, 153, 155–156, 178–179; burial customs, 180–182; education, 160, 162–163, 165; employment, 47–48, 77, 141, 145–150, 160; farming, 58; land ownership, 41–42; living arrangements, 94–95; marriage, 162–163, 179–180; organization, 140–145; relationships, 140–145; religion, 174, 176, 177
Farah, 7, 19, 42, 102, 127, 192
Farah Rud, 19, 23, 25, 35
farmer, 41, 45, 46, 47–58, 60–64, 77, 79, 80, 84, 87, 99, 105, 106, 120; housing, 90; relationship with landlord, 131–138. *See also*: class; corvée labor; landlord
farming, 51–58, 63, 90, 157, 160, 164, 182, 189–191, 194, 213; agricultural products, 58–64; methods, 51–55; recommendations, 191; tilling, 49, 52, 56–59, 123; tools, 54–55; work, 149–150, 164.
farming systems, 55–58, 62–63. *See also*: *bagri* farming; crops; farming; *galgir* farming; harvest; irrigation; *kashtmand* farming; *mamateh* farming; *pagao* farming
Fars, See Iran
Ferrier, J. P., 203
fertilizer, 51–52, 78, 99, 191
feudal system / feudalism, 37–42, 75, 99, 155, 191, 212; employment, 141, 149–150, 155, 184–185, 190, 209; feudal class, 38; feudal economy, 99; feudal power, 38, 40; oppression 139, 212
flood, 15, 18, 23, 34, 43–45, 75, 76, 77, 78, 82, 121, 126, 186, 193, 195
food, 146–149; cheese, 74, 191; cooking, 50, 94–95, 124, 144–145, 179–180; dairy products, 73–74; drinks, 50, 73–74, 111, 146–148, 157; food preparation, 50, 103; indigenous, 74; khans, 151; milk, 64, 70, 73–74, 80, 116, 140, 146, 147, 150, 156, 172, 176; milk storage, 93; oils, 112; products, 149, 50, 146, 147, 175–176, 213, 146, 149, 73, 148, 147; storage, 93, 111–112; yoghurt, 50, 73–74, 116, 146, 172. *See also*: crops; farming; harvest; marriage

galgir farming, 55, 58, 63–64. *See also*: farming systems
Galudand, 4, 63
Gardan Reg, 155
Gaud-i Zirreh, xxvi, 5, 6, 8, 13, 17, 22, 25, 27, 65, 81, 119, 121, 122, 188
gazelle, 71–73, 82
geographical boundaries, 7, 12–16, 175, 206
Ghani, Ashraf, 202–203, 207. *See also*: native ethnography
Ghaznavid, 75, 185–186; Ghaznavis era 9
Gholam Dastigir, 132

234

Index

Gholam Khan, xxii, xxiii–xxvi, 89, 123, 167
Ghur, 7, 9, 17, 27
Girishk, 33, 100, 127, 165
goat, 64–66, 70–71, 73, 97, 111, 117–118, 170
Godri, x, xxi, xxii, xxiii–xxiv, 45, 46, 47, 84, 138, 160, 169, 183
Goldsmid, Sir Frederic, 12–16, 27, 83, 204
Golichah, 187, 192
government, 38–42, 87, 100, 102, 122, 130, 132–135, 153, 154, 183, 191, 200–201; Afghanistan, xi, xxiii, 12–13, 16, 208, 212; British, 12; Iran, 11–16. *See also*: feudal power
Guludand, 44, 137, 190

Habibollah Khan, 41
Hajji Fayz Muhammad (shrine), 169
Hajji Nafaz Khan, 61, 62, 133
Hamun-i Helmand, 121, 122, 157
Hamun-i Puzak, x, 2, 19, 22, 53, 66–67, 71, 78, 98, 121, 122, 123, 186
Hamun-i Sabari, 19, 121, 186; *See also*: Sabiri Basin
harvest, 18, 52–53, 55–56, 58–64, 79, 94, 116–117, 124, 129, 145, 148, 176, 201. *See also*: crops; farming systems; food; irrigation; plants
Hauz, x, xxi, 45, 46, 47, 48, 77, 92, 96, 97, 98, 121, 125, 129, 138, 149, 160–162, 171, 183, 209–210
Hazar Joft, 57, 64, 101–102
health care; access, 165–173; birth control, 178; folk, 171–173; formal, 165–173, 184–185, 212; injury, xiv–xv, 165–166; medicinal plants, 171–173; public health, 85, 131, 165–173, 211; shrines, 167–171. *See also*: disease; medicine; opium; plants; religion
Helmand Basin, 2, 12, 15, 21–22, 23, 25, 30, 35, 42, 45, 88, 110, 191
Helmand River, xiii, xxi, xxv–xxvi, 1, 2, 4, 5, 6, 9, 13, 15–16, 17, 20, 21–22, 23–25, 26, 27, 29, 32–35, 33, 35, 42–43, 45–47, 48, 50, 52, 58–59, 71, 88, 89, 94, 121, 122, 139, 148, 156, 177, 192, 193, 209
Helmand Valley, x, xxi, xxvi, 5, 27, 66, 68, 77, 78, 79, 81, 90, 95, 98, 115, 117, 128, 129, 132, 135, 136, 150, 153, 155, 163, 165, 174, 175, 177, 186, 187, 191, 192, 207, 209–210, 213, 214
Herat, xviii, 7, 9, 11, 59, 110, 118, 127, 130, 153, 170, 203
horses, xxiii, 9, 43, 64, 71–72, 76, 81–82
housing, 90–99, 124–125, 131, 212; construction 90–97, 139, 204; elite, 90, 95–97; materials, 90–93, 98; mobility, 94–95, 98–99

hunting, 64, 71–72, 151

incense, 166–167
indigenous ethnography, see native ethnography; ethnography
inequality of roles, see women
Iran, x, xv, 4, 5, 6, 7, 10–16, 17, 18, 19, 20, 23–25, 77, 78, 87–88, 101, 121, 122, 124, 126, 127, 128, 130, 149, 153, 154, 155–156, 157–158, 180, 187, 189–190, 192, 194, 195, 205–206; government, 12–16
irrigation, 10, 18, 34, 42–55, 57, 77, 78, 123, 160, 193–194, 206; construction/maintenance 42–45; system 89, 123, 189–191, 211; *See also*: canals; crops; dams; farming systems

Jalalabad, 4, 10, 18
Jali Robat, x, 6, 119, 133–134, 154, 155, 210
jeweler, 114–116
jewelry, 114–116, 128, 129
Jui Nao, x, xxi, xxii, xxiii–xxv, 45, 46, 47, 48, 77, 85, 138, 160, 169
Juwain, 2, 11, 13, 15, 19, 23, 30, 88, 217

Kabul, ix, x, xii, xviii, xix, xx, xxiii, xxvi, 4, 6, 16, 20, 29, 32–33, 82, 83, 102, 120, 124, 127, 128, 129, 132, 151, 154, 184–185, 200, 202–203, 207, 208, 210
Kajaki Dam, xxvi, 23, 33–34, 50, 89, 123
Kanak, 66–67, 116
Kandahar, xxv, 7–8, 11, 17, 29, 33, 88, 100, 102, 106, 117–118, 122, 124, 127, 129, 130, 139, 152, 153, 155, 157–158, 192, 203
Kang, 34, 53, 56, 126
Karachi, 41
kashtmand farming, 55, 57, 63–64, 70–71, 106, 148, 181; *See also*: farming systems
Kayani, 10–12
Khalmuq, 63
khan, see chief
Khan Neshin, 5, 6, 81, 100, 101, 125, 169, 174
Khan-i Khani, 37–42. *See also*: chiefs
khanaqah (religious school), see religious education
Khash Rud, 23, 29, 34–35, 88, 191
Khaspas Rud, 35
Khel-i Bibarg Khan, x, 51, 136
Khorasan, 9
Khwabgah (R.), 27, 42, 66
Khwaja 'Ali, x, 27, 33–34, 100, 116–117, 126, 144, 147, 167, 183;
Khwaja 'Ali Bala, 126;
Khwaja 'Ali Canal, 75;
Khwaja 'Ali Pa'in (or Sufla), 126

235

Index

Khwaja 'Ali Sehyaka (Sehyak), x, xvii, xxi, xxii, 1, 4, 5, 61, 62, 65, 79, 91, 92, 93, 94, 95, 96, 101, 103, 104, 105, 106, 107, 108, 109, 112, 117, 119, 125, 126, 147, 152, 153, 155, 156, 167, 169, 172, 174, 175, 176, 177, 178, 183, 186, 187, 209–210
Khwaja Bidar (shrine), 169
Kirman, 9
Kona Qala II, 1, 4, 5–6, 133, 209
Kuh-i Baba, 29, 32
Kuh-i Khan Neshin, 5, 6, 81, 100–101
Kuh-i Khwaja, 21, 23
Kuh-i Malik Siyah, 4, 15, 16, 33, 88, 133, 172
Kuh-i Sultan, 7
Kuhak Dam, 15, 34, 87, 121, 126
Kurgani period, 38

Laki, 51, 57, 77
land, land measurement, xiii, xv, 2, 42, 55, 59, 71, 85, 137, 164; piece of, 55–57; type, 52–53
land grants, 38–39, 55, 140
Landi, 27, 63, 137, 144, 176
landowner, 2, 41, 42, 48, 51, 55–59, 60–64, 70, 73, 87, 90, 96, 120, 131, 135, 139–140, 190–191, 201, 205–206, 212; relationship w/ farmer, 131–138. *See also*: class; economy; farmer; farming systems; feudalism
Lash, 2, 11, 13–15, 19, 23, 30, 88
Lashkar Gah, x, 1, 4, 6, 7, 9, 17, 33, 52, 77, 78, 80, 82, 99–102, 112, 117–118, 127, 132, 139, 151–152, 155, 157, 160, 165–166, 185, 210, 214
Lashkari Bazar, 17–18
Lat, x, 5, 51, 99, 126, 132, 209–210. *See also*: Khel–i Bibarg Khan
left bank, xiii, 4, 5, 26–27, 88–89, 100–101, 116–117, 127, 169
literacy, 160, 163. *See also*: education; women
livestock, 32, 58–59, 64, 117, 143, 145, 157
Lop, x, 52, 99, 115, 116, 126, 167, 186

Maddi, 160, 167, 183
Malakhan, x, 6, 27, 75, 78, 100, 117, 157, 160, 183, 203
Maluchan, see Baluchan
mamateh farming, 55, 57–58, 63. *See also*: farming systems
Mamu, 134–135
marriage, xxv, 128, 140–145, 156, 157, 162–163, 174; bride gift, 179–180; bride price, 120–121, 143–144; ceremony, 179–180; cost of, 86; customs, 121, 142, 179–183; groom gift, 180, 187; Third Day, 180. *See also*: bride; bridegroom; divorce; family; wedding; women
Mashhad, 11–12, 30, 41, 127, 187
masonry, 105
Mas'ud, 9
Mateh Jat, 160
McMahon, Sir Henry, 5, 15–16, 18, 20, 23, 35, 68, 129, 204
measures and weights, xiii, xv, 53, 55, 57, 58, 60–65, 69, 70, 73, 89, 103, 116–118, 145, 151–152, 157, 176
medicine, folk, 171–173; formal, 116; *See also*: health care.
Mehrabad, 45, 160
metalworking, 54–55, 62, 103, 106, 128
military, 8–9, 12, 38–40, 77, 82, 127, 135, 193, 214–215
mills, 140, 145, 151–152; windmills, 31, 204
Mir Gadu (shrine), 169
mirab (supervisor of water), 61–62
Mogul incursions, 9–10, 38
mosque, xxii, 62–63, 99, 153, 163, 169, 174, 179, 181, 184, 185–186, 187, 209
motorcycles, 72, 78, 99–100, 154
mullah, xxii, 61–64, 143–144, 153–154, 157, 163, 166–169, 174, 178–179, 187, 205
mushrif (inspector), 61–64

Na 'Ilaj, 160
Nad-i 'Ali, 13–15, 138
Nad-i 'Ali Rud, 15, 34, 87
naswar (tobacco), 119, 128
native ethnography, 197–203; Afghanistan, 202–203; explained, 197–198; globally, 198–199; Helmand Baluch, 207–210; key issues, 199–201. *See also*: ethnography
newspaper, 102, 127
Nimruz, xxi, xxii, 1, 17, 22, 28, 35, 46, 49, 51, 52, 57, 58–59, 60, 63, 64, 66, 68, 70–71, 82, 85, 92, 96, 97, 98, 100–102, 115, 122, 127, 128, 132, 133, 143, 146, 147, 148, 149, 154, 159–160, 162, 163, 165–166, 167, 169, 170, 171, 183, 190, 212
Nishapur, 9
Nishk, 192
Nosrat ad–Din bin Bahramshah Harb, 9

occult, 166–167
Ogatay, 9
opium, 120, 151, 205, 214; addiction, 85–86, 214

pagao farming, 49, 55–58, 59–63, 205; "dead men," 56–58; *See also*: farming systems
Palalak, 63, 144
Panjdeh, 53, 68

Index

Pariyan Rud, 15, 34
Parthians, 8, 119
partition of Sistan, 12–16. *See also:* British involvement
peasants, 37–38, 40, 42, 57, 64, 90, 94, 105, 119, 124, 139, 165, 201, 206, 212
Perso-Afghan Arbitration Commission, xxv–xxvi, 18, 78, 123, 129
Peshawaran, 2, 186
pir (religious figure), 175–177, 187, 211–212
plants, disease, 54–55; food, 65; grass, 28; indigenous, 109–110, 149, 166, 172; medicinal, 171–173; shrubs, 28, 32; trees, 44, 117, 136
population, 76, 190, 192, 200, 204–206, 211, 212; composition, 41, 83–84; decline, 77, 83, 85–90, 155, 211; education, 159–160, 164; health, 165, 171, 173; public health, 85; religion, 174; size, 77, 84, 119, 122, 183, 184
pottery, 4, 6, 102, 127, 192
Pottinger, Henry, 203
prayer, 153, 163, 168, 174, 180–181, 185, 186, 187
property, 38–39, 90, 141
punishment, 12, 131–132
Puzak Basin, 21, 22, 34, 66, 87

Qala-i Fath, x, xxi, 2, 6, 27, 35, 45–47, 49, 57, 60, 63, 77, 82, 84–85, 127, 145, 149, 160, 163, 167, 171, 173, 209
Qala-i Kakh, 7
Qala-i Sirak, 165, 203
qilim, xxiv, 40–41, 94, 107–111, 118, 128, 129–130, 144–145, 149, 156

Rabi'a bin Ziyad, 8–9
radio, 102, 118, 126, 127, 149
rain, 29, 108–109, 125, 129, 187, 189
Registan, xxvi, 17, 88, 122, 129
religion, folk, 177; instruction, 163–165, 174; politics, 175; practice 174–177; religious figures, 175–177, 187, 211–212; Sunni Muslims, 174. *See also:* education; *mullah;* prayer; *pir; sayyid*
religious education, 153–154, 174. *See also:* education; *khanaqah;* religion; schools; teachers
right bank, xiii, 5, 6, 13, 25, 99–101, 117, 165, 192
rivers, 32–35, 42–46, 50–51, 61–62, 65, 75, 76, 77, 81
Rokn ad-Din Mahmood bin Harb, 9
rud, see rivers
Rud-i Biyaban, 4, 5, 6, 25
Rudbar, x, xxi, xxv, 1, 4, 5, 6, 13, 25, 27, 44, 52, 57, 63–65, 99, 115, 116, 120, 124, 126, 132, 144–147, 160, 173, 177, 186, 190, 192, 195, 209

Sa'adi Charbi, 9
Sabiri Basin, 21–22, 34, 87. *See also:* Hamun-i Sabari
Sabzgozi, 42, 44–48, 77, 85, 138, 160
Safar, 9, 52, 57, 89, 136, 167, 168
Saffarid period, 9, 10–11, 75
Saka, 7–8
sand, 10, 31, 45, 50, 59, 70, 76, 77, 79, 80, 88–90, 94, 99–100, 111, 118–119, 120, 122, 123, 126, 165, 189–191; sand dunes, 18, 26–27, 99, 127
Sar-o-Tar, x, xxi, xxiii, xxiv, xxvi, 1–2, 5, 28, 89, 120, 122, 123, 129, 143, 146, 148, 167, 186, 209
Sasanian, 8, 61–62, 75
sayyid, 166–169, 175. *See also:* religion
Sayyid Muhammad, 177
schools, 159–165, 183, 184, 209, 211; elementary school, 160; girls school, 162–163, 192; religious school, 153, 174; secondary school, 159, 160. *See also:* education; religion; religious schools; teachers; women
seasons, 28–29, 32
security, 133–135. *See also:* bodyguards; border control
Sehkuha, 22
Seljuk period, 39
Shahr, 160, 167
Shahr-i Gholghola, xxi, xxiii, 1, 2, 5, 72, 89, 181, 186, 209
Shahr-i Nao, 84, 126, 160
Shahrani, M Nazif, 202, 207
Shaparai, xv, 155–156, 209
Shaykh Hosein (shrine), 168
sheep, 64–67, 72–74, 80, 94, 108; 111, 113, 117–118, 122, 144, 145, 148, 170–171, 176–177, 204; shepherd, x, 38, 64–65, 72, 78, 80, 97, 153
Shela Rud, 5, 6, 13, 22, 25, 32, 119, 121, 122, 155, 188
Sher 'Ali Khan, 40–41
Shirabad, 34, 53
Shirak, 99, 126, 177
Shuri, 160
Sistan Basin, xxvi, 5, 18, 21, 25–27, 32, 34, 88, 122, 128, 135, 193–194
Sistan boundaries, 7–8, 12–16, 21–22. *See also:* geographical boundaries
Sistan Delta, 18, 22–28, 34, 50–51, 81, 189
Sistan Hamuns 5, 136
social class, 2, 38–41, 120, 131–133, 141,

Index

144, 145, 151–152, 174, 199–200, 211–212; relationship between farmer and khan, 131
social organization, 37–39
social system, 38–42
soil, 6, 28–30, 77, 78, 80, 123, 203, 204, 206; alluvial deposits, 23, 88; building material, xxiv, 19, 31, 67, 91, 92, 94–96, 98, 124, 125, 126, 139, 181; clay, 23, 28, 102, 145, 192; mud, 23, 31, 43, 94, 124, 139, 181; mudbrick 96, 98, 126; mud houses 19–20, 67, 91, 92, 95–96, 125; sediment, 22–27, 45, 50–51, 122
soil studies, 28
Srinivas, M. N., 198–201, 213
Sufi, 175, 177, 211 *See also:* religion

Taj Mohammad Khan, 11–12
tamarisk, xvii, 28, 73, 76, 79, 95, 96, 98, 104–105, 124; building material, 32, 90–93
Tamerlane, 10, 18, 25, 38, 43–45, 83, 162, 162–163, 189–190, 193–194. 193–194. *See also:* Timurids; Timurid Period
tanning, 111–113, 117
Tap-pagao, xxv
Tate, G.P., xxvi, 5, 7–8, 17, 35, 36, 77, 79, 81, 85–86, 120, 128, 129, 135, 154, 175, 183, 186, 205, 214
taxes, 8–9, 37–41, 58, 60–64, 75, 79, 153, 212
teachers, 159, 161, 162, 164, 184, 198, 211; male, 162 *See also:* education; literacy; school; women
Tehran, 11–12, 75
telephone, 100–102, 125, 126, 139–140
tent (*palas*), 97, 98
Third Day, 180
thorns, 28, 80–81, 150, 173; and camels 68–69; and craft use 91–92
Timurid Period, 123, 146, 169–170
Timurids, 10–12, 88–89, 119, 123, 146, 169–170, 185, 186, 194
tools, agriculture, 54–55, 53, 54, 57–58; carpentry, 103, 104; iron working, 106; jewelry, 115; tanning, 111–113; weaving, xix, 107–108. *See also:* agriculture; blacksmith; carpentry; metal working; weaving
trade, 116–118; khans, 152; routes, 25
Trakhun, 4, 6, 25, 44
transportation, 99–102; 105, 139, 211
Treaty of Paris, 15
tribal chiefs, 37–42, 182–183; tribal chieftain system, 37–41; tribal council, 39–40, 182–183; tribal law, 39–40. *See also:* chiefs; feudal system; Khan-i Khani

tribe, xxiv, 8, 11, 27, 39–42, 59, 110, 124, 135, 154, 175, 204
tribute, 8–9
trucks, 78, 80, 100, 127, 130, 157–158
Tuli Khan, 9

Umayyad, 37

villages, 76, 97; devastation, 41–42; harvest sharing, 61; life span, 98–99; marriage, 143–144; schools, 159–160; water, 45–46

warfare, guerilla, 10; tribal, 11
water, 145, as a resource, 75 , 76 , 78 , 80, 87, 147–149, 162, 169, 170–173, 186, 187, 192, 194, 195, 203; dams, 43–45; disease, 66–67; environment, xxiv, xxvi, 13, 15–16, 17, 19, 139; farming systems, 55–58, 61–62; plants, 52–55, 59, 117; water coverage, 22–23; water levels, 21–23, 87–89, 100, 121, 122, 123, 129, 191, 193; water reservoirs, 21–22, 193; water supervisor, 61. *See also:* canals; irrigation; *mirab*
weather, 50, 54, 68, 73, 80, 94–95, 111, 126, 127, 179; temperature, 28–29
weaver, 108, 110, 116, 209
weaving, xix, 104, 107–111, 118, 130, 145, 192; tools, 107–108
wedding, 62–63, 111, 142–144, 179–180; cost of, 86, 144. *See also:* bride; bridegroom; marriage
wetlands (*ashkin*), 22, 53, 66, 68, 73
Whitney, John W., xxiii–xxiv, 18–19, 36, 133, 194
wind, 18–19, 23–26, 28–32, 77, 93, 97, 99, 111, 123, 125; black winds, 32, 68; effects of, 50, 53, 54, 88–89, 153, 187, 189, 191; Wind of 120 Days, 10, 18–19, 29–30, 32, 45, 62, 88–89, 123
women, 140–145; daily life, 144–145; daughters, 141; employment, 141; status, 141; women group, 145; work, 144–145
wool, 53, 64, 69, 70, 107–112, 118, 145, 149, 156, 192

Zabul, 18, 19
Zabulistan, 9, 10
Zahedan, 18, 78, 101, 130, 162
Zamindawar, 7, 10, 27, 33
Zandak, 160, 183
Zaranj, 1, 8–10, 17, 31, 34, 42, 46, 63, 78, 97, 100–102, 117, 126, 127, 128, 130, 155, 158, 160, 165, 169, 174, 185, 195
Zaranka, 8, 17
Ziyarat-i Amiran (shrine), 169, 170, 185, 186
Zughad, 135

www.ingramcontent.com/pod-product-compliance
Lightning Source LLC
Chambersburg PA
CBHW051534020426
42333CB00016B/1915